DE VALERA IN AMERICA

Dave Hannigan is a sports columnist with The *Sunday Tribune* in Dublin, the *Evening Echo* (Cork) and *The Irish Echo* (New York). A former Irish young journalist of the year, and the author of three previous books, *The Garrison Game* (1998), *The Big Fight* (2002) and *Giants of Cork Sport* (2005). He is also an adjunct professor of history at Suffolk County Community College on Long Island. Born in Cork, he now lives in Rocky Point, New York with his wife Cathy, and sons, Abe and Charlie.

DE VALERA IN AMERICA

THE REBEL PRESIDENT'S
1919 CAMPAIGN

DAVE HANNIGAN

THE O'BRIEN PRESS
DUBLIN

First published 2008 by The O'Brien Press Ltd.
12 Terenure Road East, Rathgar, Dublin 6, Ireland.
Tel: +353 1 4923333; Fax: +353 1 4922777
E-mail: books@obrien.ie
Website: www.obrien.ie

ISBN 978-1-84717-086-6

Photographs used with kind permission: **UCD Archives, School of History and Archives
and the UCD-OFM Partnership; Boston Public Library, Print Department, Photograph
by Leslie Jones; Getty Images; Museum of the City of San Francisco (sfmuseum.org);
Tom Crowley and Noreen Moriarty.**

Cover photographs used with kind permission: **UCD Archives, School of History and
Archives and the UCD-OFM Partnership.**

Inside cover photograph used with kind permission: **Getty Images.**

British Library Cataloguing-in-Pubication Data
Hannigan, Dave
De Valera in America : the rebel president's 1919 campaign
1. De Valera, Eamon, 1882-1975 - Exile - Untied States
2. Ireland - Politics and government - 1910-1921
I. Title
941.5'0821'092

1 2 3 4 5 6 7 8
08 09 10 11 12 13

Editing, typesetting and design: The O'Brien Press Ltd
Printed and bound in the UK by J.H. Haynes & Co. Ltd, Sparkford.

DEDICATION

For my sons, Abe and Charlie

ACKNOWLEDGEMENTS

While time-wasting online a couple of years back, I came across a sepia-tinted photograph of Fenway Park packed to the rafters with people who'd come from all over New England to hear Eamon de Valera speak in the summer of 1919. Upon further investigation of the circumstances surrounding the shot, I figured there might be a book in this underexposed chapter of his career.

For sharing in that belief, I'd like to thank my publisher Michael O'Brien. He enthusiastically supported this project from the start, and made helpful phone calls about deadlines that did wonders for my work ethic. Elsewhere at O'Brien Press, a huge debt is owed to Síne Quinn, whose immense contribution to the finished manuscript went far beyond her forensic and patient editing job. Thanks also to Emma Byrne, whose exceptional work on the design of this book is evident in your hands right now.

Professor Clare Frost, of Stony Brook University, and Dr Gary Murphy, of Dublin City University, improved early drafts with their keen eyes for detail, literary and historic. I thank them both for being so generous with their time and kind with their criticisms.

While the readers of the *Irish Echo* in New York deserve special mention for furnishing me with all sorts of useful information and paraphernalia, it would require several more pages to list all the people who assisted, in some form or other, at different stages. Since pressure of space and fear of omitting anybody prevent me from doing that, I would just like to say a heartfelt thank you here to everybody who poked out an ancient book, a photograph, a bond certificate or a musty article. To my circle of friends in particular, I will be repaying your favours for years to come.

I was fortunate enough to grow up in a house that wasn't afflicted by the Civil War politics that ruled many other Irish families, so I came to de Valera with some measure of objectivity. For this and for a whole lot more, I'd like to thank my mother and father, Theresa and Denis. They are extraordinary parents and heroic people to whom I owe a debt I can never possibly repay.

I would also like to express my gratitude to my brother, Tom, sisters, Denise and Anne, niece, Kadie, Auntie Christine, and parents-in-law, George and Clare Frost.

My wife Cathy is an amazing woman, without whose love, patience and understanding, none of this would be much fun. It has also been my privilege to witness the courage with which she approaches far greater challenges than pressing book deadlines on a daily basis. Her strength in the face of adversity remains both humbling and inspirational.

I also want to thank my sons, Abe and Charlie, for still smiling at me so beatifically, even on those days when I turned into the troll in the basement office. You two are my everything.

CONTENTS

PROLOGUE

On the morning of 9 April 1885 a man named Ned Coll took his two-and a half-year-old nephew, Edward, by the hand and strode through the gates at Pier 36, on New York's North River. An Inman Line Royal Mail Steamer, the *SS City of Chicago*, stood before them. With four enormous masts for sail, two fat funnels, and an itinerary calling for a stop at Queenstown on the way to the final destination of Liverpool, it stretched over 430 feet in length along the dock, dwarfing the little boy with the tousled hair and the healthy plumpness to his cheeks.

The child's father was dead, his mother, Catherine, could no longer afford to raise him as a working single parent in Manhattan, and so it fell to a kindly uncle to ferry him from the city of his birth across the Atlantic Ocean to Bruree, County Limerick, the town from where his mother had emigrated in search of a better life. The young boy would remember nothing of the short chapter of his life spent in an apartment on East 41st Street except the leaving of it. He leaned over the wooden rails and stared wide-eyed at the broad expanse of green water the *Chicago* left in its wake.

Thirty-four years would pass before he would see his native New York again. By then, little Edward would be better-known around the world by the name of Eamon de Valera.

CHAPTER ONE

Would one not say that was a very foolish mission, indeed, a very hopeless mission from the start, to go over to the United States and to ask the Government of the United States to recognise a Government that was set up here as the result of the votes of the majority of the Irish people, by a majority of the representatives of the Irish people; to recognise the Republic which was declared here by the Irish people; that it was foolish to expect that; that, so long as Britain did not recognise it, America was not going to do such a foolish thing as to offend Britain by giving such recognition? Yes, indeed, it would have been, in ordinary circumstances, a rather hopeless mission. What inspired it? Why was it undertaken at all? Well, those of us who lived through the last war and knew what was said during the last war understand it...

– **Eamon de Valera, Dáil Éireann, 16 November 1943**

Nine days out of Liverpool, the 17,540 tonnes *SS Lapland* finally began to exit the Atlantic Ocean for the calmer, more inviting waters of New York Bay. Making its way through The Narrows and up the Hudson River, hundreds of passengers percolated to the top deck, to catch a better glimpse of the Statue of Liberty coming into view on the port side of the boat. It was a symbol of freedom, a sign the journey was nearing its end. There was cheering then. There always was once the lady of the harbour beckoned.

Manhattan lay off to their right, already steaming in the early morning of 11 June 1919, a shimmering monument to progress in the still-young century. The Singer Building, the Met Life Tower, and, larger than anything they'd ever seen before, the Woolworth, all fifty-five neo-Gothic stories of it, rising to meet them. The world's tallest building reaching farther into the blue summer sky than any edifice ever, a metaphor for the philosophy of an entire country.

From the soldiers returning from Europe to resume lives interrupted, to the immigrants dreaming their lives anew, the reactions were similar as the skyline took their breath away. Awe. Excitement. Joy. Relief. Their destination was at hand.

Far below the whooping and the hollering, Eamon de Valera remained hidden in the lamplighter's cabin. This dark, dank room had been his quarters since Barney Downes and Dick O'Neill, a pair of trusted Michael Collins's lieutenants, had smuggled him aboard back in Liverpool. Rats had gnawed through his spare clothes, brandy had helped him gain his sea legs, and Frisco Kennedy, the San Francisco-born lamp-trimmer with whom he shared the tiny space, believed the tall, gaunt stowaway was on the run for murdering two policemen. He wasn't on the run for murder. His life was way more complicated than that.

Since being famously spared execution for his part in the 1916 Easter Rising – for decades it was incorrectly assumed his American birth saved his life – he'd been imprisoned twice by the

British and embarked on a political career. In the December 1918 British and Irish General Election where Sinn Féin (the party of which he was now president) ran on a promise not to sit in Westminster but to instead establish an Irish parliament in Dublin, he was returned in absentia for the constituencies of East Clare and East Mayo. Unable to make the sitting of the first Dáil, at the Mansion House on 21 January 1919, because he was still languishing in Lincoln Jail, de Valera escaped on 3 February, following a convoluted operation involving the classic cliché of cakes filled with files and keys, and returned to Ireland.

There, on 1 April, he was elected to succeed Cathal Brugha as Priomh Aire of the Dáil, making him *de facto* leader of a rebel government seeking independence from British rule. The title was meant to denote Prime Ministerial status but the semantics mattered little out at sea where that Dáil's lack of international recognition was brought home to him every time de Valera lay down in his uncomfortable, temporary billet.

He was a man used to living in the twilight. In the four months since breaking out of Lincoln Jail, he'd gone from being on the lam in Dublin – at one point staying with the priests in Clonliffe College – to moving around the city with impunity, the British not bothering to arrest him, in case it would further burnish his legend. They had revoked his passport in order to restrict his movements, wanting him where they could keep an eye on his every move. This then was the only way to safely reach America, a fugitive secreted away on an English-owned ship, built at the Belfast shipyard of Harland and Wolff, just over a decade earlier.

He passed his days on a bunk that reeked of paraffin, nestled between ropes and paint, twitching at every strange footfall outside that might portend detection by the authorities. Even if the handful of crew members who knew his identity, sometimes smuggled him on deck at night to enjoy some fresh air as the rest of the ship slept, the discomfort, the stress and the stench were daily reminders of Ireland's lowly position in the international pecking order and the size of the task ahead of him in America.

New York was the perfect launch pad for his ambitious crusade to improve Ireland's circumstances by garnering recognition, monetary support and publicity for the attempt to break from the Empire. The newspaper and financial capital of the country, it was also a political hub and a place teeming with powerful Irish-Americans who had the resources, the influence and the desire to potentially turn his visit into a remarkable campaign for Irish freedom. All of this was underlined by the belief that the Washington government wouldn't try to repatriate him for fear of rousing the diaspora's vocal lobby.

With all the commotion filtering down from the decks above, de Valera finally peeked out through the porthole and caught a glimpse of the city of his birth, the place he'd left in the arms of an uncle before his third birthday. Thirty-four years later, he marvelled at the brightness of the sun beating down, but the eventual sound of the gangway being lowered onto the pier, at Chelsea, meant little to him. He had to sit and wait for every passenger to troop off. He needed the glorious New York day to turn into night and provide a welcoming cover of darkness before making a move. Even then it wasn't his call to leave. That decision would be made by O'Neill and Downes, men practiced in the art of transporting human contraband.

When they finally came to him that morning, he handed a note to be delivered to Harry Boland. De Valera's mission was so clandestine that not even Boland, the man he'd appointed Special Envoy to the US, just weeks earlier, knew he was coming on this particular day. Just four months earlier, the pair of them had strolled in the grounds of Dublin Whiskey Distillery, beside Clonliffe College. Back then, the talk of de Valera's pending trip to America was such he'd told Boland that very night to procure him a large fountain pen for use on board ship. Now, he was sitting tight as O'Neill and Downes headed ashore to seek Boland out in the teeming metropolis, and to hand him this missive.

Rather unexpected this! Will tell you idea when we meet. Am anxious to travel to Rochester [where his mother Catherine lived] tonight – hope it can be arranged. Want to see you before I meet anybody. I learnt a number of things since you left dealing with the matter you came to investigate. If you are watched, better not come to see me but travel to Rochester tomorrow or as soon as you can. I hope your experience did as little harm as mine has done to me. Till we meet. E de V.

O'Neill and Downes located Boland who was so shocked by the news he 'had a fit'. Then they organised the handover with the same smoothness with which they'd spirited their charge on to the *Lapland* back in Liverpool. He'd walked aboard carrying O'Neill's bag to lend authenticity to his attempt to pass as a sailor. Half an hour before midnight, he walked off on the other side of the world, wearing Downes's boatswain's jacket and carrying a heaving line (a lightweight shipping rope), for extra effect. With his eyes scanning the darkness as he went, watching for unwanted observers or British spies, de Valera was taken to the back room of Phelan's bar, on 10th Avenue, for the hand-over.

Downes and O'Neill's mission was complete. They had delivered him to Boland, a trusted friend with an impish grin, who brought him uptown to Liam Mellows's apartment on 39th Street. Mellows was another 1916 veteran who'd escaped from the British in Galway dressed as a nun. Just a dozen blocks down from the Nursery and Child's Hospital where he was born, de Valera washed, and at long last changed into fresh clothes. Boland wasn't alone through all this. He was accompanied by Joseph McGarrity, a dark-haired, moustachioed and rather dapper man with such an impeccable Republican pedigree the IRA would later use his name as an official code word for bomb warnings.

Born in Tyrone, McGarrity was a classic emigrant success story. A wealthy Philadelphia liquor merchant, he was publisher of the *Irish Press* in the city and a leading light in Clan na Gael, the American arm of the Irish Republican Brotherhood (IRB). He had been one of the financial backers of the Howth Gun-running in 1914 and his support of de Valera would prove practical, political and crucial. Bulmer Hobson, Roger Casement and Padraig Pearse were among the litany of previous visitors to his house on Chestnut Street, and de Valera himself spent several days there undercover and undergoing something of a make-over.

Befitting a self-made man, McGarrity was keen that an individual trying to pass as leader of a country should look every inch the part for the American audience. To this end, he took his guest to a tailor to be fitted for suits, then presented him with a set of fancy luggage and some astute advice. Priomh Aire might have been grammatically correct back home but here, it would have to give way to a term the locals could understand and immediately equate with power. President of the Irish Republic – it was simpler, more direct, and easier translated.

McGarrity left his prints on the younger man in other ways too. On the final day of his stay there, de Valera said his good-byes to the family and picked up his suitcase to leave. At which point, his more experienced comrade intervened and told him to put the bag down: a statesman didn't carry his own valise. 'Remember,' said the man from Carrickmore, 'from the moment you leave this house, you go now as President of the Irish Republic.'

The new title quickly caught on. By 22 June, it was being used in a report in *The New York Times* speculating about whether de Valera was in America.

'Mrs. Charles E. Wheelwright declared that she was amused when told that her son Edward de Valera, President of the Irish Sinn Féin Republic, had been in the city (of Rochester). She and her niece said they would not believe he was in the United States until they obtained direct communication with or saw him... She said she had not heard from her son since he was imprisoned. Mrs. Wheelwright said that if he has really got away, it would be more probable that her son was in Paris.'

De Valera's mother told a lie for her country. She'd already had a visit from her son. Her house had been his next destination after setting foot in New York. This wasn't the first time the pair had been reunited since the day she sent him back to Ireland all those decades earlier. Just two years after his initial departure, Catherine had returned to Bruree for a few weeks and the highlight of the visit was a day out together in Limerick city. One of his fondest childhood memories was of an American alphabet book she sent him, and as a teenager, he had written to his Aunt Hanna, in New York, beseeching her to have his mother arrange his fare to America. Nothing came of that but on a visit back to Ireland in 1907, it was reportedly Catherine who was rejected after she suggested he should accompany her back to the country of his birth.

The pair kept in regular contact by mail, even though Catherine's personal circumstances had changed greatly since the time she'd figured her son would be better off in Ireland than struggling with her in New York. In 1888 she married English-born Charles Wheelwright, and the couple had two children: a daughter, Annie, who died at the age of seven, and a son, Thomas, who became a priest. They were living on Brighton Street in the upstate New York city of Rochester when de Valera, the rebel on the run, came calling. The little boy she sent back with Uncle Ned was now a husband, a father, a politician and a notorious revolutionary.

The pair had a lot to catch up on. After the Easter Rising, Catherine had sought to clarify the name on his birth certificate in order to prove his American origins to the British.

That step later fuelled theories about whether she and Vivion Juan de Valera had been married at the time of their son's birth. Amongst others, de Valera's son, Terry, later worked diligently to try to prove his father was legitimate.

It was on Brighton Street where de Valera came closest to having his cover properly blown. All the false leads and canny propaganda counted for naught, once he was introduced to his cousin, Mary Connolly, inside the Wheelwright household. Within hours of his arrival, his loquacious cousin had told half the town that Catherine's boy, the one being written and wondered about in all the newspapers, was among them. Helpfully, Catherine herself had brazenly told the *Times* she hadn't even heard from her son since his imprisonment and discounted the idea he was even in the country.

For a man hoping to stay undercover, de Valera certainly got around in those first couple of weeks. He travelled to Boston to meet with his half-brother, Thomas (who'd also campaigned on his behalf after the Rising), and to Baltimore, Maryland, to call on Cardinal James Gibbons, the public face of Catholicism in America. He also went to Washington DC to personally thank Senator William Borah for proposing a resolution in the US Senate, requesting the Irish representatives be given a hearing at Versailles. Upon leaving Borah's office in the Capitol Building, he almost bumped into an American journalist to whom he'd given an interview back in Dublin.

A step in the wrong direction there would have ended the guessing game and deprived Harry Boland of his fun with the press. After days of speculation around New York, Boland finally made an official announcement on 22 June, declaring de Valera had, indeed, landed safely in America and was preparing for a coming-out party. His opening remarks were equal parts press release and constitutional justification.

'Eamon de Valera, President of the Irish Republic, is in his native city,' said Boland in an exchange with reporters in the lobby of the Waldorf-Astoria. 'He is here as the direct representative of the people of Ireland to the people of America. He is the elected President of the elected government of the Irish Nation, which has deliberately determined itself as a republic. He was chosen by adult suffrage through the peaceful democratic machinery of the ballot.

'Nominated by no small group of special interest, nor yet self-appointed, De Valera was freely chosen by a three to one majority of the Irish people, as the duly accredited spokesman of the Irish Nation. He is, therefore, entitled to speak for Ireland with an authority from the standpoint of democracy, equal to that of the President of the United States or the President of France or of Great Britain. President de Valera has undertaken this journey at the request of his Government.'

Boland made these bold statements in the lobby of the old Waldorf-Astoria, the largest and most luxurious hotel in the world. It boasted a ground-floor corridor that began on 34th Street, stretched for 300 feet, and became known as Peacock Alley because society belles used to strut their stuff along the impressive amber-marble walkway lined with luxurious chairs and sofas. A place to see and be seen in the most exquisite finery, it was the preferred digs of the monarchs of Europe when passing through New York. A caller to the hotel who famously requested to be put through to the king was coldly asked by the operator: 'Which one sir? We have two here today.'

For a group trying to convey some legitimacy to their enterprise and to lend a certain gravitas to the mission, it was also the logical, if slightly bizarre, choice for de Valera's lodgings and headquarters during his stay in America. In this gilded age palace, Boland spun lines about the extent of his knowledge of de Valera's whereabouts, offered a conspiratorial wink in response to questions about the circumstances of his arrival in the country, and outlined a brief biography. *The New York Times* reporter found him 'soft-spoken except when Great Britain and Ireland are mentioned. Then his broad, thick hands close, his chin is thrust forward and he isn't soft-spoken at all.' As the warm-up act, he gave an eloquent performance liberally mixing historical exactitude with obvious untruths.

Several times he professed to have no knowledge, at all, of de Valera's movements, yet he also assured reporters, in the next breath, that he definitely wasn't in New York, Philadelphia or within five miles of the hotel on that particular day. This duplicity was a continuance of the stringent effort to keep him out of the public eye until the time was right. This tactic extended even as far as McGarrity's *Irish Press* running a bizarre report on 21 June that de Valera was supposedly in Switzerland on secret business. As an attempt to distract from his true activities, the stratagem worked well.

Aside from coming laced with denials, Boland's own rhetoric was of a quality designed to constantly emphasise and re-emphasise the proper legal credentials of de Valera, and to counter any prevailing image of him as an improperly-franchised man on the run from a legitimate authority: the British government.

'His presence is intended to mark, in a conspicuous manner, the esteem in which the Irish people hold the people of America. His personal connection with this country, coupled with his well-known affection for it, in addition to his qualifications as a statesman, make him a suitable Ambassador. The visit of the President of the Irish Republic to America at this time is fraught with grave importance. He comes with a plan of reconstruction for Ireland, and will endeavour to interest American industries in the broad field of Irish commerce. He will float in America a bond issue of the Irish Republic that will start the new republic on a financial plane equaled by few and excelled by none. He will appeal to official America to stand by the Irish Republic and recognise it before the world…'

'President de Valera, having completed his work in Ireland, decided with the approval of his Cabinet, to come to America to plead the cause of Ireland before this great Republic. He had unbounded confidence in the American people and he feels certain that America will insist upon her war aims being enforced and he knows that America will not permit the people of Ireland to be the only white people in Europe, or in the world, condemned to slavery.'

Between Boland publicising de Valera's intention to make the Waldorf-Astoria his base and his actual arrival, more than a thousand telegrams and sacks of post for him arrived at hotel reception. One letter reached him, though it had been simply addressed to 'Hon. Eamonn (sic) de Valera, Elected President of Irish Republic, New York City.' The advance billing had worked to such good effect that every Irish man and woman in the five boroughs was talking of little else but the confirmation that de Valera was actually here, in their midst. The city hummed with rumours and exaggerations, tall tales and short stories about his whereabouts and ambitions, until the moment of revelation was finally at hand.

CHAPTER TWO

Press reports indicate Valera (sic) now in the United States. How did he get there? Is Department likely to get him a passport to return here?

- Cable from John W. Davis, American Ambassador in London to US State Department in Washington, 23 June 1919

Shortly before six o'clock in the evening of 23 June a dilapidated taxi cab pulled up in front of the Waldorf-Astoria Hotel with a sign saying 'Help the Irish Republic' pasted on to its windshield. Several hundred people – including an estimated thirty priests and one man clad in garish green from head to foot – already gathered around the entrance burst into cheers which ended as quickly as they began. At the hotel windows, staff and guests turned away disappointed too. De Valera wasn't in the car. The celebration had been premature. The mounted New York police officers in attendance were not yet required for crowd control. From within the building all the while could be heard the sound of an orchestra softly playing songs from the Great War.

Finally, an enormous touring car pulled up and there, plain, visible, and in the flesh at last, was de Valera. A mere glimpse of the man claiming to be President of Ireland sent the audience into a noisy frenzy. Flanked by a Carmelite priest, a pair of Judges and a who's who of Irish-American politicos, he emerged and doffed his Panama hat in acknowledgment of the warm welcome received.

Taller than most of those waiting to see him had expected, this bespectacled man stooped slightly as he moved, the way bigger people sometimes do to conceal their true height. Neatly coiffured, he cut a professorial figure in a staid tweed suit, offset by the fat knot of a blue tie. As he made for the door of the hotel, an elderly woman marched past the police cordon, flung her arms around his neck and after kissing him heartily, declared: 'Thank God you are here Mister President.'

He laughed, then appeared to quicken his step towards the entrance, and the crowd cheered some more. Inside, a fresh round of applause broke out among those politely sipping tea in the hotel lobby as the exotic new guest and his growing entourage strode past towards the elevator, on their way to the rooftop to pose for photographs.

In the most famous shot taken that day, de Valera stood in the centre of the frame directly behind John Devoy. His left hand was placed on the shoulder of the editor of the *Gaelic American* newspaper and unofficial leader of Irish-America in an affectionate manner that belied their future rancorous dealings. The pair were flanked on one side by Harry Boland and Liam Mellows, on the other by Diarmuid Lynch and Dr Patrick McCartan, another member of the first Dáil who'd preceded Boland as official envoy to the US.

It was quite an illustrious line-up. McCartan was a qualified doctor then editing McGarrity's *Irish Press*; Lynch, elected for Cork South-East in absentia in 1918, had reputedly been the last man to leave the GPO in the Easter Rising; Mellows, acknowledged as the leader of the 1916 exiles, commanded the Western Division of the IRA when it briefly took over Athenry during the same conflict, while Boland, another veteran of that rebellion was honorary secretary of Sinn Féin and has been described by some as the most influential Irish revolutionary of the period. All their CVs of course paled next to Devoy's, the only man in the picture not looking directly into the lens. With the solid grey beard and thatch of somebody approaching his seventy-seventh birthday, Devoy stared off to the right like a cantankerous grandfather underwhelmed by the excessive fussing of sons and grandsons milling around his house on a holiday.

The one-time French Foreign Legionnaire wore the solemn visage of a man who'd seen it all before throughout an epic career touching on almost every major event in the previous half-century of Irish history. A Fenian organiser and political prisoner, as far back as the 1860s, a key figure in planning the 1876 escape of six Fenians from an Australian penal colony aboard the *Catalpa*, and crucial adviser to Michael Davitt and Charles Stewart Parnell on 'The New Departure', Devoy had been so successful turning Clan na Gael into the voice of Irish-American nationalism that Padraig Pearse described him as 'The Greatest of all the Fenians'. Almost completely deaf, he'd reached a stage in life where he was a silent, frustrated bystander at meetings, yet still held enormous sway over his constituency through the pages of the *Gaelic American*.

The sepia portrait is of a group of men, full of purpose, united by a common cause that spans the generations and the ocean. Of course, the irony is the snapshot – and in particular the vignette of de Valera touching Devoy's shoulder – prefaces the inevitable split in the movement. Over the course of the next year, the united front put forward for the benefit of cameras would begin to crack rather spectacularly, Devoy and de Valera becoming such mortal enemies that the members of the supporting cast would have to choose between the two.

Ominously for their future relationship, one account of Devoy's first meeting with de Valera paints them both sitting in complete silence, each refusing to make the first move. Another theory holds Devoy was impressed with de Valera's performance on arrival but wasn't best pleased that upon setting foot in New York, he'd holed up with McGarrity rather than paying his respects first to the elder statesman. But nobody was envisaging any dark days ahead on this particular evening.

After a brief visit to the palatial suite that would be his home for most of the next eighteen months – New York papers would dub it 'The Irish White House' and de Valera 'the Irish Lincoln'– he repaired downstairs to the Gold Room, where around a hundred insiders had gathered for an unofficial reception that preceded his formal press conference. It was here he was formally introduced by Justice Daniel F. Cohalan, leading light in the Friends of Irish Freedom (FOIF). An organisation set up in America in 1916 'to encourage and assist any movement that will tend to bring about the national independence of Ireland', Lynch served as its secretary, but Devoy and Cohalan were the dominant figures.

'For the first time in Irish history we have the President of the

Irish Republic on American soil,' said Cohalan. 'He is here as representative of the Irish people. He represents no party nor creed. He is the chosen leader of the people of Ireland – President de Valera.'

Demonstrating the type of efficiency that would be a hallmark of the trip from this point on, typed-up copies of his first speech in America were distributed to journalists before de Valera ever opened his mouth, the diligence necessary he warned 'so that British propagandists cannot misinterpret what I said.'

He prefaced his initial remarks by apologising to the journalists present for the elaborate cat and mouse game surrounding his arrival and peregrinations to that point. Still, he couldn't resist teasing them and adding to the myth-making by playfully suggesting he might have come to the city by air rather than sea. Having further justified the secret portion of his sojourn by claiming it was private rather than state business, he announced his future availability and openly canvassed newspaper support for the cause. He flattered the reporters by telling them he knew well the best way to communicate with the people was through the medium of the printed word rather than via meetings with politicians.

With the reporters suitably buttered up, de Valera served the main course, a speech reiterating his position as the elected head of an elected Irish government, recounting the sins visited upon the country by the British, and declaring himself head of 'a republic established by the people in accordance with the principles of self-determination'. The latter phrase was chosen because it was the very cornerstone of the platform on which President Woodrow Wilson had placed America in the post-war negotiations at Versailles – the conference to which de Valera had been denied access.

He went on to draw an equally clever and lengthy analogy between the situation in Ireland in 1919 and that which pertained in America, before, and during, its own War of Independence from Britain, nearly a century and a half before. This was the recurring theme of an oration perfectly pitched to appeal to the locals' sense of historic liberty, and powerful enough to make the front page of the following morning's *New York Times* beneath the headline 'De Valera Comes Here To Get Help for Sinn Feiners'.

'The very same catch cries and the very same tools were used by the English government against the leaders of the American Revolution as are being used today against us,' said de Valera. 'But your leaders acted and so we have acted. They proclaimed their independence and their republic; we have proclaimed our independence and our republic. They fought; we have fought and we are still fighting. They were called traitors and murderers; so are we. The men who established your republic sought the aid of France. We seek the aid of America. It is to seek that aid that I am here and I'm confident that I shall not be disappointed.

'I come here entitled to speak for the Irish nation with an authority democratically as sound as that which President Wilson speaks for the United States or Lloyd George for England or Clemenceau for France. I come directly from the Irish people to the people of America, convinced that the American people, and consequently the American government, which as a government should reflect the people's will, will never consciously connive at, or allow itself to be made a party to, the suppression of the natural, God-given right of the Irish nation to its liberty. The great American nation, nurtured in liberty, has been liberty's most consistent champion. It has never been appealed to in vain.'

Beyond his pre-cooked monologue, there were questions from the floor too. Many of the press found him evasive, failing to elaborate too much on his future plans beyond an intention to visit Congress in Washington. Given his birth just a few blocks away, he was inevitably asked whether he was an American citizen? 'I ceased to be an American,' he replied, 'when I became a soldier of the Irish Republic.'

That sort of pithy remark exhilarated the crowd gathering for the post-press conference festivities. They deemed his debut performance such a critical success that before the official welcoming reception ended, Justice Cohalan requested all present to line-up and march in single file past the president so he could shake their hands. Some lingered longer than others. A priest from Bruree, the Limerick village where de Valera grew up, had too much drink on board and held him captive in a corner for a time.

Those in the inner circle repaired to de Valera's suite when the official reception ended where some, including Devoy, stayed talking and drinking until four in the morning. At one point in the evening however, McGarrity, Mellows, McCartan and de Valera left the hotel and took a spin through Central Park in an open-top Victoria carriage. After all the subterfuge, the gentlemen leisurely enjoyed the fresh air of a glorious summer's evening in New York. He was out in the open – at last. As they trundled along, de Valera rubbed the back of his head and half-sniggering, wondered aloud about what might happen when the news filtered back to Dublin that 'I came out in the press as President of the Republic.'

Following that tumultuous opening night, the extent to which the circumstances of de Valera's arrival in America continued to fascinate can be deduced from a story out of the upstate New York hamlet of Middletown. A week before de Valera's debut, residents there had been baffled by the arrival of an Irish stranger in their midst.

A mysterious salesman had suddenly appeared and caused quite a stir. A tall, clean-cut, lean character, he carried two large suitcases of Irish linen and cloth, was well supplied with cash, and gave his name as John James Mahoney. He did the rounds of the local tailors while holding forth in an Irish accent on the quality of the materials he was trying to peddle. Wanting to be above suspicion, he'd even visited police headquarters to show receipts for his goods, because a large quantity of similar linen had been recently stolen in nearby Maybrook. 'It will wear like a lady's tongue,' answered the inscrutable visitor when asked by a potential customer about the feel of one of the cloths.

Was this enigmatic Willy Loman with the thick brogue really Eamon de Valera on the way back to Manhattan from his mother's house in Rochester? That's what the people of Middletown wanted to know when they saw the headlines a few days later. The story is relevant only because it demonstrates the aura of intrigue that attended his every move in those first days after his emergence. Two hours north of Manhattan, Middletown created and held fast to its own mythical encounter with New York's flavour of the month. Others bought into even more outlandish tales.

One especially popular account of his journey had him escaping Ireland by seaplane, rendezvousing with a waiting yacht offshore, and then sailing across most of the Atlantic Ocean. The story continues that near the American coast, another seaplane came to shorten the last leg of the journey. A tad more dramatic than simply stowing away on an English liner staffed by men sympathetic to his cause, the racier version of events gained such credence that journalists repeatedly asked him to verify the story about the air-sea exploits.

His first response to the question was to smile enigmatically. What else could he have done upon hearing such a ludicrous yarn – in one telling the boat was actually described as the Irish presidential yacht – being appended to his legend. For fear of compromising the crew who had delivered him safely to New York, his initial grin gave way to the sort of evasion only likely to amplify the myth. 'I can't say one way or the other regarding any theories you may have of how I came here,' said de Valera. 'Because, you see, if I eliminated one after the other, you'd finally have me cornered on the right one – and that wouldn't do at all.'

He spoke while seated at a desk in the presidential suite at the hotel. Upon entering in early morning, reporters found him still in his shirt-sleeves; unlikely garb for a statesman about to conduct his first raft of interviews. De Valera apologised for his informality (the *New York Times* interpreted the lack of a jacket as a sign of his democratic nature!) by explaining he'd been attempting to negotiate a mountain of correspondence since first light. After the euphoric welcome and festive mood of his opening night on Broadway, there was now much less glamorous work to be done behind the scenes.

Just three days before the formal signing of the Treaty of Versailles in France, he handed New York journalists copies of a 17 May letter that the Government of Ireland had delivered to the French Prime Minister, Georges Clemenceau, in Paris, asserting that Britain had no right to commit Ireland to any international agreement. De Valera also vigorously denied reports that it was regular infusions of Russian and/or German money that had revitalised the Sinn Féin party. There were other matters to clear up too, not least of which was answering a few thorny questions about his own legal status.

Was the fugitive worried about the possibility of the US government doing England's bidding and placing him under arrest down the line? 'The American people would never stand by and see me persecuted by British tools. When I came over here, I had all intention of observing the laws of a government of the people, by the people and for the people. An Irishman will only refuse to obey the laws imposed upon him in his country by a foreign power.'

Did he see himself as an Irishman or an American then? 'I am an Irish citizen in so far as I am willing to lay down my life for the Irish Republic.'

Apart from clarifying his personal status again, there remained the small matter of the loan he wished to raise to fund the fledgling Republic. As soon as he announced the target figure of $5 million, questions arose about the legality of that enterprise because raising money to fund political aspirations in another country specifically violated US law. For the moment, he sidestepped the morality of the issue by declaring glibly: 'When municipal and international law conflict with humanity, I regard them as no law.'

Joe McGarrity and a famed New York lawyer named Martin Conboy would eventually come up with a legal formulation to circumvent the legal obstacles. For now though, the press seemed more concerned with the exact purposes to which any cash might be put. Was the money destined for Sinn Féin's own coffers to help it dominate Irish politics? Could he assure Americans it wouldn't be used to purchase guns and ammo? 'The money is not to be used for any party but for the development of the Irish commonwealth,' he explained. 'We will have to equip consulates and embassies in the various countries, France and Switzerland. The money will not be used as former money raised in America was used – for political fights between parties. It will be used for purely national purposes.' He expanded the parameters of the loan by declaring portions of it might also be raised in Australia and Canada, countries he asserted contained plenty of supporters of the Irish cause. The mere mention of Canada in the context of the loan raised the unfortunate spectre of a peculiar episode from Ireland's recent past, one that involved both fund-raising and military action.

In 1866 a group of Fenians in America had raised $500,000 through a bond issue in $20 denominations, and used it to finance an ill-fated invasion of Canada by an army made up largely of Irish veterans of the American Civil War. Intended to strike a blow against the British Crown, the attack on the colony (according to popular lore the Battle of Windmill consisted of a lot more wind than mill) degenerated into something of a farce, a couple of days after the invaders had planted a Fenian flag in Fort Erie, Ontario.

Originally sold to the public as an investment to be redeemed six months after Ireland gained its independence, the Fenian bonds which financed the whole imbroglio presented a serious conundrum for de Valera. If Ireland was now, indeed, a republic as he claimed, would its government be prepared to pay up to the subscribers from half a century previous? 'We acknowledge the indebtness of the Irish nation,' said de Valera. 'And the payments will be met out of the new bond issue. Or notes of the present bond issue will be exchanged for the old bonds.'

While de Valera entertained journalists, councillors down at New York City Hall unanimously adopted a resolution offering him the freedom of his hometown. Plans were also announced for a nationwide tour to take him across the country, hopefully garnering recognition at every turn. An invitation to speak at a mass meeting at Fenway Park, in Boston, the following Sunday was eagerly accepted and, in between entertaining a constant stream of visitors to his quarters, he continued to meet every reporter's query with measured and precise responses, designed to best explain Ireland's quandary to the American audience.

'Today, Ireland is being governed absolutely for the benefit of England. What news is received in this country regarding Ireland is sent to you through tainted channels. The British Government by military force virtually has possession of the machinery of the government and prevents our Deputies from carrying out their form of government. The occupation of Ireland by the British is similar to what the German occupation of Belgium was – they control the machinery of government by military force.

'Our first duty as the elected Government of the Irish people will be to make clear to the world the position in which Ireland now stands. There is in Ireland at this moment only one lawful authority, and that authority is the elected government of the Irish Republic....'

Over those crucial first few days, de Valera was constantly on message, reiterating again and again for the American press the extent of the legal and moral authority he claimed to possess. Such diligent repetition was necessary because, for all the boisterous cheerleading of an Irish-American community agog at his arrival, there was no shortage of those willing to question his position and deny his right to represent anybody.

Reverend DD Irvine, pastor of the First Methodist Episcopal Church of Richmond Hill and a transplanted native of Bangor, County Down, telegrammed the Waldorf-Astoria, challenging de Valera to a public debate about 'the Irish Republic'. Somebody who would prove a dogged opponent of the republican cause throughout the visit, Irvine was eventually removed from his own position for 'immoral behaviour' in 1921. Ironically, one of his misdemeanours was using the office from which he published an anti-Sinn Féin paper for liaisons with a woman, who was not his wife.

There were other critics too. In an editorial, *The New York Times* lambasted de Valera for comparing Ireland's situation to those of newly-liberated countries, like Poland, Greece and Hungary, arguing that he possessed no moral right to speak of those situations when he advocated remaining apart from their struggle during World War I.

'Poland has been freed from alien rule, Greece has been freed from an autocrat, certain fragments of the Latin races have been freed from the Hapsburgs within the last two years,' wrote the *Times*. 'Where was the Irish Republic in those days? Many thousands of Irishmen – men like Tom Kettle and William Redmond – were dying for the freedom of the world; and for the sake of those men, if for no other reason, justice is due to Ireland. But where was the Irish Republic? The Irish Republic came in on what looked like the winning side; and now that contrary to all expectation of those days, the Kaiser has been beaten, it is still trying to be on the side of the winners.'

The letters page of the same paper also played host to a variety of censorious comment. Sir Charles Carrick Allom, a renowned English architect and airplane manufacturer, who'd been knighted for his work on Buckingham Palace, wrote a bracing attack on de Valera and the Roman Catholic priests he claimed were devoted to teaching sedition in Ireland. Two days after de Valera was feted at the Waldorf-Astoria, Allom was ejected from the St Regis Hotel following a loud argument in the lobby with a pair of sixteen-year-old girls who had set up a stand there to collect for Clan na Gael's Irish Victory Fund. Angry at a Sinn Féin emblem on full display, Allom asked to see the manager and discovered, to his chagrin, the hotel was staffed and run by people sympathetic to the cause he abhorred.

Just a few hours after that fracas, at a location a mere thirty blocks to the south of the hotel, de Valera was guest of honour at the graduation ceremony in the Grammar School attached to the Carmelite Priory on 29th Street. Unremarkable from the outside, the Priory was an institution that, for generations, had offered shelter and succour to Irish rebels passing through New

York, served as a temporary arsenal for weapons destined for the boat to Ireland, and would eventually be described by de Valera himself as 'the cradle of Irish independence'. It was even where he slept the night before his debut at the Waldorf-Astoria.

Armagh-born Fr Peter Magennis was rector of the parish, national President of the Friends of Irish Freedom, and a vigorous campaigner for all things related to his homeland. When Sean Nunan, clerk of Dáil Éireann, arrived in New York off the *SS Aquitania* on 22 June (to take up a role as de Valera's secretary) and couldn't locate Harry Boland, he was directed to the Priory and given bed and board until the party met him there. Predictably then, de Valera's presence at the graduation was treated with great pomp, and his arrival heralded by thousands outside the auditorium waving Irish and American flags in greeting.

'Many of your names are Irish and from that I know that either your parents or their parents or more remote ancestors came from Ireland,' said de Valera to the students sitting before him. 'For seven hundred and fifty years, Ireland, the home from which your people first came, has been struggling to win the kind of freedom that you enjoy, just think of it, three hundred years before Columbus discovered America…I come here to ask the people of America to help.'

That same day, Woodrow Wilson's private secretary Joseph P. Tumulty had sent a cable to the American president in Paris. It contained a couple of *New York* press reports which were advocating some sort of independence for Ireland and a note: 'Frankly, this represents the opinion of the average man in America, without regard to race or religion. The arrival of De

Valera (sic) in America is going to intensify the feeling and the Republicans will take full advantage of it. Now that the League of Nations is on its feet, we should take the lead in this matter.'

Tumulty was right. The arrival of de Valera was about to bring all sorts of attention to the Irish cause. Rather quickly.

CHAPTER THREE

That we declare ourselves unreservedly in favour of the independence of Ireland and demand that our government recognise the Irish Republic.

– resolution passed at Fenway Park, 29 June 1919

All Saturday afternoon long, people had been gathering in and around Boston's South Station. They'd travelled from every corner of the city, and as the crowd thickened in the Great Room, it became apparent the station once regarded as the largest in the world would not be sufficient to hold the number of people arriving in droves. Some wore straw hats and clothes usually only taken out of the wardrobe on Sunday mornings for mass. A lot of them were still carrying the sweat and grime of a day's work; afraid to go home and change lest they miss the show in the interim.

By the time the clock on the granite façade above the front entrance ticked past six, there were an estimated crowd of 25,000 milling around, inside and out; an excited mob desperately waiting for the arrival of this man they'd been hearing of since 1916, and reading avidly about for the past few days. Eventually, some could stand it no more. A couple of hundred of the most anxious managed to break through the security cordon of police and made their way down the side of the train tracks. It was dangerous – stupid even. But they wanted to get the first glimpse of the Knickerbocker Express carrying de Valera from New York. They wanted to see the myth made flesh.

The 1:00pm out of Grand Central was running approximately thirty minutes behind schedule, through no fault of the driver. The delay was the result of carrying an in-demand passenger up through the towns and cities of New England. At New London, Connecticut, a routine stop turned into an impromptu pep rally when 1,000, or so, members of the FOIF swarmed de Valera's carriage and demanded a speech. How could he refuse a group who had met his train with a flurry of Irish and American flags? Following a short introduction *as Gaeilge*, he segued into English for a brief oration punctuated by shouts from the crowd along the platform.

'I've been to Old London and I'm glad to be in New London. I knew that Ireland had many friends in this country but I never knew until I got here how widespread the feeling among the American people was that Ireland is entitled to her liberty. You are a liberty-loving people....'

At this juncture, a voice declared 'We'll free Ireland' and everybody present roared their approval. After a pause to allow the cheering to die down, de Valera pressed on.

'We understood in Ireland that the people of America entered the war to make democracy safe for the world and to free small nations which were struggling to be free. We knew that at least one of America's associates in that war was not sincere in her protestations about freedom for small nations, and that is the reason why we refused to believe her word. England didn't have to go to war to free one small nation. She could have set Ireland free without entering a foreign war if she wanted to.'

'To Hell with England,' went the cry from the throng surrounding him, and the cheering was amplified once more. Finally, de Valera, carrying an enormous bouquet of yellow and white roses, presented to him by the city Mayor Frank Morgan, shook as many outstretched hands as he could, before clambering back on board the train to continue his journey north – his every step dogged by more backslapping and applause.

He retreated from the tumult to the relative safety of the car occupied by his entourage. Apart from the ubiquitous Harry Boland, there was Sean Nunan, Miss Martin, an American woman retained as official stenographer during this portion of the trip, Joseph F. O'Connell, a former Democratic Congressman for Boston who'd been sent to New York as envoy of the Fenway Park organising committee, and Reverend Thomas J. Wheelwright, de Valera's half-brother.

Any hope of spending the journey working on his speech was undermined by the alacrity with which word of his presence spread through the train once it left New York. There had been a steady stream of visitors wanting to shake his hand and make his acquaintance. A visit to the dining car gave him further evidence of his growing fame, his fellow diners staring at the new celebrity in their midst.

If the New London cameo had put the Express behind schedule, the crowd waiting at Providence, an hour or so up the tracks, was three times as large. However, the Rhode Island authorities had been a little more safety conscious and better-prepared.

They had restricted those trying to see de Valera to a fenced-off area and only official members of the Providence welcoming committee were allowed inside the barrier to gain access to the train. They were soon joined inside the velvet rope by a large contingent of Boston politicos and dignitaries, who'd travelled down to accompany their distinguished visitor back up north to South Station, in Boston.

Some of the political representatives probably made the journey out of pragmatic motives. What better way to impress constituents than for them to see their local councillor exiting the train on the shoulder of the man of the hour? Many though had purer motivations. When Dr James T. Gallagher, a veteran of Irish causes through the decades, was introduced to de Valera, tears ran down his cheeks as he proclaimed: 'Thank God I've lived to see a President of Ireland. God Bless you.'

There was no shortage of blessings or of those qualified to give them. A large gaggle of priests had boarded at Providence. Among them was Fr Liam O'Connell, of Philadelphia, who'd made the expedition from his home town to personally extend the best wishes of the clergy from that city.

With the security arrangements precluding him from properly alighting to answer the repeated calls for a speech from those stranded on the outside looking in, de Valera moved to the back of the train from where he spoke briefly to a small group of Rhode Islanders who'd gathered there. When it came time for the train to continue on its way, he waved theatrically to those precluded from getting close enough to hear him and the chaos was such many of the Providence officials found themselves unable to disembark. They were carried off to Boston, where by now South Station was bulging at the seams.

Twenty minutes before seven, the man of the moment finally reached his destination but it was well past the hour by the time most of the crowd even caught a glimpse of him. Upon reaching the door of the carriage, de Valera was met by a phalanx of photographers with still and moving cameras, recording umpteen handshakes with various Boston luminaries. He stood on the top step posing for pictures for a full fifteen minutes, satisfying the media's demands. In some photographs, he wore the rigor mortis grin of somebody newly conscious of the importance of public image. In others, the warmth of his smile reeks of a man happy with his move from the shadows and the clandestine to the glare of the flash bulbs and spotlights.

After the barrage of cameras, de Valera began the long march towards his car. A band led the way but even their lusty rendition of 'Amhrán na bhFiann' (the Irish national anthem) was almost drowned out by the rousing ovation sound-tracking his every step.

The formalities of the occasion weren't to everybody's liking and merely applauding wouldn't do for those intent on shaking his hand or slapping his back. Many in the crowd repeatedly rushed the police line to try to get a close-up look at their hero. These surges were contained and the constabulary finally delivered the tall, still smiling figure to the automobile waiting outside. The size of the multitude surrounding the vehicle can be gleaned from the fact the following morning's *Boston Globe* photograph of the event carried a helpful arrow pointing to the exact spot in the heaving mass where the car was located.

'It was with the greatest difficulty that the distinguished

visitor was gotten through the crowd,' wrote M.E. Hennessy in the *Boston Globe*. 'The police did their best to restore some kind of order in the carriage concourse but men and women lost their heads and crowded about his motor car. Finally the start was made and the motor procession crept through the immense throng which filled Summer Street and Dewey Square until there was barely room enough for the autos to proceed…The women marched with the men in the streets, following his auto and cheering him at every step, waving Irish and American flags, and shouting in English and Irish: "Welcome! A thousand welcomes to Boston! God bless and preserve Ireland's saviour and leader".'

Evincing a teacher's typical eye for a learning opportunity, de Valera asked the Americans sharing the car ride with him if they had recognised the air being played by the band back at the station. When they confessed ignorance, he related the story of the provenance of 'Amhrán na bhFiann' and how it had come to be regarded by the people as the national anthem of the nation that wasn't of course yet a nation in the eyes of the world.

At the entrance to the Copley-Plaza Hotel, there was more mayhem. An estimated 6,000 had eschewed the South Station arrival in order to stake out the best spots at the venue that would play host to a banquet in his honour that evening. This crowd was soon joined by thousands more who'd accompanied the motorcade, and by the time de Valera reached the sanctuary of his room, he was feeling the ill-effects of all this adulation. He told Joseph F. O'Connell his right hand was actually hurting from the intensity of all the handshakes. O'Connell duly noted his complaint and the welcoming committee soon made an announcement requesting people: 'not to express in their hand-clasp with President de Valera all their enthusiasm for the cause.'

De Valera needed to be in peak condition for his first major public speech of the campaign the following afternoon at Fenway Park. Built by Charles E. Logue, a Derry-born contractor, it was ordinarily home to the Boston Red Sox, who during the 1919 season drew an average of around 6,000 fans to games. Even the day nine months earlier when the team, including one Babe Ruth, clinched the World Series with a 2-1 victory over the Chicago Cubs, just over 15,000 were present to celebrate what would be its last such triumph for nearly nine decades.

For the appearance of de Valera at a public rally organised at less than a week's notice however, it was still expected that maybe 25,000 people might show up come Sunday afternoon, this being the self-styled most Irish town in America, after all. By lunchtime on what turned out to a perfect summer's day, it became clear from the enormous throngs milling along Lans-downe, Van Ness and Jersey Streets that as many as twice that number were going to attend.

In the seven years since it opened for business, Fenway had never hosted anything quite like this. A full hour before the scheduled start of 3.00pm, police began to block off entrances for fear too many people were pushing their way into the venue. Thousands were already too late for the show and confined to eavesdropping the action from outside; disappointed that they missed a colourful and unique spectacle.

Many of those standing on the green sward in the outfield carried signs voicing their support for Ireland or displeasure with England. 'England is disqualified and unfit to rule Ireland' read the banner from the Boston Gaelic School Society. 'We demand England withdraw 140,000 soldiers from Ireland' went another. Everywhere, tricolours and stars and stripes fluttered cheek by jowl. It seemed no group saw fit to parade into the venue without prominently waving both flags, fully symbolising their twin allegiances.

All over the stadium, Irish Volunteer Bands from every corner of New England were in full voice. For a time, each played to their own tune, causing quite a cacophony until somebody in authority finally managed to coalesce their efforts. Together, they then launched into a symphony of greatest Irish hits that only served to inflame the passions of the waiting attendance further.

At various junctures, dozens of men in uniform – from organisations like Charlestown's John Boyle O'Reilly Guards and Lowell's Wolfe Tone, Sheridan and Meagher Guards – stood anxiously, awaiting the arrival of the keynote speaker. Several of these Irish societies were unable to fulfill their great ambition of forming a guard of honour through which the star might walk to the stage that had been erected over home plate. Their best efforts were thwarted by the unruliness of a crowd electrified by the sudden sight of three mounted policemen beginning to clear the narrowest pathway to allow de Valera and the welcoming committee to navigate through the multitude.

As they negotiated the narrow canyon of people, the crowd surged forward from both sides to try to catch a glimpse of their hero. Women fainted in the crush, several appeals were made to try to calm the masses, yet still they pressed forward. Even when de Valera finally reached the stage, reporters stationed at tables directly in front of him found themselves immediately under siege as men clambered over them in a quest to get ever closer to the action.

Once some sort of order was restored, de Valera took his seat on a platform boasting a soldier on each side. One bore aloft a tattered stars and stripes carried by the 101st Division when it fought the Germans at Argonne, in France, the previous year, the other held fast to a tricolour. If the presence of the flags denoting the nation of his birth and the nation which he now claimed to lead made the location especially fitting, the self-styled President of Ireland was actually mixing in rather nefarious company. In a city where politics has always been something of a bloodsport, the line-up of esteemed Bostonian dignitaries alongside him on the stand represented a veritable rogues' gallery.

District Attorney Joseph C. Pelletier was already under investigation and would eventually be disbarred by the Massachusetts Supreme Court for criminal conspiracy. Former Mayor James Curley was the son of Galwegian immigrants whose nickname 'The Rascal King' only hinted at the corruption and scandal that attended every stage of his illustrious political career. Curley's successor was on the podium too, one Andrew Peters. An undistinguished holder of the office, Mayor Peters would earn a dubious footnote when he was later exposed as a paedophile. As he sat in Fenway that day, he was already sexually involved with a twelve-year-old girl.

They weren't the only ones with colourful reputations surrounding de Valera either. Dan Coakley, a prominent member of the Boston Bar Association, had earned a fortune of money and the soubriquet of 'The Knave of Boston' through his devotion to the art of bribery. His particular modus operandi was luring extremely wealthy men into compromising positions with prostitutes and then getting photographs of the scene. Coakley was the first official to speak. He rose and introduced Thomas H. Mahoney as the presiding officer of the meeting.

In the middle of this motley crew then sat de Valera, smiling in most photographs, obviously and inevitably impressed by the enormous show they were staging in his honour. How much did he know of the personal foibles of the characters in his midst? Well, the quality of de Valera and Boland's intelligence about so much else in Irish-America suggests they must have realised they weren't exactly hanging with choirboys. Given the dimensions of this theatrical event he may not, under the circumstances, have been able to afford to care about the morality of the men behind it. This lavish promotion garnered international headlines and the perfect high-profile start to his trip. That the individuals responsible weren't the most wholesome bunch didn't figure in the contemporary newspaper reports.

'To say that it was thrilling is putting it mildly – it was electric,' wrote A.J. Philpott in the *Boston Globe*. 'The heart and the head of the people of Irish blood were in it. In Eamonn (sic) de Valera was personified the fulfillment of their hopes, and the very mystery which attaches to this man, who was comparatively unheard of until recently, somehow fulfilled the dreams of the race – that some great figure would arise at the crucial moment and lead Ireland to freedom. In the thoughtful, militant, cleancut face and gaunt personality of de Valera, there is somehow also personified that new spirit which has come to Irishmen everywhere in which the demand has superseded the appeal for justice in Ireland.'

The almost-religious flavour of Philpott's appraisal was in keeping with the mood of the occasion. There was no shortage of clerical input.

'Fellow Americans – Before proceeding to say prayer I would wish to convey to the President of the Irish Republic the kindest wishes, the highest consideration and the blessing of his Eminence, the Cardinal Archbishop of Boston, the great Irish leader and prelate,' said Fr Philip O'Donnell reciting the opening prayer as representative of Cardinal O'Connell, who had a prior engagement in Chicago that weekend.

'We thank thee O God, father of our people, that we have lived to witness this day and are able to be here in the great historic city of Boston to have heard the President of the great Irish republic. Our fathers longed and prayed and suffered for this day. All of us from childhood days have knelt and prayed to thee O god that some day the land of our race and the cradle of the race might be free and independent among the nations of the world; and today we thank thee O God that we are so near to the consummation of those wishes and those prayers…

…There is no other nation whose people have gone out in the world and spread the religion of Christ as have the people of the Irish race. Even in the days of her greatest suffering, the sons and daughters of Ireland went out to educate the world and teach them the knowledge of their Heavenly Father. We ask Thee in the name of all that is pure and holy to favour this people, who from the beginning have believed in the doctrine that the love of country is one with the love of God, and who have set an example of piety and virtue to all other races of the earth. Amen.'

This abridged version of O'Donnell's supplication captures the essence of a prayer that set the tone for so much of the speechifying that followed. In a brief offering, Mahoney made the first of many references to Boston's outsized role in American history, and also took a couple of crowd-pleasing swipes at the proposed League of Nations and England's putative place therein. Mayor Peters (watched by his doting wife Martha, and interrupted briefly by the thunderous sound of tables collapsing beneath the weight of spectators) continued to bang the drum about Boston's contribution to the fight for freedom and, at one point in his soliloquy, turned to de Valera to assure him he was welcome in the city.

The similarities between Ireland's struggles and America's own quest for independence nearly a century and a half before were echoed again and again. Former Democratic Congressman Eugene F. Kinkead (a native of Cork and a major in the American military intelligence division during World War I) placed the Irish cause in the context of the Paris Peace Conference, and pointed out how Irish independence was in keeping with President Woodrow Wilson's beloved doctrine of self-determination. Harry Boland went to one of Wilson's predecessors in his own particularly feisty contribution to the fare.

'We come to you to ask you to see to it that we are not the only white race condemned to slavery,' said Boland, introduced to rapturous applause as a member of the Irish parliament, director of elections and somebody who had fought alongside Padraig Pearse in 1916. 'We have come here to rouse the Irish people in America and to bring them to reclaim the debt which America owes Ireland. It is a grand thing to be a successful rebel. [George] Washington in his day was a rebel. Washington in his day was an anarchist…Washington was all that was evil in England, just as our president is the worst evil in the English empire today. Yet, Washington won, was a successful rebel and today is proclaimed the father of his country.'

Boland tugged at the heart strings and most probably could be accused of flirting with racism by dropping the white slavery line, but it was Senator David I. Walsh who stole the show from de Valera. The son of Irish emigrants, Walsh was the first Irish Catholic to reach the Senate from Massachusetts, had previously been the first Irish Catholic to govern the state, and during a quarter of a century in Washington was fervently pro-Irish. One historian described him as possessing a 'Boston Irish Catholic's hatred of perfidious Albion'. This was certainly a day when he lived up that billing.

'As I looked for the first time in the face of that great leader, my mind went back to another great man,' said Walsh, recalling a meeting with de Valera during his pre-coming out visit to Washington. 'There was something about that form. There was something about that face. There was something about that intellect. There was something about his cause that made me think of him as I thought of that great American who 57 years ago came into American life and by his strength and leadership broke the shackles of slavery of 3,000,000 black men. So the Lincoln of Ireland will take the shackles of tyranny from the limbs of the sons of Ireland. Thin and lean in stature, angular in form and features, bright and clear in intellect, born in lowly, humble circumstances, you can be the next Lincoln…'

For this sort of rhetoric and a whole lot more about how Ireland's cause should be America's too, Walsh earned enormous applause and piqued the interest of the British secret service. According to one biography, the British began keeping a file on him from that point on. After he was exposed as a regular visitor to a gay brothel in Brooklyn in 1942 – an outing that played some part in him losing his Senate seat four years later – one conspiracy placed British spies at the centre of the scandal. That was a story for another day. For this one, Walsh had whipped the crowd into a frenzy, his delivery and content pitched so perfectly that the only problem was de Valera subsequently failed to match his performance and was actually outshone by the warm-up act.

Before he could even try to match Walsh's epic performance, de Valera had to wait some more. John H.H. MacNamee, a former mayor of Cambridge, Massachusetts, and Treasurer of the Irish Victory Fund announced – just to make the event even more like mass – a collection was to take place. The Haverhill Friends of Irish Freedom handed over a cheque for $10,000. The Fitchburg Friends' branch managed a quarter of that sum. For smaller denominations to go towards the Fund, established earlier that year for 'educational' purposes, a hundred women were then dispatched through the crowd to gather contributions.

Prior to beginning his prepared remarks, de Valera admitted the quality of the previous orators made him briefly consider not speaking at all. Of course, that was not an option to the tall, slender figure now barely visible to those spectators bobbing up and down in the sea of straw hats that stretched to every corner of the stadium. The impressive view from the dais led him to apologise in advance that his voice would not carry to the outer reaches of the venue. After a cursory nod to the magnificence of the crowd, he began his own attempt to make headlines.

'I do not fear for a moment that the people of America will make a shuttlecock of our cause, to pass it from party to party. I know they will not do this. I believe that Americans can differ as to the policies about America but they are united in the cause of liberty. And I came here to this grand free land knowing that if the Irish question were by any means to be made a question of parties, it would be only in this sense that the parties vie with each other as in who could help Ireland best? Now I shall not attempt to plead Ireland's cause with you. It was sweet to my own ears, sweeter than I could tell you, to listen to Ireland's cause being pleaded by Americans, and I hope that on all the platforms on which I shall stand it will be the people of America pleading Ireland's cause, and I shall be there only to represent Ireland.'

At one point, he made an issue of telling the audience he was reading directly from the page for fear of being misquoted. Again and again throughout his time in America, he would constantly remind audiences that Britain was capable of twisting his words. The main thrust of his argument though centred on the signing of the Versailles Treaty. Since it promised to protect each member against external aggressors, Article X of that agreement was perceived by de Valera as guaranteeing England's right to rule Ireland. He didn't much care for a League of Nations without Ireland involved either.

'Peace was nominally signed between the two great countries yesterday – I think this was what I heard shouted out in New

York by a newsboy before I left – peace that will cost us 20 wars instead of the one it nominally ended. The British minister said a few days ago that there were 23 wars going on at the present time, and this is the peace treaty that the world has been asked to look forward to as the treaty that would establish everlasting peace. It is a mere mockery, and it will remain this unless America takes up the responsibility for the world to which her traditions entitle her, that at this moment is freely offered to her by the common consent of mankind. The present opportunity is never likely to occur again. The idea of a community of nations recognising a common law and a common right, ending wars among nations as municipal law has ended private war among individuals, is today a possibility, if America does what the people of the world pray and expect America will do.

'To lose this moment would be a disaster that it would be impossible to repair. If America disappoints, then the right-minded, the good and the just in the world will be thrown back into a cynical and sullen despair. Democracy dies or else goes mad. A new 'holy alliance' cannot save democracy. A just League of Nations founded on the only basis on which it can be just – the equality of right among nations, small no less than great – can. America can see to it that such a League is set up and set up now. She is strong enough and it is her right, in consequence of the explicit terms on which she entered the war.'

His thoughts on the Paris Treaty and his description of America as 'the hope of the world' led the coverage in the following morning's *Boston Globe* and *The New York Times*. It was the perfect ending to a tumultuous week that began with wild rumours of de Valera's whereabouts, and ended with him feted by the people of Boston in perhaps the most overt display of Irish-American unity in history.

The morning after Fenway, de Valera's dance card remained full. After several delays prompted by well-wishers arriving at the hotel trying to meet him, he departed the Copley-Plaza in a convoy of seven cars. His vehicle was at the front, the American flag billowing on one flank, the Irish tricolour on the other, the by-now familiar symbols of the relationship he wanted to foster between the countries. His first stop was across the Charles River, a formal welcome reception in his honour at Cambridge city hall where the inevitable mob of supporters surrounded the cortege upon arrival.

Between that engagement and fulfilling an invitation to speak at the Massachusetts State Legislature, he took in several sites around the Boston hinterland that boasted links to the American Revolution. A natural tourist's impulse? Hardly. Given how much Boland and himself had sought to establish the parallels between America's historic struggle for independence and Ireland's present in their speeches the previous day, this was smart politics. What better way to bolster the links than to be seen paying homage at some of these hallowed grounds?

Beyond clever tactics, it was also good copy for the journalists accompanying him. Every stop served only to reiterate how de Valera and the movement he represented were merely tracing the footsteps of so many American icons.

He laid a wreath by the Washington Elm, the tree in Cambridge Common beneath which George Washington had taken formal control of the Troops of the United Provinces of North America on 3 July 1775. Another wreath was left at the

Minutemen Monument, on the green in the town of Lexington, commemorating the Massachusetts militia who famously pledged to be ready to fight the British at a moment's notice. Yet another flower arrangement was taken out when the party reached Bunker Hill, the spot where in defeat the Americans had inflicted huge casualties on the British and established, for once and for all, their own fighting credentials.

It was at Bunker Hill, surrounded by children, some of whom were holding the hem of his coat, that de Valera planted a wreath decorated with Irish and American flags at the base of the monument. In a delicate piece of theatre, he then produced a blank card from his pocket, etched the date in the top corner and wrote the sentence 'The liberties of my country are safe' beneath. He signed his name and carefully attached the card to the flowers. The fact he had inked the very words Washington uttered upon hearing the militia had fought the British made it into the following morning's papers. Contrived or not, that little dramatic cameo was further amplified by one of his pithier quotes.

Towards the end of a short address giving tribute to the Irish who had died for the cause of American freedom, he returned to the recurring theme of the trip. 'Ireland has had her Bunker Hill, she now awaits her Yorktown.'

Invoking the location of the decisive Franco-American victory over the British in the Revolutionary War was in keeping with his mood. At the state legislature – where he encountered boisterous scenes on the floor of the house as senators and congressmen enthusiastically waved tricolours and led cheers for the new republic – de Valera cited Robert Emmet, the 1848 and 1867 insurrections, and the events of Easter Week by way of illustrating Ireland's repeated attempts at replicating America's triumph. He also reminded his audience the union between Britain and Ireland was not a voluntary one.

'There is no question of Ireland's secession. If a young lady were carried into the harem of a Turkish chief and she tried to get a release, would you call it a trial for divorce?' That was one of his snappier lines. The rest of the speech contained the usual diet of heavyweight geo-political analysis.

'When you speak of the Ulster question, that means a small fraction of Ulster, not half of Ulster, a matter of four counties in Ireland where the opponents of a republic are in a majority. The ideal democracy contends that majorities must rule. I hold that minorities have their rights, and that when a minority is nervous or anxious about the rights being interfered with, it has the right to look for guarantees from the majority. But it has no right to impose or try to impose a permanent veto on the will of the majority. It is pretended that this question is a religious question. I deny it. There is no question of religious differences dividing us in Ireland.

'It happens that the majority of that minority are Protestants; it happens that the majority of the majority are Catholics. But there is surely nobody going to say that they are back in the old days of religious prejudice. That would have died all over the world were it not England's special interest to keep it alive. England has quite continually, by all the artifices she could command, tried to keep it alive in Ireland. But I am happy to tell you she has not succeeded. We are getting more and more to regard ourselves as brothers, with a common country to love and a common country to serve. The proclamation of the Irish republic guarantees equality of rights without consideration of party, class or religion to every citizen of the Irish nation...'

Watching all this from the overcrowded public gallery was John H. Bartlett, Governor of New Hampshire. He had accompanied de Valera throughout the day and once all engagements were fulfilled, the official convoy headed north to spend the night in Bartlett's home state. Among those travelling in the party were Inspectors Smith and Concannon of the Boston police department. From the moment he stepped off the train at South Street, they had been by his side as the official security detail. More than once, he pointed out this made a huge change from having police hunting him down like a criminal in other countries. If the presence of two armed guards appeared like the accoutrement of a head of state, de Valera also somehow succeeded on his trip through New England in leaving the impression he was a man of the people.

'There is a simplicity to him that is very marked,' wrote James T. Sullivan in a gushing column in the following Saturday's *Boston Globe*. 'He was right at home with the women and children at Washington Elm...While hearty welcomes please him, he is not seeking adulation. That is the secret of his success. He is at home with the peasantry and they are at home in his presence. He has their confidence; they have his. He is fighting their cause and is not concerned with what enemies say about him. He considers himself a means to an end.'

CHAPTER FOUR

The whole trouble is to organise the sympathy for our cause which is widespread and harness it to a definite purpose. The press is not hostile but the English are massing their forces against us. I have to watch W (President Woodrow Wilson) very carefully. He could do us great damage were he to come out openly hostile. I am waiting till we have got the people properly first – then were he even to attack it would not be deadly…

**– Letter from Eamon de Valera to Arthur Griffith,
9 July 1919**

The car bearing President Woodrow Wilson on his homecoming parade through New York slowly wended its way along Fifth Avenue, heading towards a grand reception in his honour at Carnegie Hall. Fresh off the *USS George Washington* from France, Wilson cut a triumphant figure in a silk top hat and black tails, standing up in the back seat to acknowledge the adoring crowds that lined the Manhattan streets. The city was in a celebratory mood with hundreds of thousands of people gathering to pay tribute to the man credited with winning the war and bringing peace to the world. The crowd roared as the car moved, and children were lifted onto shoulders to catch a glimpse of the beaming hero as he passed by, repeatedly doffing his hat.

De Valera watched the festivities from a window of the Waldorf-Astoria on 8 July, just yards away from the party, far removed from the mood. He was sitting at a table with Liam Mellows, Frank P. Walsh, a labour lawyer from Kansas City, and Edward F. Dunne, former Governor of Illinois. Still smarting from the American President's refusal to admit an Irish contingent to the Paris Peace Conference, this small gathering was discussing the wider political implications of the celebration outside.

Dunne and Walsh had formed two-thirds of a committee called the American Commission for Irish Independence, which had been dispatched to France earlier in the year to try to negotiate safe conduct for a delegation of de Valera, Arthur Griffith and Count Plunkett to gain a hearing for the Irish claim. Blame for their failure to do so was placed largely at Wilson's door. The president had been unwilling to apply the principle of self-determination – a keynote in his iconic Fourteen Points speech to the US Congress back in January 1918 – to the Irish case.

A committed Anglophile, Wilson had a troubled history with the Irish-American community. Always regarded as excessively pro-English, many resented his attacks on the culture of hyphenism among immigrants during the 1916 presidential campaign, and also felt he could have done more to assist the cause of those captured during the Easter Rising. Even before heading to Europe, Walsh had been part of an Irish-American committee that met Wilson at the Metropolitan Opera House to personally beseech him to introduce the Irish question on the agenda in

France. He hadn't promised the representatives anything on that occasion and was as good as his word.

There's a school of thought that argues Wilson had come to think the Irish question was an internal affair to be resolved by the British Empire, not to be interfered with by foreigners, and definitely not the business of a conference to redraw the map of Europe. Whether he had any real intention of ever raising the touchy subject at the negotiating table, the so-called Big Four of Italy, US, UK and France had, in any case, agreed that representatives of small nations could only be heard by unanimous consent of all of the quartet. Wilson wasn't moved to action even by the 6 June resolution of the US Senate (as put forward by Senator William Borah), urging its own President over in Paris to assist the Irish cause.

Five days after that 60-1 vote had taken place in Washington, Wilson did give Walsh and Dunne a thirty-minute audience, after which the Irish-Americans issued a statement saying the President had assured them he would do what he could 'unofficially...in the interest of Ireland'. Ultimately, Wilson was never going to risk promoting the Irish cause for fear of causing a huge rift with Britain, a more powerful and important ally at such a crucial juncture in his career and in history. Less than a month after all that came to naught, Walsh, Dunne, Mellows and de Valera sat in the Waldorf-Astoria staring out at the man receiving a hero's welcome and wondering about their own next move.

It came just two nights later. Smaller in scale than the estimated half a million people who'd cheered the American president all the way from the pier at Hoboken to the stage at Carnegie Hall, the occasion of de Valera's first public speech in the city was still a spectacular affair, during which Wilson was delivered a noisy riposte. Twelve thousand people had shoe-horned their way into Madison Square Garden, by the time Fire Chief Kenlon belatedly ordered the doors locked. Almost half as many again were stranded outside, where they stayed and held vigil throughout; all made their disdain for Wilson known by joining in the frequent jeering of his name.

For this meeting organised by the FOIF, de Valera and his entourage of Dunne, Walsh and Michael J. Ryan (the third member of the American Commission for Irish Independence) was escorted into the hall by soldiers from the 69th Infantry Regiment of the New York National Guard, a largely Irish outfit renumbered the 165th Infantry after America entered World War I. In anticipation of his arrival, the crowd was warmed up by several fife and drum bands playing Irish melodies. When de Valera finally entered the arena, the largest attendance ever to fill the venue went berserk for a full nine minutes, cheering and waving the tricolour flags that had been issued upon entry. Outside, their cheers were soon echoed by those who'd come too late to the party.

But this was no party, it was a gathering with a serious political motive. That much was demonstrated almost immediately as John J. Finnegan, a tenor on loan from St Patrick's Cathedral, sang a version of 'The Star-Spangled Banner' that included the third verse in which the English are reminded: 'Their blood has washed out their foul footsteps' pollution. No refuge could save the hireling and slave, from the terror of flight or the gloom of the grave'. During World War I, it had become so customary to omit that stanza from the song in view of the two countries fighting side by side that the sanitised version was even taught in schools.

As MC, Justice Cohalan was cheered to the rafters. He swiftly turned the volume up with an attack on Wilson that included a popular swipe at English Field Marshal Sir Douglas Haig, which drew the first sustained cacophony of boos. After outlining the purpose of the meeting – to welcome the president of Ireland, to hear the Paris report from Messrs. Walsh, Dunne and Ryan, and to protest the League of Nations – Cohalan introduced Fr Francis Duffy and the jeers turned to resounding cheers.

As chaplain of the 165th Infantry during its campaign in France, Fr Duffy proved an inspirational presence to his men on the battlefield by always going where the fighting was fiercest. Awarded the Distinguished Service Cross and the Distinguished Service Medal, he would later be commemorated with a statue erected in Times Square (considered by some as Duffy Square), and was played by Pat O'Brien in the 1940 movie *The Fighting 69th*. A philosopher and teacher, Duffy's war record had made him as popular a figure with the general public as he'd been with his fellow soldiers, and he assured his audience those men had gone to Europe in the belief they were fighting for America and a free Ireland.

'It was not us who introduced this principle of American protection to foreign lands: it was President Wilson,' said Duffy, the very mention of the president's name was a signal for a sustained outbreak of hissing and booing. As the thousands around him displayed their anger and disdain, the priest's face betrayed no emotion whatsoever. He continued:

'After reading the declarations made by the President I felt that the question that would arise in many minds would be "What about Ireland?" Now whether the President will come around to accord with his own principles I do not know but we do and we will stick to it. We are determined that the republic which was kicked from the Peace Conference door like a beggar, will have its place when kingdoms that oppressed it are down in the dust.'

That set the tone for the rest of the warm-up before the main event. The mere mention of de Valera's name unleashed another torrent of emotion and noise. One estimate put the ovation at ten and a half minutes; another timed it at closer to fifteen. All observers agreed it was loud and so long that eventually, the band had to be asked to stop lest the cheering and the chanting of 'de Valera, de Valera' continue on indefinitely. At the first semblance of order, two men carrying the American and Irish flags appeared and stood either side of de Valera and suddenly the band couldn't be controlled anymore, launching into 'Amhrán na bhFiann' and causing further mayhem.

'This,' said de Valera when the reception finally subsided, 'is New York's recognition of the Irish Republic.'

The niceties over, he eventually got down to business and took up the argument begun by Duffy, placing the Irish situation in the context of the Versailles Treaty.

'What do the Irish people want? They want their country. Yes, their country, every inch of it, from the sod to sky, to have and to hold for themselves and their heirs in the Irish nation. Is there anything incomprehensible in this demand, anything surprising in it, anything unreasonable or extreme in it? Are the Irish people some inferior race, some degraded branch of the human kind, destined to find its natural good in servitude, and purposely left by the Almighty without the feelings, aspirations and instincts which He has implanted in the minds and hearts of other peoples?...

'The fathers of the Irish republic were Orangemen, or rather were Protestants. I have not forgotten that the idea of this republic was founded in the north, and I am certain that if England's interfering hand were taken away, the appearance of division would disappear. And when I mention Belfast, it will be news I'm sure to New York, to tell you that in that city there are more Irish nationalists than in Cork. Irishmen want their country. It is rightfully and lawfully theirs. Irishmen want their freedom: freedom to live their own lives in their own way: freedom to develop along their own lines: freedom to express their own national individuality in government, trade, art and literature: freedom to raise their own institutions in accord with their own genius: freedom to come out once more into the big world to share its activities, to act and to be acted upon, and to contribute their quota to human achievement. Freedom...freedom from the rule of the baton and the bayonet, from rifles, from machine guns: freedom from police spies and police perjuries, from the invasions of their homes without writ or warrant: freedom from murder by their government agents: freedom from invented crimes and imprisonment without trial. And not least, freedom from the infamous libels spread by the organised official propaganda of the English government in order to hide the true nature of their rule in Ireland, throw dust in the eyes of people and cover up the truth.'

To illustrate the last point, de Valera held up a couple of

clippings containing what he perceived to be the dastardly work of English operatives trying to undermine his own work.

'I have here a couple of specimens of the methods England employs in her propaganda of falsehoods. These leaflets in my hand purport to be an extract from *The New York Times* (the mere mention of which drew a chorus of hissing disapproval to match that earlier launched at Wilson). I do not know if it is. But whether it is or not, it is a lie, an English agent lie: I know no stronger adjective to apply.

'It gives a description by a priest of the heart-rending scenes in Queenstown when the *Lusitania* was sunk, and without stating it, implies that this priest, who is given as Father Browne, nephew and secretary of the Bishop of Queenstown, accused us Sinn Féiners of looking on, and when their assistance was wanted, begged for, denying it, that they refused to dig graves or permit those who might have been inclined to help from doing so, and puts it down to Sinn Féinism that the graves were left unidentified and that the bodies were put into two trenches.'

Two months later, the photographer Father Francis Browne also personally rebutted the allegation which had appeared in the *Times's* letters page with a missive of his own to the paper.

Forty-eight hours after that tour de force, 10,000 people greeted de Valera off the train at La Salle Station, in Chicago, with (the by now expected) mixture of passion and fervour. The events at Madison Square Garden however, had turned into a public relations disaster because the hissing and booing of President Wilson's name made the front pages. No country enjoys the sight of its leader being jeered by immigrants and so, almost immediately upon arrival in Chicago, de Valera set about repairing the damage, issuing a statement distancing himself from the crowd's behaviour and speculating that it might actually have been the handiwork of enemies of the Irish cause.

'I would be deeply humiliated if my presence here in this country and my advocacy of the just and reasonable claims of the Irish people should be made the occasion of any demonstrations of hostility to your President,' he said, returning to the topic at a luncheon that day. 'He is your President, and whilst as Americans, you have a right no doubt to criticise, you will forgive me for saying I feel it is not in good taste before a stranger... As I have pointed out, one or two in a meeting can make a great noise, and it would be a very obvious device for those who are opposed to our cause here to send agents for that purpose.'

De Valera was speaking at a luncheon in his honour at the Congress Hotel, where his first attempt to deliver a speech had been interrupted by six guests who manhandled him up on to their shoulders and insisted on chairing him around the dining room. As they paraded him up and down between the tables for fifteen minutes, he got into the spirit of the impromptu celebration himself, enthusiastically waving a tiny stars and stripes in one hand, and a tricolour in the other.

The only interruptions to his own speech, after that initial demonstration of adulation, came when certain sentences elicited supportive shouts of 'Down with England', 'Long live de Valera' and 'God Bless Ireland'. His conciliatory tone towards the White House didn't prevent him either from using his first platform in the Midwest to link Wilson's beloved doctrine of self-determination with the plight of Ireland. He did have the good sense to soften up the locals first before having them digest the point.

'The spirit of (Abraham) Lincoln and (Owen) Lovejoy (a beloved pastor, politician and anti-slavery agitator in Illinois) still lives in the people of the state that gave them to the world. You are not like those whom Lincoln ironically derided as upholders of that great principle that: "if one man makes a slave of another it is nobody else's business". In demanding recognition for the Irish Republic, we are simply demanding recognition of the principle of government of the people, by the people, for the people.

During the luncheon, he'd been shocked to recognise a familiar face among the crowd. Catherine O'Connell was an eighty-year-old woman from Limerick, who he recalled meeting as a young boy in Bruree. Later that night, when the scions of the local Irish-American community would have preferred him to sit around the Congress Hotel (the usual accommodation for any American president passing through Chicago) talking business with them, he went to 3148 Fulton Street to drop in on his compatriot for a chat.

In another delightful cameo, Mary Keelty Sullivan, an eighty-four-year-old native of Ballymote, County Sligo, insisted her grandchildren bring her from Clinton, Michigan to see and hear de Valera that day. Her reward was a private audience with him and a photograph of the pair that made the front page of the *Chicago Herald Examiner*, beneath the headline 'Age and Youth Clasp Hands for Ireland.'

After using his first public appearance in the city to start the political argument and then continue the damage control regarding Madison Square Garden, de Valera embarked on a sightseeing tour of the north side, and on the way back through

Lincoln Park stopped to pay homage to the man after whom the park was named. At the Lincoln monument, he placed a wreath beneath Augustus Saint-Gaudens' famous statue of the sixteenth president of the USA rising from his chair as if about to speak. Just like in Boston the previous month, de Valera enclosed a card upon which he had written: 'That a government of the people, by the people, and of the people, may not perish from the earth.'

There were other more high-profile stops on his itinerary too during his three days in Chicago. Wearing a cap and gown, he was conferred with an honorary Doctorate of Law by the president of DePaul University, Reverend Francis Xavier McCabe. A call to Archbishop Mundelein, a man beloved by Chicago Catholics for his leadership of the church there, yielded an official welcome from the future cardinal: 'I am certainly delighted that the first president ever to enter my house is an Irish president.'

In a move designed to bolster the notion that the Irish Republic he now claimed to represent, aspired to be an ecumenical nation, he also met with a group of Lutheran Church leaders at the hotel and assured them full religious liberty would be guaranteed in the new Ireland. Equally spiritual in a different way was a brief sit-down with Colonel Richard O'Sullivan Burke, an iconic Fenian who'd led the prison-van rescue half a century earlier that culminated in the hanging of the Manchester Martyrs.

As he was being honoured and celebrated at every turn in Chicago, news of de Valera's reception in America was beginning to cause an impact 3,000 miles away. At an Orange march in Holywood, in Belfast, on 12 July, Edward Carson was criticising his activities.

'There is a campaign going on in America at the moment, fostered by the Catholic Church, which will soon be joined by the Germans and their friends, in order to create a great anti-British feeling...I am not going to submit to this kind of campaign whether for friendship or any other reason. I seriously say to America today: "You attend to your own affairs; we will attend to ours. You look after your own questions at home and we will look after ours." We will brook no interference in our own affairs by any country, however powerful.'

From Carson's point of view, things quickly got worse with de Valera being the keynote speaker at a mass meeting on Sunday afternoon in the Chicago Cubs' baseball park, a venue better known today as Wrigley Field. If the crowd of 25,000 was significantly less than turned out in Boston, they were, if anything, even more enthusiastic. In what the British Consulate described in a dispatch to London as 'a very impressive display of humanity', de Valera received a standing ovation that lasted more than half an hour.

'In ecstacy, 25,000 Chicagoans of Irish birth and blood bade him welcome,' wrote the *Chicago Daily Tribune*. 'For thirty-one minutes they cheered. For more than two hours they shouted and sang songs of Irish freedom. Through it all they clasped the green, white and orange banner of the "Irish Republic" as a cherished emblem. De Valera appeared almost awed, yet he yielded gracefully to the crowd's whim while Mayor Thompson brandished the American and Irish flags, while aged men and women who were born Gaels wept, and while a band blared melodies known as Irish.'

Chicago Mayor William Hale ('Big Bill') Thompson was such

a renowned Anglophobe that during the war he'd been dubbed 'Kaiser Bill'. A controversial figure constantly fighting allegations of corruption and mismanagement during his time in office, he warmed up the crowd by wading into Wilson for his failure to assist a country, which by Thompson's reckoning had contributed one-third of the American army in the Revolutionary War. The very mention of the American president's name brought forth some predictable hissing, but the mayor was the least effective of the warm-up acts. It was former Governor Dunne and Frank P. Walsh – both liberally sprinkling their speeches with mention of their recent experiences in Europe – who whipped the audience into a frenzy that culminated in another lengthy ovation for de Valera.

After beginning with his customary introduction *as Gaeilge* – a touch that one reporter noticed caused some expatriates on the field to shed tears – de Valera quickly got down to the heavy lifting, arguing trenchantly against Article X of the Versailles Treaty. His intent was to outline how the provision by which all members of the League of Nations vowed to adhere to a principle of collective security and to protect each other's territorial integrity effectively meant any Irish attempt to break away from Britain would require the rest of the League to assist in the crushing of the rebellion.

'Now that article, if the treaty is accepted in that form, means for us that we are to be cut off from the sympathy that you here are giving us; from the practical, material and moral aid of other countries that sympathise with our cause, and I may say, every country on earth except the one holding us in subjection sympathises with us....We ask you to make representations to your government to ask them to see that Ireland by that covenant is not put in the position to which she will be consigned to the mercies of England.'

Apart from articulating the need for the American people to pressure its politicians to recognise the fledgling nation, he ran through a familiar checklist about the legality of the elected government in Ireland, its readiness to govern and the desire of the majority for independence from Britain. With every paragraph of his speech punctuated by degrees of applause and cheering, he also appealed to America's sense of righteousness to assist in the removal of the oppressor.

'I might be asked why I have come to America first. Well I think the reason is obvious. But it is not so much that here in this country there is a large portion of men and women of Irish blood. It is not even because we recognise that here we have a liberty-loving people but it is because we know that this nation is big enough to be able to stand up and follow its own will, irrespective of whether John Bull likes it or not.'

At the baseball field, de Valera was preaching to the choir. More importantly from a propaganda point of view, the entire speech was reprinted in the following day's *Chicago Daily Tribune* and a large portion of it made papers from New York to Los Angeles. The propaganda war had begun, in earnest by then, as the counter-attacking by London was also impacting in American newsrooms. On 14 July, the last day of his stay in Chicago, de Valera awoke to discover the *Chicago Daily Tribune* was carrying a map of Ireland in which Ulster is shown to be an entirely Unionist province. It ran in several papers all over the country.

'An Ulster man is as much an Irishman as a Munsterman,'

said de Valera in an address to the Chicago City Council where he met the issue head on. 'In this morning's Tribune was a map purporting to show Ulster as entirely Unionist. It did not mention the fact 14 of the seats there are Sinn Fein and twenty-three Unionist. We stand ready to give every man in Ireland equal rights.'

Then to the war again.

'The Irishmen in the English army were deceived, for the devil is no less the devil if he puts a holy motto on his banner. Ireland remained out of the war because we knew we were not strong enough to see to it that we would be fairly treated at the end of the war. If we had gone in, England would have made it appear we were in as England's partners and therefore content with English occupation.'

After he spoke, the enormous, wide figure of Councillor John 'Bathhouse' Coughlin (so called because he began his professional career as a masseur) rose to propose a motion wishing 'de Valera Godspeed on his mission'. It was unanimously adopted. At 7.00pm that evening, a large crowd thronged La Salle Station in the rain to wave de Valera off, as he caught the Overland Limited of the Chicago, Milwaukee, St Paul Railway to San Francisco.

CHAPTER FIVE

....Let no man write my epitaph: for as no man who knows my motives dare now vindicate them. Let not prejudice or ignorance asperse them. Let them and me repose in obscurity and peace, and my tomb remain uninscribed, until other times, and other men, can do justice to my character; when my country takes her place among the nations of the earth, then, and not till then, let my epitaph be written.

– Robert Emmet, speech from the dock, Dublin, 19 September 1803

The car journey from the San Francisco Ferry Terminal to the St Francis Hotel, on Powell Street, was interrupted by an earnest deputation from the Ancient Order of Hibernians (AOH). They requested the driver turn the engine off so they could have the honour and privilege of dragging de Valera's vehicle the rest of the way to his destination. Ropes were quickly attached and six proud men then hauled the automobile to the haughty establishment overlooking Union Square that was to be his base in California.

Traffic slowed to gawp and passersby stopped to stare at this bizarre spectacle as it moved along. Most of the bemused onlookers didn't understand that for expatriates and second-generation Irish who never thought they'd live to see anybody able to claim to be president of the country, the symbolism of this arrival was too good an opportunity to pass up.

Ten thousand others had crowded around the entrance and lobby of the hotel in anticipation of Eamon de Valera's west coast debut. Among that vast attendance was a group of young girls wearing traditional Irish costumes. Each carried a basket full of petals and the moment their quarry began to make his way through the throng, the girls streamed the flowers in his path. A garland of roses was produced and placed upon his head, and his progress into the hotel was soundtracked by a loud encomium from a Miss Peggy O'Neill, who informed him: 'We hail you as the true representative of real democracy. Our joy at receiving you is beyond expression because you come from a country under whose government the women have the same constitutional rights and share equal privileges with men.'

It was Thursday evening, 17 July, and there ensued four more days of constant adulation and loud acclaim. The name of the city had changed but the song remained the same. Everything he did was news. Everywhere he went became an event. The final leg of his journey through the wharf, ferry and train terminal known as the Oakland Mole had even been filmed and was almost immediately being broadcast in local theatres alongside the first footage of Jack Dempsey relaxing at home following his recent dethroning of world heavyweight champion Jess Willard. Heady company for a politician to be keeping on any bill, there were plenty other acknowledgements of his growing celebrity too.

Before a packed high mass in St Peter's Cathedral on Sunday morning, de Valera was escorted to his seat by a guard of honour from The League of the Cross Cadets, and, according to newspaper reports, afforded 'all of the ritualistic courtesies due the Catholic head of a sovereign people.' The sermon that day was delivered by Fr Augustine, a Capuchin Friar from Dublin, who had ministered to the Easter Rising veterans awaiting execution at Kilmainham Jail back in 1916. 'The Lord is the strength of his people. Spare oh Lord thy people. Never did I feel the truth of those words so fully as I did in those dark days of 1916,' said Fr Augustine. 'When I heard those words on the lips of a blind woman, I knew that God had spared the Irish people and especially the distinguished man in our midst today.'

The distinguished man also received an honorary doctorate of philosophy from St Ignatius University, a Jesuit college now known as the University of San Francisco. At Shellmound Park, in Oakland, a crowd of 20,000 feted him during a festival of Irish dancing and sport. In City Hall, Mayor Jim Rolph – the son of an English immigrant – and the Board of Supervisors awarded him a gold plaque. At every turn, de Valera followed up expressions of gratitude for the warmth of the welcome with a reminder of the business at hand.

'The main thing I want to get in this country is recognition of the Irish republic. We have a nation big enough and resources big enough to look after ourselves. I would rather go back to Ireland without a penny piece and the recognition of our republic through this country than I would if you were to give me all the gold you possess…This cause, if it triumphs, means really the triumph of everything America went into the war to obtain.'

That was an extract of his comments when receiving the fancy bauble from Rolph, but during a packed itinerary there was plenty more where that came from and no shortage of high-profile platforms on which to speak. The most picturesque of them came on Sunday morning, at Golden Gate Park, where de Valera unveiled a statue of Robert Emmet, another set-piece laden with symbolism and historical symmetry.

The famous Irish sculptor Jerome Connor (born in Kerry and residing in Washington) sculpted four identical bronzes of Emmet, each seven feet tall, using only sketches from the patriot's trial for treason and his famous death mask. The original was commissioned by a group of Irish-Americans in Washington DC in 1916, and can still be seen on Embassy Row there. One copy is in St Stephen's Green, in Dublin, and another resides in Emmetsburg, Iowa, a town settled by Irish immigrants in the late 1800s. The model in front of which de Valera posed with a cast of San Francisco's 'great and good' was gifted to the city that year by Californian Senator James Phelan.

'I thank the citizens of San Francisco that here, facing your Golden Gate, you have erected a statue of Liberty as glorious as that on your eastern coast in New York Harbour,' said de Valera. 'That statue represents the spiritual ideal. This statue represents the temple of a real, individual spirit who fought for liberty and whose soul is a true spirit of liberty. This man died that the idea of a free Ireland, an Irish Republic, might live....Thank God our country has been saved from a compromise which might have endangered forever the writing of the epitaph of Robert Emmet. You may recall his speech from the dock and it will confirm the truth that that tyranny remains the same. His character was impeached. He was called a traitor to his country, an emissary of a foreign power....We pledge ourselves to go on unceasingly until in a united, free Ireland, the epitaph of Robert Emmet can be written.'

Even six thousand miles from home, de Valera wasn't beyond the remit of British influence. Shortly before he arrived in San Francisco, an American federal agent had visited the St Francis Hotel and discreetly asked the management to stop flying the Irish tricolour from the staff outside the building. By way of justification, he explained Washington had not yet officially recognised the country the flag was supposed to represent. In actual fact, the government's representative had been prompted into this action by the complaints of Captain Arthur Snagge.

A naval attaché of the British Embassy, Snagge had checked out of the hotel in great umbrage at the mere sight of the billowing green, white and orange flag earlier in the week. Once safely out of town, Snagge later released a statement pointing out that Major M.M. Sissley, assistant provost marshal for Canada, had declared the establishment out of bounds for all British and Canadian soldiers after learning about the flag. The local Irish community responded with predictable outrage to all of this. Under the leadership of City Supervisor Andrew Gallagher, they held what the local papers described as an 'indignation meeting' to call attention to this attack on Ireland.

Others were more direct in their response to any perceived British influence. When de Valera spoke to a crowd of workers at the Bethlehem Ship Yard, a man in attendance took advantage of a lull in the speech to shout 'God Save the King': brave and/or foolish. What happened next was best captured by a report in the *Oakland Tribune*.

'Never, witnesses say, did anything ever staged to make famous the name of Donnybrook Fair have anything on the events that fill the minutes immediately upon the impact of that paean to Britain's ruler upon the eardrums of those assembled to demand freedoms for Ireland. Somebody swung on the jaw yet unclosed from the utterance, from another quarter came a second blow and the eager feet performed jigs upon the prostrate form of the man whose sentiments dominated his discretion. Then came a detail of police and after some struggling the cops rescued the man, took him into the cafeteria of the yard, gave him emergency treatment and escorted him to safety. It was said the man was not an employee of the yard.'

Beyond the impromptu theatre of an angry mob setting upon a discordant voice in the crowd, the trip to the shipyard had a more serious purpose. It was the chosen location for de Valera to make his pitch to organised labour.

'... I believe that I know what I'm saying when I say that Irish labour is heart and hand with American labour in wishing that the ideals for which the war was fought should really be accomplished ... What we want is what your representatives at the convention of the American Federation of Labour voted unanimously that we should have, and that is recognition; and we feel that we should have that recognition because the government we will set up is based on the one solid basis and that is the will of the governed...'

'... you believe in a League of Nations. So do we. But it must be a real League of Nations. This present one is going to bind the shackles together not only on nations but on individuals...We will fall behind the American nation in any movement to improve the conditions of labour the world over. I thank you for giving me this opportunity to speak to you and I assure you there is no audience I am more honoured in appearing before. I was brought up in a working home and I am therefore in my heart a worker, as I have always been a worker, though mostly with my brain. But I am a workingman and am proud to be with you.'

With other sections of the community, de Valera didn't have to go for the hard sell. A group of Indian immigrants known as the Hindustan Gadar Party, established in 1913 with the intent of fomenting rebellion against the English crown in the Raj, sought him out to award him an engraved silver sword and a large silk tricolour. At the presentation, the Indians cited the common cause and common enemy shared by Ireland and India, and what they perceived as both countries' indisputable claims to nationhood.

'I take it that the sword represents the sacred idea of the struggle of both our countries for their freedom,' said de Valera, 'and the sword is really a sacred weapon for such a righteous cause.'

Other less contentious organisations around the Bay Area were anxious to be associated with de Valera as well. The Red Cross invited him to Letterman Hospital, where he visited with soldiers still recovering from injuries sustained in World War I. The Little Sisters of the Poor escorted him around a home for the aged, where he was made an honorary member of the Sunshine Club, and presented with a gold medal. And then, there was the AOH. It formally adopted a resolution to petition the President of the United States and the Congress to recognise Ireland as a free and independent nation, and de Valera's address to its 53rd biennial convention in the city drew an attendance of 12,000.

'Ireland can win what it must have by enlisting the support of the democratic peoples everywhere. We are in a big contest. In the broadest sense, this is a battle for democracy. Now is the time to make the world safe for democracy. In Ireland, as elsewhere. If America leads the way, the democratic peoples of England and France and Spain and all the nations of the world will rally with you.

'It would be an act of despair in God's justice and goodness if we were to think our cause a failure. In order that Poland might be freed, three mighty empires had to fall. With the triumph before us, no one can feel that Ireland is going to fail. It may be necessary to have another period of conflict and world strife to change the old order but it depends on America whether that period will be necessary.'

On Monday, 21 July, a detail of 300, or so, accompanied de Valera to the train station to wave him off as he started his journey back across America. The first leg of the trip took him to Salt Lake City, in Utah, where on the afternoon of 24 July, the magnificent pipe organ in the Mormon Tabernacle at Temple Square blared out a selection of hymns before deviating into a tune not usually heard in the venue. A haunting version of Thomas Moore's melody 'Let Erin Remember The Days Of Old' was played in honour of a tiny audience gathered in the cavernous home of the Church of Jesus Christ of Latter-Day Saints to witness the performance.

The recital had been specially-organised in honour of de Valera and his travelling party by the local reception committee. A little musical treat after so much politicking. He spent just sixteen hours, in total, in Salt Lake, a low-key and hastily-arranged stop, still long enough for him to speak at two separate functions in the Hotel Utah, and to compare his mission to Benjamin Franklin's activities, as the newly-independent America's representative to France 140 years earlier. He also received a visit from the state Governor Simon Bamberger.

'The people of Utah sympathise with the people of Ireland and hope they will achieve their independence,' said Bamberger, a German-born immigrant, who'd become just the second Jew to govern a state.

From there, the delegation headed north to Montana, a territory boasting a unique and historic connection to Ireland. The strength of that special bond was obvious to de Valera when he stepped from the train at Butte, a remote mining town to which the Irish had been flocking in search of their fortunes since the Great Famine. The Anaconda Copper Mine Band played a selection of Irish and American songs as Lieutenant-Governor W.W. McDowell, deputising for Governor Sam Stewart, greeted the new arrival, and hundreds swarmed the platform to try to touch his shoulder or clasp his hand.

Following McDowell's formal address of welcome, Miss Mary Cosgrove presented a green, white and orange bouquet of flowers to the esteemed visitor, on behalf of the ladies of Butte. Befitting an outpost where one in four residents was Irish, and neighbourhoods went by names such as Cork Town and Dublin Gulch, the place was in festive mood as de Valera stepped into Sheriff O'Rourke's car for a parade to the Finlen Hotel. Thousands accompanied the cortege through packed streets and the highlight of the short trip came outside the courthouse.

There, a choir of 300 schoolchildren was standing on the

steps. Conducted by Mrs Harte-Parkes, the students serenaded the guest of honour, who stood upright in the vehicle to thank them for their efforts. The mood of the whole spectacle reminded one of de Valera's colleagues of a certain kind of Irish event.

'The meeting in Butte was somewhat reminiscent of an election meeting at home – there were so many first generation Irishmen working in the mines – mainly from around Allihies in West Cork,' wrote Sean Nunan of the rapturous reception.

An estimated ten thousand people crowded into Hebgen Park that night for a rally, where the Irish cause was eulogised by local judges, clergy and of course, de Valera himself. Resolutions were adopted at the meeting in support of Ireland's quest for recognition from the American government, and at a banquet in the Silver Bow Club, where hundreds had to be locked out because of excessive demand for tickets, Mayor T.W. Stodden presented de Valera with the Freedom of the City and W.W. McDowell presented him with the Freedom of the State.

'They tell us that the Irish cannot govern themselves,' said the Lieutenant-Governor turning to de Valera as he spoke. 'I can tell you Mister President that while I know nothing of what the Irish do in Ireland, in this country they run the American government.'

W.W. McDowell also extended an invitation to address the joint houses of the Montana Legislature, the sort of generosity that might have been expected from a man whose initials stood for William Wallace. De Valera endeared himself to the locals with a nugget of his own: 'When we were in prison in Lincoln, England,' he said, 'the Irish prisoners used to gather in the evening and sing "The Star-Spangled Banner". It spelled hope for them.'

While that sort of poignant memory was elevating his standing in Montana, word of his presence, less than 300 miles from the Canadian border, elicited a different response from the authorities there.

'If Mister de Valera, President of the Irish Republic, visits Canada, he will be arrested and handed over to the British authorities,' reported the *Montreal Gazette* on 29 July. 'While the government has made no official pronouncement on the subject there is little doubt of the course that will be pursued if the Sinn Fein leader comes to this country. One minister has stated that on the arrival of Mr. de Valera he would soon realise that this country is British and no sanctuary for fugitives, political or otherwise, from British justice. The Sinn Fein leader is a political prisoner who escaped from custody.'

On the very day that story appeared, de Valera was in fighting form as he stood before the joint assembly of the Montana Legislature in the capital city of Helena. 'Since America won her independence, there have been five revolutions in Ireland seeking her independence, and there will be another if we cannot get it by peaceful means.'

Even before speaking, he had reminded his audience of the mutual heritage shared by Ireland and the state of Montana by laying a wreath at the foot of the statue of Thomas Francis Meagher, which stood sentry on the lawn outside the state house. In doing so, he paid homage to a figure with an epic biography and a very special footnote in Irish history. Together with William Smith O'Brien, Meagher had brought the redesigned

Irish flag, the first tricolour of green, white and orange back from France in 1848.

Transported to Australia after that year's rebellion, Waterford-born Meagher escaped from Van Diemen's Land (Tasmania) to New York, rose to the rank of Brigadier General in the Union Army in the American Civil War, and later became acting-Governor of the then territory of Montana. Along the way, he picked up the nickname 'Meagher of the Sword' and it was with just that weapon in hand, sitting astride a horse, that his likeness was cast in bronze in 1905. Fourteen years later, another Irish nationalist was telling the people of Helena the story of the flag Meagher had introduced to the country of his birth.

'It was hard for the people of Ireland to give up the harp on their flag. But they did this so that their new flag in colours of green, white and orange should typify the union of their north and south, irrespective of religion. It is hard to be misunderstood by those one loves, and this is the position in which the majority in Ireland find themselves in relation to those of their own race and kin who form the minority…There are among the Irish minority a few who love their British citizenship and are loath to give it up. To those we have made the fair proposition that it is but a short distance across the channel to the shores of England, and they are at liberty to move over; and that the Irish republic will see that they are recompensed for any material holdings they leave behind.'

That particular explanation was given at a formal banquet held at the Rose Room that evening where Governor Stewart delivered the official welcome for de Valera. On what appears to have been a more jovial occasion, the relentless parade of speeches by dignitaries was punctuated by a sing-song featuring standards such as 'When Irish Eyes are Smiling', 'Mother Machree' and 'The River Shannon'. Amid the entertainment, de Valera personally requested a rendition of 'Believe Me, If All Those Endearing Young Charms', a ballad Thomas Moore supposedly wrote about his wife.

CHAPTER SIX

The reception accorded to President de Valera in U.S.A. had exceeded anything they had expected. No envoy from this country had ever been received in the way that their President had been received. As regards the Loan issue in U.S.A., President de Valera had asked for discretionary power to increase the amount of the issue originally decided on. He was at present in conference with a number of American Bankers, arranging preliminaries as to the issue of the Loan.

– **Arthur Griffith, statement to Dáil,
19 August 1919**

In the course of just twenty-three days, de Valera had travelled 6,000 miles across and back the width of America, and delivered seventeen major public speeches, and a host of smaller ones to aggregate crowds nearing half a million people. The cross-country trip had been hugely successful in terms of promoting awareness of his presence and garnering crucial column inches for the cause in newspapers from California to the Carolinas. After so much glitz, glamour and adulation however, he returned to New York on 3 August to begin the more mundane, but no less important, task of sorting out the proposed bond issue. All of the theatrical set-pieces would count for naught if the money didn't come rolling in.

On just his second day at the Waldorf-Astoria back in June, he'd sat down to fully appraise the most prominent figures in Irish-America about his fundraising intentions regarding a bond issue. He quickly discovered this wasn't going to be the most straightforward aspect of his stay. At a meeting where the line-up included Joseph McGarrity, John Devoy, Justice Cohalan, and Justice John W. Goff, he saw troubling signs of opposition to the idea; obvious personality clashes between certain characters, and the very real possibility local enmities, which had been brewing for a while, could yet spill over into something toxic. By one account, de Valera was even offered $250,000 right there and then to abandon the loan idea and return home with that money to the Dáil. It was not something he wanted to consider. 'I have a mandate from my people,' he said, 'and I intend to go ahead whether I succeed or fail.'

The most serious and logical objection to his plan came from Cohalan and had a justified legal basis. Since the Republic de Valera represented wasn't formally recognised by the American government, it did not exist in the eyes of the law and therefore any attempt to sell bonds in it contravened 'blue-sky statues' designed to protect the public from fraudulent schemes. To circumvent this problem, it was decided, after much argument and debate, that the loan would be raised by selling 'bond--certificates' rather than 'bonds', and those selling them could not be known as 'bond sellers'. A linguistic solution to a legal problem achieved mostly through the work of McGarrity and renowned New York lawyer Martin Conboy; independent advice on the matter was also sought from Franklin Delano Roosevelt.

After serving as assistant-secretary of the Navy (1913-1920), Roosevelt returned to his old position as partner at the New York law firm of Emmet, Marvin and Roosevelt, a company founded by Robert Emmet's brother Thomas, back in 1805. The future thirty-second President of the US met with de Valera, as a lawyer, and signed off on the legality of the new formula in which the retention of the word bond was especially crucial. That was the term used by any nation when selling itself in the world of international finance and for a parliament seeking recognition, it was essential to be seen as operating by the customary principles.

The legal wrangling was only one issue. There was also the matter of an ongoing and similar financial campaign. Back in February the Irish Race Convention, in Philadelphia, a gathering called to provide moral, fiscal and political support for the first Dáil, had spawned a money-spinning effort of its own titled 'The Irish Victory Fund.' Under the auspices of the Friends of Irish Freedom, that appeal ended up collecting $1,005,080.83 in just six months. A hugely impressive tally, the problem was that to avoid confusion with the bonds, de Valera asked that the fund be shut down as of 31 August to clear the way for the new initiative. Hardly the sort of request likely to endear him to those more established in American society, especially when the quibbling on certain points reached inane proportions.

'I remember him coming out from a conference, which had lasted over four hours, over the wording of a circular advertising the bonds,' wrote Patrick McCartan. 'President de Valera had written the circular and used in it the words "peasants" and "steers". Cohalan contended that the term "peasant" was associated in the American mind with "peon" and conveyed the idea of an inferior type of humanity and that the word "steer" was also objectionable to Americans. President de Valera maintained that "peasant" had a poetic flavour and "steer" was expressive: and as he met me, he voiced his satisfaction that he had held out, and not given in to Judge Cohalan.'

There is an undercurrent in all of the rows that the legalistic posturing and the squabbling about minor details were simply manifestations of the simmering tension between de Valera on the one side, and Cohalan and Devoy on the other. The grand old men of Irish-America felt the 'new boy' was attempting an old-fashioned and pretty blatant power grab. What else to think when somebody is trying to gain control of the financial arm of any movement? Of course, de Valera viewed it quite differently. He was the leader of Ireland and saw the management or at least the oversight of a campaign intended to materially assist his country as his natural right.

'Considerable difficulty in getting the bond issue started,' he wrote to Arthur Griffith. 'Am trying to get the Walsh-Ryan-Dunne Commission [The American Commission on Irish Independence] to take it over. If I fail will take it up directly myself and organise....The bond issue will be for 5 or 10 million dollars not yet decided which.'

To add another layer of intrigue to proceedings, McGarrity, de Valera's confidante, had fallen out with Devoy and Cohalan back in May, their row centring on the portion of 'The Victory Fund' that should be sent to Ireland. Despite that old enmity further affecting the ongoing deliberations on the bonds, the existing fund was closed as requested. On 9 August Friends of Irish Freedom (FOIF) secretary Diarmuid Lynch wrote to all branches of the organisation advising them of the need for a 'whirlwind finish' to the campaign.

Given that the FOIF also advanced a loan of $100,000 to the bond scheme to help with the initial expenses and were continuing to fund de Valera's expensive and extensive travels, the pushing through of the loan against such weighty opponents represented a definite victory. Yet, it was a win in a single battle rather than a war, as the entire quarrel had done little for the movement except boldly delineate where the lead characters now stood in relation to each other. Devoy and Cohalan were on one side, de Valera and his allies on the other, and everybody else around them would ultimately have to choose between the two.

Somehow, amid all that tumult, the formal announcement that the American Commission on Irish Independence had opened a New York headquarters to deal with 'the work of floating the ten million dollar Irish Republican Bond Issue' came on 23 August. McGarrity had procured an office in Room 404 of the Stewart Building at the southwest corner of 37th Street and Fifth Avenue, where the first two storeys were a women's department store. Their fund-raising target had ballooned from the initial figure of $1,125,000 decided upon by the cabinet in Dublin, because McGarrity had persuaded de Valera that aiming higher would ultimately yield more. Asking for ten million dollars was settled on as the best way to get five million.

In between bickering about language, struggling against the leadership of the quasi-nation that was Irish-America, and learning the intricacies of commercial law, there were still meetings for de Valera to attend. The success of the loan would depend largely on his ability to whip up publicity and engender a positive feel for the cause in as many places as he possibly could. With a much longer national tour mooted for October and November, he spent the remainder of August and September travelling up and down the eastern seaboard, where surprisingly he began to hear some discordant notes about his presence.

'Of course you know and I know that there is no Republic of Ireland and we know de Valera is no more President of such a republic than you are King of Siam,' said former Justice Robert Carey, when resigning from a committee set up to welcome and give the freedom of Jersey City to de Valera. 'In my judgment, more extended liberty for Ireland is not to be obtained by these fancy parade performances which are seized by local politicians purely for personal effect and purposes.'

Carey was not alone in this type of view either. Judge Martin T. Manton of New York denounced de Valera as 'a half Spaniard attempting to mislead the American people... permitted to land on our shores and by speech and conduct make propaganda to arouse Irish sentiment.' If the rantings of members of various benches made for colourful copy, there were more pointed public snubs as well. Governor Westmoreland Davis of Virginia introduced him to a crowd of 3,000 in Richmond, but refused to address him as president. Likewise, Mayor William F. Broening of Baltimore didn't give him an official reception in Maryland and called him only 'visitor' when they were introduced.

Still, de Valera drew sizable crowds in both places and in Baltimore met again with Cardinal Gibbons. A champion of immigrant rights and a man once described by President Theodore Roosevelt as the most venerated and respected citizen in the country, Cardinal Gibbons had spent his childhood in Westport, County Mayo, in the 1840s. Growing up in the one of counties most affected by the Great Famine had a huge impact on Gibbons. 'I recall how the United States came to the aid of Ireland at that time,' said Gibbons. 'I shall never forget the arrival of a ship filled with corn.'

'Yes,' replied de Valera. 'And when that ship arrived it passed a ship leaving the coast of Ireland loaded down with wheat and oats which was being taken away by England.'

De Valera never passed up an opportunity to score points against the enemy, and another wonderful chance to do so came his way that same month.

'The Mayor of Newport and Governor of Rhode Island sent me invitation to go to N'port,' wrote de Valera to Arthur Griffith on 13 August. 'I am waiting till the Crown Prince of England gets there and he waiting till I leave there – meanwhile all the ball dresses of the aristocracy who were ready to receive him are getting musty – most amusing. The battleship is the compromise.'

The future King Edward VIII never made it to Newport on his late summer and autumn jaunt through Canada and North America. He spent a few days in New York that November, and even dined at the Waldorf-Astoria more than once. By then, de Valera was in the midst of his second nationwide tour and 3,000 miles away in California. For all the bravado in the mid-summer missive to Dublin, de Valera had far more pressing matters on his mind when he did arrive in Rhode Island on 12 September.

That very day, the British government moved to suppress the first Dáil and launched a series of raids on Sinn Féin operatives all around Ireland.

Having first refused to comment upon arrival in Providence that evening, de Valera finally issued a statement at midnight responding to the news from Ireland. Curiously, he substituted the American term Congress for Dáil, in what may be deduced as a hasty attempt to make it easier for his audience to grasp the significance of the British actions.

'The war front is now transferred to Ireland where the one-time Commander in Chief in France, Lord French, and the former Chief of Staff, Sir William Robertson, are now in command. If law and order is all that is wanted in Ireland it can be had within twenty-four hours. The alien government of Britain has only to withdraw its army of occupation. This occupation is the cause of disorders. Let the will of the Irish people prevail. This suppression by armed force of the Congress of Freely Appointed Representatives of the Irish People is a commentary which Americans will understand on England's desire to "make the world safe for democracy".'

In an effort to emphasise the genuine nature of the government being put down by the British, he outlined the recent decrees of the Dáil with regard to matters, such as: industry, fishing, forestry and farming, and claimed the work of 'material reconstruction' is what motivated the suppression – and not the upsurge in violent reprisals around the country. While Ernest Blythe and Padraig O'Keefe, Sinn Féin members of parliament for Monaghan North and Cork North, were arrested, and Michael Collins had to flee a safe house swarmed by soldiers and police then, de Valera pressed on with his itinerary.

Rhode Island Governor R.L. Beekman held an official reception at the State Chamber, and Providence Mayor Joseph Gainer welcomed him to City Hall, where he spent nearly a full hour just shaking the hands of well-wishers. If this was the usual work of personally promoting the cause, it did lead to an unfortunate contrast between his own situation and that of his colleagues back home. On Saturday, 13 September, as military lorries packed with prisoners arrived in Dublin from all points of the country, de Valera was sailing down picturesque Narragansett Bay on his way from Providence to Newport aboard the *Editha*, one of the most opulent sailing boats yet made. It was no wonder O'Keefe would later accuse him of going to America to get away from trouble.

A gigantic 138-footer with a permanent staff of ten, the *Editha* was capable of reaching twenty-five miles an hour under steam, and had been commissioned by the wealthy industrialist John H. Hanan as a gift for his wife Edith. Irish-born but New York-bred, Hanan accrued a fortune in the shoe business and married into a family that traced its ancestry in America all the way back to the *Mayflower*. Edith was the leading socialite in a town that was a haven for the East Coast elite and their palatial residence 'Shore Acres' was renowned for hosting the most lavish parties every summer.

There's no evidence de Valera enjoyed that type of hospitality but he did find time while there to spend an hour being chauffeur driven up and down Ocean Drive, a neighbourhood known for its spectacular rows of mansions. And the newspaper photograph of him alighting, at his ease, from a Gilded Age yacht would have done little for his image back home, had it made its way across the Atlantic. In a town with a sizable English population, the build-up to his visit had been predictably hallmarked by regular letters of protest in the local papers – but he still had a packed itinerary.

After being formally welcomed to City Hall, there was a luncheon party in the Hill Top Inn, an evening banquet at the Newport Beach Dining Room, and the by-now de rigeur visit to a battlefield in Portsmouth, where the Americans had engaged the British in 1778. There, he was serenaded by a choir of local school children and received a guard of honour from World War I veterans. There was more adulation at a mass meeting of 4,000 at Freebody Park, where he declared: 'We will resist as long as the spirit of manhood is left in us. Our spirit is something that bayonets cannot drive out.' Later that night, a British flag was torn down from the front of a building in Thames Street and burned on the beach.

Following mass at St Mary's on Sunday morning, de Valera boarded the *Editha* again for the trip back up to Providence, where a crowd had gathered to greet him on the dock. With a slew of police inspectors installing themselves as his personal troop, several hundred uniformed Irish volunteers and a brass band marched with him along the two and a half miles to Melrose Park, a route lined with thousands more cheering spectators. Upon arrival at the baseball field, he discovered a stadium full of tricolours and supporters – who wouldn't allow him to speak until several minutes of sustained ovations had passed. By the time he did talk, he was in crowd-pleasing form: 'I ask the American people if this is the time for your country to adopt the attitude of Pontius Pilate, to wash its hands of all concerned in Ireland's claim to freedom?'

'No!' responded the 15,000 people gathered before him.

Beyond that entertaining set-piece, he delivered an up-to-date précis of the situation in Ireland, made the case for the legitimacy of Dáil Éireann, and reiterated his ongoing appeal to the people of America for help. Formal resolutions were then adopted protesting the suppression of the Dáil and expressing 'unalterable opposition to the proposed League of Nations.'

Somewhere in the schedule, time was found for a trip to Central Falls, just north of the city, to meet James Wilson. The ninety-year-old was the last surviving member of the six Fenian prisoners who'd escaped from Fremantle, Western Australia, aboard the *Catalpa* whaling ship in 1876. Upon reaching America, the Rhode Island chapter of Clan na Gael had sold him a house for $1, where he lived the rest of his days. More than half a century separated them in age but the pair had much in common, having served time for the same cause at a couple of the same jails in Ireland and England.

Ironically, when de Valera was sitting down for a symbolic meeting with an iconic figure, who owed his freedom to John Devoy's audacious planning and financing of the *Catalpa* rescue, relations between the two leaders were taking a turn for the worse. In the aftermath of the suppression of the Dáil, Joseph McGarrity and Patrick McCartan had convened a protest meeting at New York's Lexington Theatre on 14 September. Headlined by Frank P. Walsh, a raucous evening culminated in a resolution asking the US Congress to cut off funds to the British government. A logistical triumph given the speed at which it was pulled together, the event also garnered favourable column inches.

In a calculated snub, the organisers had neglected to inform Devoy or Judge Cohalan about it or to formally invite them. Insult was then added to that injury by a subsequent decision to bill the FOIF the $1515 it had cost to hire the Lexington Theatre.

'The latest development in the effort to sidetrack us was the meeting at the Lexington Theatre on Sunday evg. last,' wrote Devoy to Cohalan. 'All our men went to it and made it a great success because of the announcement from the altar and the big ads in the paper. It was started, managed and carried out by Joe [McGarrity], Dr. McC[artan], and [William J.] Maloney, and they sat on the platform together with an unmistakable air of ownership. For the first time we have proof that they worked with Maloney...They did not tell a single one of our men a word about it. I knew nothing at all about it except through a notice in the evening papers.'

The role of Dr William J. Maloney (who set up the American Committee for Relief in Ireland) in the affair peeved Devoy most. Born in Edinburgh to a family with County Down connections, Maloney had been injured fighting for the British Army in the Dardanelles, and though an enthusiastic supporter of Irish independence since arriving in New York, his past life was enough to have him viewed with some suspicion. Devoy went farther than most, believing the Scot was a plant by British intelligence, a spy working hard to destroy the movement in America from the inside. That charge would never be proven. In any case, by the middle of September, Maloney was just one facet of the ongoing decline in relations between de Valera and Devoy. There would be plenty more for them to argue about beside the controversial Scot, as the gap between the two different generations of Irish leaders began to widen irrevocably.

CHAPTER SEVEN

The American Legion of Pennsylvania on Saturday branded Eamon de Valera self-styled President of the Irish Republic as a traitor to America, his native land, and termed the public receptions in his honour a repudiation of the cause for which our comrades fought and died. There was a storm of applause from the floor when the resolution was adopted. It declared that de Valera is an American and should have served in the army or navy and that he should not be accepted or recognised by any city in America.

– *The Agitator* Newspaper, Wellsboro, Pennsylvania, Wednesday, 8 October 1919

A second cross-country trip, a two-month odyssey that Frank P. Walsh described 'as the largest-speaking tour ever undertaken in the United States', began on 1 October in Philadelphia. A city with a rich Irish heritage, and one which played such a huge role in America's own story of nationhood, it made a logical starting point. Here was a place so rife with symbolism that on the very first day, in a departure from the usual protocol, the case holding the Liberty Bell was specially opened to allow de Valera to actually touch the famous old cracked object, which was associated in the American popular imagination with the Declaration of Independence and, later, the Abolitionist movement.

'This shrine is not a shrine for America alone,' said de Valera speaking in front of the bell. 'It is the shrine of freedom, the freedom that is America's and that, God grant, may be Ireland's. It is the symbol of liberty to all the world. ...It is a matter of great pride to know that Irishmen had a part in the establishment of such a shrine, that Irishmen, as your mayor has told me, signed that famous Declaration of Independence. They were great men who awoke liberty on this spot. I'm sure that if those men were alive today they would say that Ireland should be free'

Charles Thomson from Maghera, County Derry, physically wrote out the first Declaration of Independence, Strabane native John Dunlap printed off the first copies of the document, and Thomas Fitzsimons, another Irishman, was among the first signers of the United States Constitution. With those sort of tangible links, it was inevitable de Valera would be feted on his visit to Independence Hall where Thomas C. Nolan, a twelve-year-old boy whose mother was once arrested for hitting Lloyd George over the head with a picket sign, stepped forward to present him with a red, white and blue floral replica of the bell.

'I think the greatest day in my life was the afternoon you spoke at St. Joseph's College,' wrote Nolan in a letter to de Valera fifty years later. 'I was there as a student of the Gesu Parish School of which the college was also a part, and I was able to say (in truth, I boasted) that I knew you and had presented you with the floral liberty bell; I was (or believed myself to be) the hero of the school.'

From the moment the New York train had pulled into North Philadelphia Station shortly before midday that Wednesday afternoon, de Valera was engulfed by thousands more just like Nolan. Despite teeming rain, a convoy of 300 cars festooned with Irish flags and colours were waiting upon arrival to escort him. As the party blared their horns on the way through the city, they passed the Baldwin Locomotive works, where employees were gathered outside in great numbers to cheer him on. Some even rushed towards the car in an attempt to shake his hand.

That first day, de Valera spoke at both a luncheon and a banquet at the Bellevue-Stratford Hotel, and delivered another soliloquy after visiting the statues of President George Washington and Commodore John Barry, the Wexford native whose contribution to his adopted country's quest for independence from Britain earned him the title 'Father of the American Navy'.

'We Irishmen know the meaning of statues. We have erected many statues to our patriots: they are statues of men whom the world has said have failed, but to us they have not failed. Their immediate object may have remained unaccomplished, but they kept alive the fire of patriotism. Your statues tell you to keep alive that which your heroes have done. Ours tell us to strive to bring the glory of success that noble work which they have striven for, and in which they have failed. The determination of the Irish people has been aroused in the cause of freedom. They shall strive until it is achieved, and it is an inspiration that will lead us to that end that I and all my people find in the memorials of Philadelphia dedicated to the glorious cause of liberty.'

At the cemetery on Fifth and Arch Street, he placed a wreath on Benjamin Franklin's grave, and reminded his audience that back in 1778 the great American statesman had argued the case for Ireland's freedom, pledging to its people: 'that means will be found to establish your freedom in the fullest and amplest manner.'

'The patriots of Ireland are one in spirit with Franklin,' said de Valera. 'I hope my mission in America will be as successful as his.'

All of the historical analogies and high-profile tourist stops were merely a preamble to the main event of his Philadelphia stay. On Thursday night a spectacular torch-lit procession brought him north from his luxurious room at the Bellevue-Stratford, then regularly listed among the world's most finest hotels, to his appointment to speak at the Metropolitan Opera House. With a bodyguard of American soldiers striding either side of his car, there were more than 3,000 uniformed veterans of World War I and Irish associations of every stripe marching, waving Irish and American flags. A constant cheering sound-track was punctuated only by the sound of schoolchildren reciting a chant.

> One, two, three, four
> Whom are we for?
> De Valera, de Valera
> Rah, rah, rah

The parade took so long that some of the speeches had to be cut short. With the Opera House already packed to the rafters upon his arrival, a second outdoors overflow meeting was also hastily arranged to cater for the thousands who couldn't get in to hear the guest of honour. Having received a fifteen minute ovation when he first took the stage indoors, de Valera ended up speaking to both audiences and, in the constant drawing on America's own history to bolster his arguments, quoted at length the message George Washington had sent to the people of Ireland back in 1788.

'Patriots of Ireland! Champions of liberty in all lands. Be strong in hope. Your cause is identical with mine. You are calumniated in your day. I was misrepresented by the loyalists in my day. Had I failed, the scaffold would be my doom but now my enemies pay me honour. Had I failed, I would have deserved the same honour. I stood true to my cause even when liberty had fled. In that I merited success. You must act likewise.'

A huge crowd accompanied de Valera to the station on Friday morning to wave him off on the 10.25 train to Pittsburgh. If the first leg of the trans-continental journey had gone swimmingly, the second would be a little bumpier to negotiate. Upon arrival in the place known as the steel city, his welcoming committee was a loud and enthusiastic 10,000 strong and his first speaking engagement at Syria Mosque and Memorial Hall again required an overflow. The problem was that as de Valera was talking there, the state's own branch of the American Legion – a co-operative organisation formed earlier in the year by World War I veterans – was adopting a resolution condemning him and those who feted him.

That was a significant development because it was the first inkling of serious, organic opposition towards de Valera from a grass-roots body. Though some within the Legion ranks in Pennsylvania spoke out against the motion afterwards, it cast a shadow that would become visible regularly as the tour headed west.

Fortunately, there was no such opposition at his next stop in Youngstown, Ohio. There, he happened into the middle of the Mahoning Valley steel strike, a dispute entering its third week. Significantly, all strikers' meetings were cancelled that weekend to allow the protesting workers to instead go to the open air meeting at Idora Park where de Valera spoke. That sort of accommodating attitude set the tone for a five-day jaunt through Ohio that encompassed stops at Cincinnati and Columbus, where poor advance organisation meant the meetings didn't match the warmth of the receptions. All others also suffered by comparison with the events in Cleveland.

Five miles outside a town where Mayor Harry Davis would award him the freedom of the city, de Valera's party was met by a convoy of 500 other cars and yet one more parade was formed. This particular cavalcade was monitored on its progress by an airplane flying overhead distributing papers advertising his appearance at a mass-meeting that night. Once the city line was reached, an escort of mounted police moved in to accompany him on the way to the public square where a twenty-one-gun salute was given in his honour.

The most striking thing about this welcome was how it contrasted with that received by King Albert I of Belgium in Cleveland, just twenty-four hours earlier. On an American tour designed to promote his own country's forthcoming national loan, the monarch who'd tried rather heroically to stand up to the German advance in 1914 was afforded the usual courtesies of a head of state. But there was no twenty-one-gun salute in his name and far less pomp and ceremony accorded his stay. De Valera was obviously a little more box office and the city a little more Irish than Belgian.

From Ohio, they pushed on westward, stopping at Louisville, Kentucky en route to Indiana and engagements in Indianapolis, Fort Wayne and Valparaiso. The last of these was perhaps the most symbolic. At almost every venue in the first fortnight of his trip, de Valera had been trying to counter the argument that the Irish problem was a sectarian divide motivated by hatred of Protestants. The invitation to speak at and collect an honorary degree from Valparaiso University, a small, Protestant institution in the mid-west, represented a chance to debunk that myth by his very presence alone. Of course, less than twenty-four hours after that cameo, de Valera was in another corner of Indiana, entering arguably the most famous Catholic college in America: Notre Dame.

'Mr. de Valera will be entertained in South Bend on the 14th by the United Irish societies of the city and has accepted Father Burns' invitation to address the students of Notre Dame the next morning,' went a report in *The Notre Dame Scholastic* on 5 October 1919.' Elaborate preparations are being made at the university...If the necessary arrangements can be made, the students will be asked to turn out en masse for a parade, and the school's newly-organised band will be expected to add "tone" to the reception.'

Even though de Valera arrived one day later than originally planned, the necessary arrangements had been made. The same paper subsequently reported that he 'received one of the greatest ovations that Notre Dame has ever accorded a visitor'. This enthusiastic reception was not surprising, especially when the campus had just started offering classes in both the Irish language and Irish history.

An estimated 1,600 students greeted him upon arrival, standing in formation to spell out the letters U N D (University of Notre Dame) with their bodies, and repeatedly chanting his name. Once the adulation died down and the introductions were over, he laid a wreath at the statue of Father William Corby, a former president of the university, who also served as chaplain to the Irish Brigade during the American Civil War. Attached was a note reading; 'From Eamon de Valera in loving tribute to Father Corby- who gave general absolution to the Irish Brigade at Gettysburg.'

There was more diasporic history on the agenda too. He inspected the extensive 'Gaelic Collection' in the Notre Dame library where the sword of General Thomas Francis Meagher, the driving force behind the Irish Brigade, was on view. He also planted a tree in the quadrangle as a memorial of his visit before delivering a stirring address at Washington Hall that covered everything from justifying the events of Easter 1916 ...

'In the first place, our rising was not really a rebellion but simply another battle in a long-continued fight which has never been given up. Secondly, the object of war is not always simply to beat the enemy in the field. The object in the main is the acquiring of a political result...'

... to his belief that the enemy of my enemy is my friend ...

'As a matter of fact, England would be far more secure with Ireland a free nation than she is in her present situation. At present we will join with every enemy England has. Our present position is the gravest danger England could have. We welcome the attack of a foreign power on England even if it means conquering that country and incidentally, ourselves…'

….to the impact of English policy on the Irish population…

'Seventy years ago, our population was five-eighths that of England. She considered this as a menace too grave to be allowed to continue and by persistent oppression she has succeeded in reducing our population by half…'

The speech was rapturously received by the 1,200 students and faculty packed into the hall to hear him. Those who spent time with him, in closer quarters, were equally taken with his persona.

'His personality made even a deeper impression – his gravity when speaking of serious things, his reverence when referring to holy things,' wrote the editor of *Ave Maria* on campus. 'Few failed to observe how recollectedly he said grace at table, and how thoroughly absorbed he seemed to be while kneeling before the blessed sacrament. A good as well as a great man, a leader who inspires the highest respect and the fullest confidence…'

In an interesting addendum to this visit, de Valera left one curious legacy. At this time, the college's famous grid-iron team had a number of interchangeable and equally popular nicknames, including 'Ramblers', 'Nomads', 'Hoosiers', and 'The Fighting Irish'. The last moniker had a couple of theories claiming to explain its origin. Some contend a group of rival fans once chanted 'Kill the Fighting Irish' at Notre Dame during a close game, more trace its emanation from one of their own players making an impassioned halftime speech calling for increased effort on the grounds that most of the squad were of Irish descent. All agree about when it became predominant.

'De Valera's visit applied momentum to the Fighting Irish nickname and the Scholastic began employing it in game accounts,' wrote Murray Sperber in *Shake Down the Thunder: The Creation of Notre Dame Football*. 'After the 1919 game over Army [which took place three weeks later], the student reporter wrote that the "game unmistakably rebranded the Notre Dame warriors as 'The Fighting Irish.' "

Nothing near that tangible came out of Detroit, his next stop after South Bend. Although Mayor James J. Couzens awarded him the freedom of the city and he went down a storm both at a mass meeting and in a smaller speech before the Chamber of Commerce, a private sit-down with Henry Ford, the son of an Irish immigrant, didn't yield anything concrete.

In a letter to Arthur Griffith back in August, de Valera wrote about the need to get big American businessmen interested in the industrialisation of Ireland and mentioned Ford as a prime example of somebody with potential given that he already had a factory in Cork. Early in October, various newspapers also reported that Ford was thinking of establishing a steamship line to Ireland. Against that background, de Valera must have been hopeful when they met that good things could happen. Instead, they appeared to spend much of the encounter in a rather heated debate about the League of Nations. Consequently, de Valera left disillusioned about the motoring scion's interest in Ireland's independence, and the proposed steamship line never happened.

From Detroit, the itinerary headed back to Chicago. There, a committee from Milwaukee was waiting to bring the intrepid travellers to Wisconsin's largest city. De Valera drew 7,000 to the auditorium there, but it was where he went afterwards that made this particular state so memorable.

At midnight on Friday, 17 October he left Milwaukee, taking the overnight train to the Chippewa reservation in Spooner, in the far north-west of Wisconsin. The last leg of the trip was a thirty-four-mile drive through spectacular pine forests. Upon arrival de Valera was greeted by what the *Irish Press* in Philadelphia described as 'three thousand red men'. There followed a ceremony during which he was made a Chief of the Chippewa Indians. The first foreigner to be so honoured, he was given the title *Nay-naw-ong-gay-be,* which translates as 'Dressing Bird' or 'Dressing Feather'. It was also the name of one of the historic tribal chiefs who signed the 1854 Treaty between the Chippewa and the US Government.

If the photograph of de Valera in full headdress is the moment from his day on the reservation that has endured through history, the contemporary newspapers ran with a more formal shot of the visitor shaking hands with Chief Wolf and Padis Kedanyeve, the Chippewa's principal medicine woman. If the purposes of this entire sojourn in America were fund-raising, battling for recognition, and raising the profile of the Irish cause, the photo opportunity that allowed headlines, such as, 'Chief of Ireland now Chief of Chippewas', certainly came under the latter heading. Apart from a colourful picture, it also offered a chance to link the Irish cause with that of another downtrodden people who had been wronged by a larger power.

'The ceremony took place in an open field at which there were Indian dances and speechmaking,' wrote Katherine O'Doherty in *Assignment America.* 'Another Chief, resplendent with headdress of feathers reaching to his ankles greeted Mr. de Valera in Chippewa; next came the Head Man of the Tribe, Joe Kingfisher, who presented the Irish Chief with a handsome beaded tobacco pouch and moccasins.'

Kingfisher saw a kindred spirit in the man before him: 'I wish I were able to give you the prettiest blossom of the fairest flower on earth,' he said, 'for you to come to us as a representative of one oppressed nation to another.'

De Valera also received an elaborate wampum belt and, according to one Chippewa oral history he, in return, gifted his hosts a number of rifles. If he did, that detail was left out of the official account of the trip, thus avoiding headlines linking the Irish government with arming the Indians.

'In later years Father spoke again of his time with the Chippewa in Wisconsin,' wrote his son Terry de Valera. 'As part of the initiation ritual, the chief of the tribe and the chief elect had to draw a little blood, then to mix the blood to signify their brotherhood. This did not appeal to my father, so he somehow managed to avoid this part of the ceremony without causing offence.'

The party dined on wild rice and venison, smoked the traditional pipe of peace and attended a mass, celebrated by Father Philip Gordon. One of just two Native American priests in the country at the time, Gordon was a famous Chippewa who used his collar to fight for better rights for his fellow Indians throughout his life. Somewhere along the way – most likely at a military college full of Irish-Americans – he also developed sympathies for Ireland and was instrumental in organising de Valera's visit to his tribe.

The mass was held to commemorate those Indians who had been killed on active service during World War I, and de Valera – his speech interpreted for the locals by Ira Ishas – was politic enough to reference their sacrifice in his own speech too, before asking for help for his Ireland. 'I call upon you,' he said, 'truest of all Americans, to help us win our struggle for freedom.'

The Chippewa paraphernalia ended up being put to good use later in the de Valera home where his sons saw them as exceptionally authentic toys. 'My brothers and I were delighted,' wrote Terry de Valera. 'We could play Cowboys and Indians with real things. Ruairí always insisted that we took the Indians' side.'

CHAPTER EIGHT

Robert E. Lee never advocated leading a force shooting from behind trees at the Yankee Army. When he surrendered his armed forces in the field, he surrendered them and came back into the American union as well as he could, reconciled to the situation. The Irishmen might learn a little something from us. We are nearly all glad today that there are no Custom Houses along the Ohio and the Potomac to divide the American people. The Irish might at least learn, if they have sense – and I doubt whether they have or not – that while they are seeking the freedom of a part of Ireland, they might at least allow Ulster her freedom.

– Senator John Sharp Williams, US Senate, 16 October 1919

I n between Eamon de Valera's exultant visit to Notre Dame, colourful dalliance with the Chippewa Indians, and contentious sit-down with Henry Ford; Senator John Sharp Williams made headlines with a swingeing attack on the Irish campaign in America. During a debate on the Versailles Treaty, he claimed to have been on the receiving end of several threatening letters, some signed by 'O-something or Mc some-thing' vowing to assassinate him for his opposition to the Irish cause. A Democrat from Mississippi, Williams crossed to the

Republican side of the chamber to deliver a speech in which he sought to discredit the popularly-held belief that Irish immigrants had played a key role in the American Civil War, claiming instead they had contributed hugely on the British side in the War of Independence, and were constantly promoting the fallacious notion they'd helped defeat the Confederates.

'As a matter of fact, of course, the Irish never whipped the South. They could not whip the South at any time. It is a part of the braggart nature of the Irish. They are always contending that they have done everything everywhere at every time. I am tired of this business. I am tired of this vanity and nonsense. I do not care how many Irishmen vote the Democratic ticket.'

Several senators responded angrily from the floor to these statements. There was some mudslinging about the fact Williams was himself the descendant of Welsh immigrants, but perhaps the most cogent reply came from Democratic Senator Tom Phelan of California: 'It is just as well to let it be known again that the South was fighting for slavery while the Irish have always fought for freedom.'

Williams's speech and the prominence afforded the Legion resolution in Pennsylvania offered further evidence that while de Valera continued to draw big crowds and plenty of popular acclaim, there was a counter movement also firmly in place. As time went on, the denouncing of British influence on newspapers and various journalistic misrepresentations of the Irish cause became a staple in almost every one of his speeches.

'British propaganda has sought to make Americans believe that the issue between Ireland and England is a religious one,' said de Valera upon returning to New York. 'It is a purely political struggle. Failing in this attempt at beclouding the facts, England has turned to an attack on Ireland's attitude in the war. Ireland was the most generous nation on earth for she lost 3 million men who had been deceived into thinking that they were fighting for the rights of small nations.'

He and his handlers were also battling misconceptions and lies in a more direct way. As early as mid-August, advertisements had been placed in many newspapers promoting the Irish cause and in some cases, de Valera's forthcoming appearances. Ahead of his arrival in Kansas City, a quarter page ad referenced the historic ties between the quest for American independence and Ireland beneath the slogan 'Benjamin Franklin went to Ireland, Eamon de Valera comes to America', and with copy such as: 'America appealed to Ireland in her extremity and with equal rights and in the same noble cause Ireland appeals to America now.'

Another similarly-sized announcement laid out the case for Ireland's financial independence – 'The Irish Republic Can Pay Its Way'. This ad emphasised how Ireland was more populous and larger than various other small nations, the point being the wherewithal and resources were already in place to operate as a country under its own steam without any British input – 'Judged by any standard, Ireland is equipped for freedom.'

As the entourage made its way through the heart of middle America, the pace was relentless, especially given the fact a good impression had to be made at every stop. This involved much glad-handling, smiling for the cameras and of course, speech-making. In the course of five days starting on 20 October, the party managed to hit five different cities in Minnesota, Iowa,

Illinois and Missouri. It was a punitive schedule; de Valera's diary for this period shows that amid the fanfare, there was also turmoil brewing behind the scenes because of problems with the fund-raising.

October 22nd, Bloomington , Illinois. Arrived here after tiresome journey. Not pleased with affairs in New York and Washington…Hear that Bond Drive has not been properly organised. Joe (McGarrity) and (Charles) Wheeler impatient…

October 24th, St Louis. Presidential salute of 21 aerial bombs. Arrived at 7.25am. Parade of city; 5 speeches today. Walsh (Frank P) and McS (Edward F. McSweeney) arrive. Have long chat on Bond issue. Harry (Boland) to go back to New York to see to organisation of Bonds.

Despite the concerns back at headquarters, the deteriorating situation in Ireland (where de Valera was re-elected President of Sinn Féin at an annual convention in Dublin, which had been prohibited by the British), and the ongoing criticisms from various American politicians and organisations, the cavalcade continued on regardless.

In Springfield, Illinois, de Valera was given a gold locket containing a shamrock grown on the lawn of the home of Abraham Lincoln there. In presenting it, Lincoln's grand-niece, Miss Eva Evans said she hoped de Valera would be as successful as her grand-uncle had once been. Reverend T.W. Drumm, Bishop of Des Moines, Iowa, issued a pastoral letter to his diocese, in which he outlined the similarities between Ireland and America's own struggle for independence, and urged parishioners to support de Valera. At St Paul, Minneapolis, de Valera was so moved by the experience of speaking at a military college that he said he wished to have been able to attend such an institution himself.

However, it wasn't all sweetness and light. There was always some minor furore, or other, awaiting at the next stop. Ahead of de Valera's arrival in Kansas City on 25 October, Democratic Mayor James S. Cowgill took a stand against him on account of his anti-Versailles Treaty rhetoric, refusing to formally invite him to the city, and then declining the opportunity to sit on the welcoming committee.

The Democrats were considered the party of the Irish in America, and having another high-profile member refusing to sing from the hymn sheet was a blow to prestige, and spawned more negative coverage. It was also a particularly brave move by Cowgill given that an estimated 1 in 5 of the employees of his own city hall was Irish. That statistic was borne out by the council subsequently ignoring the mayor's position, adopting a resolution welcoming him to the town, and extending all official courtesies during his stay. 'I have no objections to this man coming,' said Cowgill. 'So far as I'm concerned he is welcome to come and say whatever he desires. But it would be inconsistent for me to invite him or to participate in his reception, believing as I do.'

The party went ahead without the mayor, but the speech de Valera delivered in Kansas and the reception afforded him there, were overshadowed by the fact he happened into the middle of a murder trial in the city courthouse. On 25 October he entered the courtroom of Judge Ralph S. Latshaw, who appeared pleased by the interruption of the murder trial of a woman named Mattie Howard, charged with participation in the death of a pawnbroker. He approached the bench and shook hands with the judge, who then led him to the platform near the witness chair. Cheering broke out in the public gallery and the guest of honour spoke: 'In Ireland court trials are more or less of a burlesque,' he said. 'They put you in jail and then forget about you.'

At the end of his brief address, many people left their seats, crowded around him and shook his hand. Even the defendant, Howard, was evidently pleased by the distraction from her own woes: 'Glad to meet you Mister President,' she said, 'you're the first president I ever met. So glad you came.'

She was later convicted and sentenced to twelve years in the state penitentiary.

After Kansas, a successful swing through Nebraska, Colorado, Idaho, Montana and Seattle drew accolades and almost uniformly positive coverage at every turn. The party reached Portland, Oregon, on the night of 13 November, and though the itinerary was made up mostly of the usual set-pieces – a visit to Columbia University, a meeting with local Archbishop Alexander Christie – this leg of the journey would garner press for mostly negative reasons. This was where the real controversy about his activities in America began to gather steam.

Upon arrival, de Valera was afforded the by-then almost customary parade from the train station to the Portland Hotel, the finest establishment in the city, the same place President Woodrow Wilson had stayed some weeks earlier on his nationwide tour to convince the American people of the merits of the Treaty.

The morning after he arrived, the car charged with ferrying de Valera around town was parked out front, with an Irish flag and an American flag billowing in unison, the same symbolic pairing that had been deployed at every turn in every state since June. It just so happened that this hotel was situated across from Liberty Temple, the local headquarters of the American Legion, and some of the former service men on duty there apparently took umbrage at the commingling of the two flags.

There are conflicting versions of what happened next. In the account put forth by Ensign AT Kurtz, a veteran of seventeen months in the Navy, he led a deputation of twenty-five Legion men which approached the individual guarding the vehicle and demanded he remove the Irish flag, because it was not an emblem officially recognised by the US Government. Before an answer could even be given, the Legionnaires ripped off the tri-colour. De Valera was not present at the time of the incident, though one newspaper account claims Dr A.C. Smith, chair of the Oregon Welcome Committee, got into a shouting match with Kurtz and his cohorts.

The matter might have ended there except Mayor George L. Baker – famous for once refusing to stop the Ku Klux Klan using public buildings for rallies – then issued an inflammatory statement declaring display of the Irish flag objectionable and prohibiting it from public use for the duration of de Valera's stay. The battle lines were drawn. As de Valera was leaving his hotel on the Saturday morning, his car and others in the convoy were decorated with the two flags again crossed on the front. The only difference was they were now surrounded by a cordon of Irish-Americans, standing sentry whilst a menacing group of Legionnaires stared on from across the street.

When de Valera's car pulled away from the curb, it did so through a path created by two lines of burly men, each carrying

Irish and American flags in their hand. Even still, the drama wasn't over. Out on the road, his car was immediately followed and chased by another vehicle. One wonders did de Valera fear for his life as the other driver tried to pull alongside, drawing parallel and closer and closer with each passing yard. Eventually, one of its passengers leaned out the window but instead of brandishing a weapon, he angrily ripped off the tricolour and left the Stars and Stripes flapping alone in the wind. And presumably left de Valera and his fellow passengers suitably relieved that was all he did.

'The flag of the Irish republic was torn from my car in Portland by British representatives, not by members of the American Legion,' said de Valera. 'America is in a mesh of British propaganda. I am confident that the American Legion would vote unanimously for Irish independence if the opportunity were given.'

Try as de Valera did to play down the controversy, it was gleefully reported and occasionally distorted by the *Los Angeles Times*, a paper which had been running a fervent anti-Irish campaign for weeks ahead of his scheduled arrival in that city on 19 November. The headline 'Oregon is aroused by Insolent Display of "Republic" Traitor Banners' offers a flavour of the *Times's* attitude towards the representatives of the First Dáil. It also devoted several inches to listing the various prominent individuals and organisations throughout America who were against his visit to LA.

'Kitchener Post World War Veterans, Long Beach unanimously denounced de Valera as a slacker and a fugitive from justice... Associated British Societies of Los Angeles denounced de

Valera as a traitor to the cause of the allies... Lady's Lily Loyal Orange Lodge of Los Angeles protested the coming of de Valera to the city...Association of Naturepathic Physicians of California declared that de Valera is spreading insidious propaganda to stir up hatred between the Anglo-Saxon people.'

Although de Valera's activities in many states had an ecumenical bent to them, there was heavy advance criticism from various Protestant pulpits around Los Angeles. Pastors at different Methodist and Presbyterian Churches had condemned him in sermons the previous Sunday, with Congregationalist Dr Thomas H. Harper describing him as somebody who wanted a 'Hun invasion' of America. Some of the outspoken clergymen were on the receiving end of hate mail and angry phone calls, subsequent to their public remarks. In reply to all this, Liam Mellows countered with a bracing defence of the Irish cause in the *Los Angeles Times*, but by then the growing amounts of flak had started to have an effect.

The degree of vitriol directed towards de Valera can be traced to the publisher Harry Chandler, who a couple of months earlier had described his interest in the Versailles Treaty thus: '... as far as the *Los Angeles Times* is concerned, the League (of Nations) is not our politics now but our religion'. Chandler obviously believed this Irishman was preaching a blasphemous doctrine against the League and had to be dealt with accordingly; not to mention that his visit was being sponsored, at least in part, by a rival organ, the *Los Angeles Examiner*.

'He is the self-styled "president" of an "Irish republic" which exists only in the imaginations of his followers,' went an unbylined piece in Chandler's paper on 16 November. 'His American "tour" is being staged, not to secure real freedom for Ireland, but for the following objects: First, to stir up opposition in this country to Great Britain. Second, to defeat, if possible, the establishment of a League of Nations. Third, to raise funds for the Sinn Feiners of Ireland who slay soldiers and peace officers and who assaulted American soldiers during the war.'

When de Valera stepped off the train from San Francisco at 11.30am on Wednesday, 19 November, there were still enough acolytes in Los Angeles to offer him the usual fanfare. A crowd at the station, many of whom wore de Valera buttons on their lapels, gave him a parade through the streets in a car bedecked in Irish and American flags and bunches of bright yellow chrysanthemums.

In the lobby of the Alexandria Hotel, another set of girls in Irish dancing costumes hurled flowers in his path as he walked, and people in the lobby offered three cheers as he made his way to the elevator. There followed a successful luncheon, during which he delivered a speech regarded as merely a warm-up for his longer soliloquy scheduled for the city's famed Shrine Auditorium that very evening. Unfortunately, word reached his hosts during the banquet that the second event was going to have to be cancelled.

Although the local organising committee had paid the $250 rental cheque in advance, the Shriners – an adjunct of the Masonic fraternity, committed to philanthropy – decided to rescind on the initial deal under pressure, it said, from its own members. They claimed not to have known the exact purpose for which their hall was going to be used by the bookers, a group called the American League for Irish Freedom. Once they had imbibed a few of the *Times's* editorials, the Shriners were totally opposed to the idea of de Valera speaking before an audience of 7,000 on their premises.

'I think de Valera is here for no other purpose than to stir up animosity against Great Britain and to interfere with the ratification of the peace treaty,' said Shriner and District Judge Benjamin F. Bledsoe. 'Considering that Great Britain was defending our hearthfires for three long years before we entered the war, I regard it as exceedingly unpatriotic that we should permit de Valera to voice his opinions here.'

The rug was pulled so late that a large crowd had already gathered on the steps of the Shrine at 7.00pm, the time when the meeting was supposed to have started. The doors were locked and a contingent of police was on hand, keeping a watchful eye in case of trouble. The cops had little to do apart from listening to a few rousing speeches of protest, denouncing the Shriners and the *Los Angeles Times*. Remaining far above the fray, de Valera didn't go to the venue, and spent the night dining at the home of the Bishop of Monterey and Los Angeles, Limerick-born John Joseph Cantwell, before decamping to San Diego for more appearances the next morning.

The Shrine Auditorium represented a huge victory for Chandler over de Valera, but the American suffered a setback too that day. Back in Washington, the Senate voted to reject the Treaty of Versailles and by extension American membership of the League of Nations proposed therein.

Angered by the Shrine Auditorium debacle, the local organisers hastily rescheduled de Valera's main Los Angeles address for the following Sunday afternoon at Washington Park, a minor league baseball stadium. Perhaps motivated by the demeaning events of earlier in the week the attendance for this, the final speech of the tour, was at least double what the Shrine would have held. Pro-de Valera sources put the crowd at 20,000, the *Los Angeles Times* stated it was well over 10,000. We trust the truth is somewhere in between. What is not in dispute is that the place hosted a fitting end to this marathon odyssey.

In a display of encouragement that lent support to de Valera's almost constant refrain that the American Legion opposition to him was more the work of malicious British agents than genuinely aggrieved natives, around 600 uniformed US Army and Navy men escorted his car to the gate of the stadium at 2.30pm. Then, as a band played, a bunch of soldiers hoisted him upon their shoulders and carried him through the entrance to his seat, on a stage between home plate and second base, facing the largest grand stand and festooned in stars and stripes and tricolours.

There, de Valera sat beside Lieutenant Rene Linguard of the French army, a tourist and war veteran who'd been reportedly so angered by the campaign being waged against the Irish representatives in the press that he'd requested to be involved in the proceedings. The pair of unlikely bedfellows listened to a stirring opening address from Joseph Scott, a prominent local attorney with a colourful CV. Born in England to an Irish mother, Scott was a devout Catholic and Hibernophile, and had famously represented two union agitators who bombed the *Los Angeles Times*, killing twenty-one people back in 1911.

For several minutes, Scott lacerated the *LA Times* for its malicious behaviour towards Ireland, and then congratulated the spectators for ignoring the scaremongering and voting with their feet. At the end of his screed, he demanded and got three cheers for de Valera before introducing the headline act. As was his custom, de Valera's opening remarks were in Irish, a device he said reminded his listeners of Ireland's linguistic and historic claim to nationhood. Apart from touching the usual bases like England's lack of moral authority in Ireland, his own hopes that the American people would sway their government to recognise his country, and the will of the Irish voters, he directly addressed the growing media criticisms about Sinn Féin's absence from World War I.

'It is said here that Ireland stabbed America in the back in the late war,' he said, waving a newspaper, the *LA Times,* in his hand to show the crowd. 'We had our own war to fight, the war that was being waged by our nation against Britain before Christopher Columbus was born, before a Hohenzollern ever sat on the throne of Prussia. We have the same right to remain neutral as did Spain or Norway. Ireland was forced to pay to Britain last year 200 million dollars in tribute. They make us pay for the ropes with which they try to strangle us. Again, I repeat, England never had any acknowledged right in Ireland. We are not an English colony and what is more, we never will be. We owe no loyalty to Britain.'

At the conclusion of a speech that lasted well over an hour, de Valera walked around the edge of the field, to give the people a proper chance to see him in the flesh and to applaud him once more.

If that was the last ovation of the tour, the party which previously took time out in Colorado to visit the grave of Buffalo Bill, couldn't resist some more sightseeing on the way back to New

York. 'We stopped off at Williams, Arizona, to view the most awe-inspiring freak of nature – The Grand Canyon – a fissure one mile deep and hundreds of miles long,' wrote de Valera's secretary Sean Nunan. 'The President and I hired cow ponies and rode down the canyon, a most pleasant change from the official engagements of the past two months.'

They were perhaps entitled to their recreation, because it had been an incredible journey. By any standard of measurement, this extended cross-country jaunt was the most successful aspect of de Valera's stay in America. In terms of raising awareness and drawing the attention of newspapers and public alike, it was a fantastic achievement. For the duration of the tour, and a good while after, coverage of all things Irish, especially in regional organs, exploded.

If de Valera deserves credit for putting himself through the daily grind: the endless trains, and a draining 130 speeches; Liam Mellows was the logistical genius and chief organiser behind the entire operation.

'For Mellows, these were days of physical strain but nervous exhilaration,' wrote C. Desmond Greaves. 'He delighted in action. He would arrive in a strange town, make contact with the Irish societies, which would sometimes exist in the flesh, at other times on paper only. If they were not strong or experienced enough to make arrangements, he must book the hall, place the advertisements and move on to a fresh place without any means of control in the one he had left. He enjoyed the strange sensation of having enough money to do all that was needed.'

Travelling ahead as advance man, Mellows had to ensure that when the main group arrived, an eye-catching reception was in place and a suitable venue available for a mass-meeting. In an era of such primitive communications, his ability to pull the various threads together was hugely impressive. Mellows also had to keep de Valera (travelling hundreds of miles behind) abreast of any changes in the detailed schedule. It was also his job to research topical issues and regional hierarchies, so that the guest of honour could pepper his conversations with nuggets of local information to impress the townsfolk. When all that was done, he still, somehow, found time to pen articles for newspapers promoting and explaining the first Dáil. Given that he regularly expressed a dislike for the country he was traversing: it was a job incredibly well done.

CHAPTER NINE

To James O'Mara, TD South Kilkenny

A chara,
In connection with the flotation and subscription of the Irish
National Loan to the United States of America, it is, in the opin-
ion of the ministry, desirable that President de Valera, who for-
merly received your assistance on National Finance, should again
have that assistance. I request you therefore to proceed to the States
and place your service at his disposal.
Is mise do chara,

– Arthur Griffith, acting-President,
9 October 1919

Within weeks of receiving that letter, James O'Mara found himself on the docks at Southampton, wearing the garb of a sailor and feigning inebriation. Part of a disguise, the drunkard act ensured nobody would question why he was being half-carried onto the *SS Lapland* by the formidable pair, Barney Downes and Dick O'Neill. The ship they manned had been switched to sail out of a different English city, but the ingenious duo, who'd safely delivered Harry Boland

and Eamon de Valera across the Atlantic already that year, were still up to the task of providing safe passage to another political stowaway. They placed O'Mara in a cubby between layers of life-saving equipment, kept a watchful eye on his safety and slipped him food at regular intervals.

These were Spartan conditions with which he wasn't accustomed. A Clongowes Wood alumnus and a graduate of the Royal University of Ireland, O'Mara was twice elected MP for Kilkenny South, gained notoriety as a skilled filibusterer during debates at Westminster, and introduced a bill in 1903 to make 17 March an official bank holiday in Ireland. Having become the first major politician to leave the Irish National (Home Rule) Party for Sinn Féin back in 1907, he served as Director of Elections in the 1918 election, was returned to office by the people of Kilkenny South and appointed a trustee of the First Dáil. He had a very impressive political resume, but that wasn't the reason his assistance was so sought-after in America.

'I wish O'Meara (sic) would come over,' wrote de Valera to Arthur Griffith in a letter on 21 August 1919. 'I need such a man very badly to act as my representative on the bond question whilst I am on this tour.'

Coming from a wealthy family synonymous with the bacon business in Limerick city, O'Mara had gained international experience in that industry and also dabbled very successfully in the London Stock Exchange. With obvious knowledge of large-scale selling and an astute financial brain, he was the perfect candidate to help unravel the mess that was threatening to derail the bond issue before it even began. His presence was so badly needed that as the ship entered Canadian waters, O'Neill and

Downes acquiesced to his desire for more airy quarters. At greater risk to their own positions, they moved him into one of the lifeboats, where he lay for another ten days when a dock strike forced the *Lapland* to have to drop anchor off Halifax.

'Dad had his own kind of courage,' wrote Patricia Lavelle, 'He accepted this arduous work without question. It needed considerable courage to abandon his new house and his fishing, to leave the management of his bacon factory in Dublin, which was working full-time and over. He knew that Ireland was facing serious trouble and that, from political unrest, we were headed to actual fighting. At that particular moment his finances were fully extended, and he would have to leave mother and the seven of us to face the growing difficulties of the time.'

On 6 November O'Mara finally reached the pier in New York. Back in sailor's clothes, he took a position near the gangway assisting with the disembarkation before then promptly walking off himself. Joseph McGarrity and Boland lay waiting to spirit him away to safety. It says much about the urgency of the whole business that within a week, O'Mara had travelled another 3,000 miles by land, crossing the country to meet up with de Valera and the rest of the touring party in Portland, Oregon. Since his role in that last leg of the marathon didn't merit any mention in public dispatches, one can only assume O'Mara went that distance purely in order to speak at length to the Chief about the troublesome nature of the bond issue.

'Bonds by day and night. Bonds will be alright! Bonds not yet in sight. Talk Bonds all day and rave all night,' wrote Boland in a diary entry for 8 November, a graphic illustration of how unwieldy the whole business had become.

Somewhere between Los Angeles and arriving back in New York on 29 November, de Valera announced to those around him that O'Mara would take over the bonds completely with Sean Nunan drafted in as his secretary. The idea was to put the organisation of the enterprise on a more solid footing, and though reportedly something of a martinet around the Fifth Avenue office, O'Mara's abrupt manner, incredible work ethic and impressive array of abilities caused his fellow workers to nickname him 'Ben' after Benjamin Franklin. That word of his impressive career back in Ireland and England had followed him across the ocean seemed to have helped too.

'In Ireland, O'Mara had been a successful merchant,' wrote Patrick McCartan. 'The Irish-American leaders understood him to be a millionaire which gave him a status with them that none of the rest of us enjoyed. In O'Mara, the rank and file had confidence: they felt that the moneys he raised by the sale of bonds would go to the Treasury of the Government of the Irish Republic. And we all shared their confidence. O'Mara gave de Valera the respect and deference due to a president; and would wait patiently, with sheaves of papers in his hand, outside de Valera's door till de Valera could give him an audience.'

It was O'Mara's brainchild to distribute a couple of hundred thousand copies of Dr William J. Maloney's 'Irish Issue', a pamphlet outlining the case for the island's self-determination for which the alleged 'British agent' waived all copyright to allow it be used as a promotional tool in the service of the sale of the bonds.

The appointment of O'Mara was a wise long-term move – but not an immediate cure to all the ills besetting the drive. More needed to be done because almost six months had now passed since the grand announcements at the Waldorf-Astoria and there was still no sign of any bonds being issued.

On 2 December de Valera went to Washington to deal with other problems, at the newly-established information office there, and during the visit somehow found time to formulate a restructuring of the organisation. The new plan was to appoint a prominent chairman in each state, to head up the selling campaign, those individuals in turn would appoint officials to head up every city and district across America, and all concerned were to capitalise on the goodwill generated by de Valera in most places he'd visited. Even with the new structure in place, the launch, once touted for November, was then put back to mid-January.

In the meantime, there was plenty more work to be done in the propaganda war, new fronts in which were opening up every day. Upon returning to New York one of de Valera's first acts had been to denounce JP Morgan & Co, an American bank then running a $250m bond issue on behalf of 'the United Kingdom of Great Britain and Ireland'. De Valera repudiated the whole business 'in the name of the Republic of Ireland.' Then, there was the arrival into the city, in early December, of a Unionist deputation from Ulster, whose purpose was to alert Americans to the 'true position and dangers which threaten the churches in Ireland by the adoption of the Sinn Féin programme.'

Made up of six clergymen (three Methodists, two Presbyterians and an Episcopalian), and William Coote, MP for South Tyrone, this delegation had been wished 'Godspeed' on their mission by Edward Carson. De Valera was prompt with his welcome too. He immediately challenged his rival lobbyists to consent to the setting-up of a commission of investigation to adjudicate the rights and wrongs of his claims and theirs. He called for a five-man panel consisting of two American clergymen nominated by Sinn Féin's representatives, two by their northern brethren and an agreed chairman. He then proceeded to issue a statement in tone and texture of a kind the visitors had come specifically to counteract.

'It is admitted by at least one member of the delegation that there are two governments in Ireland today,' said de Valera in a statement to the press on 8 December. 'Now one of these governments is a government elected by the Irish people by ballot on a basis of adult suffrage, a government of the people, by the people and for the people, the other no less demonstrably so, an alien government, a government without the consent of the governed, a government maintained solely by foreign bayonets in the interests of foreign imperialism… Is it not a fact that British rule in Ireland is at present a military regime, a regime of an army of occupation comparable to the German regime in Belgium when the Germans entered into effective control of Belgian territory? Is it not a fact that the movement for Irish independence has had for its most distinguished leaders during the past century and a half Irishmen who were not of the Catholic faith?'

He also invited Coote to debate him in any public forum on the issue of Irish independence, an offer that was not accepted.

'The case is before the American people,' said Coote. 'They are the jury and I am one of the attorneys. De Valera is the opposing attorney. I can see no benefit to the case by indulging in an argument with him.'

Some in the Irish community regarded the Protestant delegation as direct emissaries of Lord Beaverbrook, the Canadian-born newspaper mogul, who'd served as Britain's Minister of Information, and disseminator of propaganda to allied countries during World War I. Back in September, he had used his *Sunday Express* column to advocate the use of the strong Methodist and Presbyterian presence in America to counteract the excitement being engendered by de Valera and 'to crush the American Sinn Féiners as a cartwheel crushes a toad.'

During a two-month tour that brought them the width of the country, the most publicity Coote's party received was when a group of Sinn Féin sympathisers repeatedly tried to disturb a meeting at the Grace Episcopal Church on West 104th Street, in Manhattan. As Reverend Frederick Harte was speaking about the situation in Ireland, a man jumped up from a pew, walked up the aisle and shouted 'Down with the lying ministers! Hurrah for de Valera'. There ensued several more unruly disruptions before members of the NYPD finally removed the agitators. It was an embarrassing episode that de Valera condemned immediately as unrepresentative of Sinn Féin's attitude.

'We stand for freedom of speech and freedom of the press everywhere,' he said. 'We welcome the advent of these men from the north-east corner of Ulster.'

The proscription of Sinn Féin in Ireland on 25 November exacerbated the situation back home, and December quickly turned into as hectic a month for de Valera as any since he'd first walked off the *Lapland*. Apart from Coote's delegation and the ongoing bonds drama, there was growing unrest between himself and the doyennes of Irish-America, John Devoy and Justice

Coholan. If the arguments over the parameters and legalities of the bond certificates and the way in which they cut across the Friends of Irish Freedom's Victory Fund had caused bad blood, talk of a rival organisation strictly to run the bonds drive further worried the established leaders of Irish-America; not to mention the Lexington Theatre incident back in September. Consequently, at the National Council meeting of the FOIF on 10 December in New York, Devoy requested de Valera state 'the exact truth of the situation'. A précis of his attempt to clarify the state of their relationship is contained in the minutes for that gathering.

'As far as himself (de Valera) and his colleagues were concerned any accusations as regards lack of support were false; Judge Cohalan and John Devoy had given him every assistance in their power; that he had had several conferences with them and always found them ready with advice and help; nobody had tried to trip him up and he hoped there would be an end to all such mischievous statements.'

If that's an accurate representation of his speech, de Valera was at best being political and at worst downright hypocritical. Dealings between the Irish-Americans and the Irish were increasingly fraught because de Valera wanted more autonomy than was available within the strictures of the Friends of Irish Freedom, a pre-existing organisation that had been founded and was still ably led by Devoy and Cohalan. Relations were complicated by a number of other factors. The Friends boasted huge financial resources and – in the absence of any bond revenue as yet – were actually supporting the visitors from Ireland. Their end of year accounts for 1919 show that a vast sum of

$26,748.26 was spent on de Valera's travelling expenses alone, a figure that, according to inflation calculators, would translate as $365,483.42 in today's money.

If that didn't cause enough difficulties, there was also the timing of the annual convention. It came just two days before de Valera was back in Washington for a House Foreign Affairs Committee meeting where one of the chief witnesses would be Cohalan. This was hardly the time to be going public with any grievances. 'Peace?' wrote de Valera beside the listing of that event in his diary.

The House Committee was considering the Mason Bill, a piece of legislation aimed at directing the US government to spend $14,000 annually on the salaries of a Minister and consuls for the new Irish Republic. Introduced back in May by Representative William E. Mason, Republican, Illinois – it was of course about much more than the money. For the House to agree to those funds being appropriated for that purpose would amount to a Congressional recognition of the Irish Republic. The hearings took place on 12 and 13 December against a curious backdrop. The Treaty and League of Nations had been defeated for the first time in the Senate, just a few weeks earlier, and President Woodrow Wilson was incapacitated following an October stroke – the true debilitating effects of which were concealed from the American people for the rest of his time in office. In any case, *The New York Times* felt the bill had little chance of success, and the hearings were merely a cosmetic exercise to appease Irish-American voters heading into an election year.

'The claim of the Irish republic to recognition as an

independent government was brought to Congress again yesterday and was debated in militant fashion throughout a tempestuous all-day session of the House Committee on Foreign Affairs,' went an Associated Press report on the front page of *The Washington Post*. 'A crowd which jammed the committee room and blocked adjoining corridors punctuated the proceedings with hoots of disapproval as the opposing speakers presented their arguments, and many times threw the session into disorder by yelling gratuitous advice to committee and witnesses. It included many leaders of the cause of Irish freedom in this country and manifested in many ways its sympathy with the plea for recognition.'

Cohalan was joined on the witness stand by Frank P. Walsh, and Boland sat with the pair, often leaning in to offer advice and clarifications to assist them with their answers. The opposing testimony was provided by Professor George L. Fox, a lecturer at Yale, and Rev. Dr George T. Lemon of Albany, secretary of the National Orangemen's Association. During what was a tumultuous affair, Cohalan grabbed most of the headlines and plaudits from the Irish-American lobby by baldly asserting his belief that America should be prepared to go to war with England, even if it meant forcing the recognition of Ireland.

Representative Tom Connally of Texas (Democrat): Supposing we should pass this resolution and Great Britain should take offence at it, and our action should eventuate in war; as an American citizen would you be willing for America to go to war to maintain the freedom of Ireland?

Cohalan: I am going to answer your question and there will not be any doubt as to my reply. I say yes... I insist and I reiterate that, as an American citizen, I would be in favour of absolutely doing that which was just.

It's fair to assume de Valera must have been in two minds about Cohalan's show-stopping performance. He had travelled down to Washington, as well, but didn't appear on Capitol Hill that day. Perhaps the decision was made that it would have looked decidedly unpresidential for a man claiming to be the leader of his own country to be sitting in the cheap seats during the hearing, as a boisterous crowd waved tricolours and hurled insults at their opponents. The supporters were at their most uproarious after one Congressman asked Walsh how the Irish Republic was being run at all if its president was roaming America. The noise that ensued spared him from answering the question, although somebody on the floor did shout out that America was still governed while Wilson had been in Paris.

De Valera cropped up too when James S. McGraw, a Presbyterian minister from Pittsburgh, read into evidence the resolution passed by the American Legion in Pennsylvania, declaring that de Valera had used his influence to handicap the cause of Great Britain and the Allies in the war, and protesting against his activities in the United States. Still, the star turn was provided by Cohalan.

'We point out that in no country since the armistice was signed has a plebiscite been taken except in Ireland, and that there with a political unanimity which can be found in no other quarter of the world, the people decided by a popular vote of almost four to one in favour of the establishment of a separate and independent form of government,' said Cohalan. 'A recognition of the republic of Ireland by the United States of America would give the people of England the opportunity of bringing their government to see that it was the part of wisdom to agree with our view and to leave the government of Ireland to the people of Ireland.'

Even though the matter of the Mason Bill would drag on well into 1920 and ultimately die on the committee room floor, Cohalan did a fine job that day articulating the kind of argument which de Valera had made his own stock-in-trade over the previous six months. Afterwards, Dr Patrick McCartan practically ran towards the judge to shake his hand and congratulate him on his display – it was a hugely symbolic gesture given they were both on different sides of the growing chasm. With the developing tension in the movement, it's fair to assume de Valera must have been conflicted by the news of such a virtuoso performance. The natural inclination to share McCartan's undoubted pleasure at seeing the Irish cause so properly represented at such a crucial forum must have been laced with concern about an increasingly troublesome ally stealing the limelight. If nothing else, Cohalan's impact that day gave weight to his own belief that he was the unofficial leader of 20 million Irish-Americans.

On 22 December, Lloyd George outlined the parameters of a new Government of Ireland Bill in the House of Commons. Speaking just three days after the failed IRA assassination attempt on Lord French, Lord Lieutenant of Ireland, at Ashtown, in Dublin, had garnered international headlines, the Prime Minister outlined a plan proposing two parliaments for the island, one in Dublin to govern twenty-six counties, another in Belfast to govern a six-county Ulster. In an explanation, arguably designed to impact directly on de Valera, George compared the prospective powers of each body to those of the state legislatures in America, and warned that any attempt at secession from Britain 'would be fought with the same force and determination as the northern states fought the southern states during the American civil war.'

That very night, de Valera was back in the spotlight himself, drawing a crowd of 8,000 to the Broadway Auditorium in the upstate New York city of Buffalo. Introduced by Reverend William Turner, the Kilmallock-born Bishop of Buffalo, who took the opportunity to slam the 'pro-British faction in this country which is spreading anti-Irish and anti-American propaganda', it was de Valera's response to the new bill in London that dominated the coverage of his appearance.

'I have not seen Lloyd George's latest plan for two parliaments in Ireland and before reading it in detail, I cannot, of course, comment upon it in detail,' he said. 'All I can say is that the Irish people have accepted and acted upon the principle of self-determination, and have shown that what they want is an independent Irish republic, free from the domination of any imperial authority. We deny the right of any foreign statesman to dictate to the Irish people what form government they shall live under. It is my belief that this new parliamentary plan, outlined by the British Prime Minister, is nothing more than another attempt of British politicians to fool the Irish people.'

From Buffalo it was a short spin across to Rochester, where de Valera was going to spend Christmas with his mother for just the third time in his life. The strengthening or the reawakening of the bonds between Catherine and her boy must have been an inevitable byproduct of this entire episode. There are conflicting reports about the true nature of their relationship. If it was very obviously not a standard mother-son arrangement, the pair appeared to forge a special sort of bond that endured spending decades apart, and up until her death in 1932, she also campaigned for him at several crucial junctures in his career.

'There is ample evidence to show that a truly loving and lasting relationship existed between Kate de Valera and her son,' wrote Terry de Valera, and while obviously not a wholly objective source, he based his opinion on the evidence of a stash of letters exchanged between the pair.

The warmth and security of a familial atmosphere during the holiday season must have provided some welcome respite from his gruelling schedule. It was also a measure of how much his world had turned in just twelve months. De Valera had spent Christmas 1918 in Lincoln Jail. Seven months into his stay there, he had just been returned in absentia for both the Mayo East and Clare East constituencies in the General Election that give birth to the First Dáil. That he'd whiled away Christmas Eve there writing a coded letter he hoped would help speed along his escape from the prison summed up his position. One year on, he was writing more prosaic letters to the Irish people.

'Greetings to the persecuted people of Ireland from the many millions of Americans who love liberty and who love people everywhere who will not be denied liberty,' wrote de Valera in his 1919 Christmas message sent back to Arthur Griffith and the citizens of the Republic. 'Work and pray and endure yet a little while. The year 1920 may see the Republic of Ireland officially recognised by the United States, and then final victory after seven hundred and fifty years. Everyone, colleagues, and self are doing our duty.'

The one thing that hadn't changed between this Christmas and the last was his absence from his own family. Between stints in jail, time on the lam in Dublin, and his departure to America, he had only lived with them continuously for eleven months since the Easter Rising – more than three and a half years earlier. By now, Sinéad de Valera had borne him six children, two during his time in prison, and all of whom were under the age of ten. It was quite a brood for a woman to deal with on her own.

'Another New Year's night away from you and the children – I hope you are not as lonely as I am,' wrote de Valera to his wife on 31 December 1919, from the Shoreham Hotel, Washington. 'This separation is the great sacrifice and I know it is hard on you. When playing with the youngsters at Joseph McGarrity's, I felt more lonely than ever.'

She remained at the family home in Greystones, County Wicklow, where Michael Collins paid almost weekly visits to update her on the state of affairs in America and eventually, he would organise a false passport and her passage across the Atlantic. Collins always included a report on the family's welfare in his missives to de Valera and ironically, given the impact the McGarrity children had on the absent father, even waxed lyrical about how much fun he had playing with the de Valera children.

CHAPTER TEN

We, the members of our city's municipal body, the Board of Alder-
men, appreciating the spirit of the American Government which
has ever extended its protection and sympathy to all lovers of
democracy who have been compelled to seek either assistance or an
abode of safety, and recognizing in the person of Eamon de Valera
the right to seek our appreciation as the legally and sovereignly
elected President of the Republic of Ireland, and desiring to recip-
rocate the solicitude and comfort bestowed upon a foreign Ambas-
sador from these shores in the person of Benjamin Franklin by the
people of Ireland, hereby cordially and with deep concern for his
Honor's welfare, tender unto him the freedom and welcome of our
city and its citizens, and urge our fellow-citizens to join us in
those, our heartfelt felicitations.

- Resolution of New York Board of Alderman,
27 June 1919

From very early on Saturday morning, 17 January 1920,
a crowd began to gather near the foot of the marble
steps leading up to New York's City Hall. Some of
them carried Irish tricolours in their hands. All were anxiously
waiting to see Eamon de Valera finally arrive to receive the

freedom of the city. Six months had passed since a vote had been taken in favour of conferring such an accolade and now the formal ceremony would serve as the opening salvo in a nine-day promotional frenzy called 'Irish Loan Week' during which, at long last, the bond certificates would be sold.

By the scheduled starting time of midday, an estimated 1,000 people were milling on the steps and the walkways in front of the impressive façade. Among them were nine pipers, who marched up and down in military formation blasting 'The Wearing of the Green' and other Irish tunes. One of them even had an ornate old dagger protruding from the top of one of his pipes. Whether that was meant to be a historic symbol of Ireland's struggle or a convenient weapon in case of trouble, isn't clear. What can be said for certain is that the soundtrack was merely one layer of the inevitable colourful pageantry.

By the time de Valera's cortege of cars swung into City Hall Park, escorted by Colonel A. E. Anderson and a number of other veterans from the 165th Regiment, children from the Carmelite School were standing sentry along the steps, each boy and girl wearing traditional Irish costume. He walked this welcoming gauntlet to rousing cheers, and was met at the door of the building by the mayor's secretary John H. Sinnott. As they strolled through the rotunda together, the corridors were suddenly thronged, and the reception equally noisy and welcoming for an entourage that read like a who's who of the city's Irish. In spite of the growing tensions between them, John Devoy and Justice Cohalan were there for the centre-piece event of a bond campaign they had fervently opposed.

It was Sligo-born William Bourke Cochran who formally

presented de Valera to Mayor John F. Hylan in the aldermanic chamber. A former Congressman acknowledged by judges, including his friend Winston Churchill, as one of the great orators of the age, Cochran had distinguished himself over the previous decades with some fiery speeches denouncing Imperialist atrocities around the world. The sixty-five-year-old attorney had also been Grand Sachem of Tammany Hall - the powerful Democratic Party machine that controversially and rigorously controlled New York politics and patronage for more than a century and a half. The Irish-American Tammany was wholly responsible for Hylan holding the city's highest office in the first place, and he performed his duties admirably when it came to eulogising his guest and lending official legitimacy to his activities in America.

'It is a privileged honour, personal as well as official, to greet most cordially in the person of Eamon de Valera, the President of the Irish Republic,' said Hylan. 'I do so officially as Chief Executive of the city of New York, in concord with the resolution of the board of Aldermen calling on me as mayor to convey to him the welcome, in addition to the freedom, of the metropolis of the western world, the city of New York. The performance of this official duty also gives me personal satisfaction as an American citizen who feels that self-determination in principle and practice should not be denied to the people of Ireland.

'The question that must be answered sooner or later is why Ireland, alone among the smaller nations, should be excluded from a just and legitimate share in the triumph of the late war. Your own enthusiastic and most sincere reception throughout our glorious country, and may I say your dignified campaign of education, coupled with a masterly presentation of safe and sane governmental policy, have not failed to impress the American people with the justice of Ireland's cause and with the ultimate realisation of her national liberty and aspirations.'

Hylan went on to laud the contribution of the fighting 69th and, showing perhaps the impact that de Valera's constant referencing of it was having, he even made mention of Sinn Féin's thorough triumph in the 1918 General Election. Any joy at his labouring of such an overtly political point on behalf of his visitors had to be tempered by the knowledge that, just two months earlier, Hylan had waxed even more lyrical when granting the freedom of the city to the Prince of Wales during his tour of America and Canada. Although *The New York Times* mentioned that slight contradiction in its coverage on Sunday morning, nobody dared mention that anomaly on the day. It would have been out of sync with the celebratory mood.

Upon accepting the scroll from Hylan, de Valera began his response 'Mr Mayor' but was allowed to go no further than that. Somebody in the crowd yelled out a demand for three cheers for the mayor, and duly received just that amount. De Valera started again but with similar results. This time the three cheers were requested for Frank P. Walsh, the veteran campaigner whose attendance was also deemed worthy of recognition. There followed yet one more noble call for Bourke Cochran. Finally, at the fourth time of asking, the native New Yorker who'd returned to claim its ultimate municipal honour was allowed to speak.

Eschewing the opportunity to mention this incredible journey of a nervous child on a dock waving goodbye to his home and leaving his mother behind, de Valera stuck instead to the usual staid pleasantries. He thanked Hylan: 'Mr. Mayor, I feel that to be received by the Chief Magistrate of New York is always a high honour' and then adhered to the script:

'That expression of sympathy which your action and that of the Board of Aldermen so clearly conveys will be appreciated by the Irish people for whom it is intended and by the rest of the world, on whom its significance will not be lost... the whole people of the fair island, your neighbour over there across the Atlantic, yearns with a yearning that only those who have long been denied liberty can understand.'

Beyond the predictable platitudes of the acceptance speech, de Valera began the hard sell. Under the aegis of Walsh's American Commission on Irish Independence, the body that had gone to Versailles to fight for Ireland's place at the treaty negotiations; an estimated one million canvassers nationwide were about to approach the Irish-American community to buy bonds for the cause. An impressive figure when published in the newspapers that week, it was also, of course, a hugely exaggerated one. After Hylan backed up his words with the purchase of the first bond-certificate to be issued, de Valera clarified for reporters, at City Hall, the exact nature of what was being sold.

'It will be distinctly understood by each subscriber to the loan that he is making a free gift of his money. Repayment of the amount subscribed is contingent wholly upon the recognition of the Irish Republic as an independent nation. Each member will receive a certificate of indebtedness of the republic, signed by myself, or my deputy, which certificate is non-negotiable and non-interest bearing. The certificate will be exchangeable at par for gold bonds of the republic upon presentation at the treasury of the republic after freedom is obtained. The gold bonds will bear 5 per cent interest from the date of the recognition of the republic and will be redeemable at par one year after the same date.'

Twenty-four hours later, de Valera was the main attraction at a mass meeting at the Lexington Theatre on 51st Street, a three-hour event designed to generate more publicity for the bonds issue. Presided over by Cochran and officially blessed by Father Duffy, there was an eclectic list of speakers, including Judge Cohalan, Rabbi David Klein from the Bronx, and Nancy O'Rahilly, wife of The O'Rahilly, founder of the Irish Volunteers who was killed in the Easter Rising. During his own contribution, Cochran read a letter of support from Archbishop Hayes that included a cheque for $1,000 to pay for his own personal bond.

'After a very satisfactory conference with Mr. de Valera, President of the Irish Republic, I am convinced that his program for the agricultural, industrial and commercial development of Ireland is entirely practical and constructive,' wrote Hayes. 'If England would but approach in a large Christian spirit the dilemma the Irish problem has evolved, Erin would prove more than generous and noble as a friendly neighbour, would never allow herself to be the pawn of any foreign power, and would be foremost to maintain the highest standards of Christian civilisation. With these world facts before us, Ireland would be welcomed as one of the most conservative forces of our distressed times.'

When the headline act finally approached the stage, a small African-American boy presented him with what the papers called 'a hillcock of roses', the auditorium turned into a sea of green, white and orange flags, and delivered an ovation that lasted six and a half minutes. As was now his custom, de Valera began the speech in Irish but by the time he reached the most crucial point, was speaking in a tongue understood by all present. 'We have issued bonds, and these bonds are bonds of the Irish people,' said de Valera, reiterating his point from the previous day. 'These bonds will be profitable in the end. Those who buy them will have a personal share in the Republic of Ireland. We aren't so much interested in the bonds as we are in the by-products of them, such as the devoted help they will inspire.'

If de Valera appeared to be going to great lengths to remind his market this wasn't exactly a sound financial investment, that much appeared to have been lost on this particular audience, as representatives of the various boroughs of New York all boasted about the grand sums they would raise. Once John J. Rooney, chairman of the campaign in Manhattan, announced his team had already received pledges of $500,000 and were confident of eventually doubling that, Joseph J. Finnegan guaranteed Brooklyn would yield sales of a million dollars too. Slightly more conservative spokesmen for the Bronx and Queens estimated their corners of the city would bring in $250,000 and $200,000 respectively. Altogether the figures made for good copy and lent weight to the belief that a target of $10m nationwide was attainable. However, there was discontent within the ranks.

'I feel it somebody's duty to protest against the financial appeal being made by the so-called "president" of the mythical "Irish Republic", de Valera,' said Alderman W. F. Quinn, a New York politician of Irish descent, who denounced the scheme with a swingeing statement that very day. 'This man no doubt is sincere in his dream of freedom, and as there is nothing dearer to an Irishman's heart than the freedom of the Old Sod his appeal no doubt will have tremendous effect… A bond issue is a financial lien against a tangible property. The misty dream of a deluded agitator is not and never can be called security for a bond issue. If this man de Valera is sincere let him tell the truth about these subscriptions for Irish freedom.

'It is not a subscription to a bond issue but a financial gift to the man who thinks he is going to free Ireland by travelling around the United States, having his expenses paid by appealing to the sweetest sentiments of the most generous race on earth, aided and abetted by a bunch of political bronco steerers who have been fooling the Irish and the Irish descendants in this city for years… Good Americans, including Irish and Irish descendants, don't forget that this man de Valera is doing almost identically the same thing in this country that we are deporting the radicals for.'

Less than a month earlier, the anarchist Emma Goldman and 248 other foreign-born radicals (dubbed 'Reds' by the press for their union activities) had been deported out of New York on the SS *Buford*, at the behest of attorney general, A. Mitchell Palmer, nicknamed the Fighting Quaker. De Valera was in no such danger, as even before the public relations triumph of the bond launch, 1920 had gotten off to a very promising start. He'd been feted by the New York Chapter of the Knights of Columbus, drew huge crowds while receiving the freedom of the Connecticut state capital Hartford, and even found time to visit a cousin, Sr Mary Bartholomew, at a convent near the city.

At a gathering of Congressmen in Washington DC which he

attended, Representative Isaac R. Sherwood of Ohio, a former general who'd fought in forty-two battles of the civil war, had described him as 'the greatest moral hero around the world'. There was another honour bestowed too. In mid-December Joseph McGarrity's wife had given birth to the couple's sixth child, they christened the boy Eamon de Valera McGarrity, and asked his namesake to serve as godfather. His trip down to Philadelphia for the ceremony became an occasion for political comment when he was asked his opinion on the failed assassination attempt on Lord French. 'It did not shock me more than an attempt to assassinate General Von Bissing [Germany's tyrannical military ruler of Belgium between 1914 and 1917] by the Belgians would have shocked me during the war. Lord French is the head of the military occupation in Ireland by a foreign power.' Again, he drew a comparison between prevailing conditions in Ireland and the suffering of the Belgians when the Germans rolled through, the sort of image that might resonate with the American public.

All these happenings were only preambles to the serious business of the bonds. After the Lexington Theatre, he headed north to the New York state capital of Albany. There, he had lunch with Democratic Governor, Al Smith - later to earn his place in history as the first Roman Catholic to run for President - and was given a public reception at City Hall by Mayor James R. Wyatt. Twelve thousand people filled the city Armory on Washington Avenue to which de Valera had been escorted by a band and a group of ex-US servicemen.

'The Republic of Ireland is not seeking establishment,' he told that audience. 'It has been established. It is established. What the

Republic seeks is formal recognition of its existence by other nations.'

De Valera didn't shy from the issue of talking money and its political implications either.

'When England borrows money from the United States, she pledges the security of Ireland, as well as England, to make good that loan. In Ireland, a huge army of occupation is maintained. That costs money and the money comes through the loans granted to Great Britain by the United States.'

All of this was designed to make sure that the crowd departed this and every public engagement roused enough to put their money where their mouths were. Some had already been moved simply by news of de Valera's travels throughout the country. The New York office received a subscription in writing from a man in Juneau, Alaska. A Greek waiter in Manhattan who'd grown enamoured of the cause bought eleven bond certificates worth hundreds of dollars. From Ireland, Archbishop William J. Walsh, of Dublin, had sent a cheque for 100 guineas - reproduced in McGarrity's *Irish Press* for all to glory at.

They were inundated too by requests from people wishing to exchange Liberty Bonds, purchased to help finance the Allied cause in World War I, at face value for the Irish equivalent. This strand of the business brought with it unforeseen trouble. 'The near illegality of the whole bond-certificate sale carried with it some danger of government restriction,' wrote FM Carroll in *American Opinion and the Irish Question, 1910-23*. 'A Boston publisher and bookseller wrote to President Wilson to ask if the government had given tacit approval to the Irish bond-certificates by allowing them to be exchanged at par value for Liberty Bonds. Frank P. Walsh was eventually sent a stern note from the secretary of the Treasury warning that such practices must stop. The feeling in the State department was that the administration was allowing an outrageous situation to develop.'

Opposition was coming from other angles too. A, by now, familiar nemesis, Mississippi Senator John Sharp Williams, wondered if de Valera and his fellow travellers could be federally indicted for 'missions of military enterprise against the dominions of a foreign state at peace with the United States'. Just to put Williams's continued attacks on the enterprise in some context, he also regarded the Fifteenth Amendment to the US Constitution - the one allowing former slaves the right to vote as - 'one of one of the greatest crimes in political history.' Still, he must have enjoyed *The Wall Street Journal*'s conclusion about the Irish fund-raising.

'More than one inquiry has been directed to this paper as to the status of the so-called "bonds" of the equally so-called "Irish Republic",' mused the *Journal* on 4 February. 'Are these being sold to Irish domestic servants, and others of a like or lower standard of intelligence, as a legitimate investment for money in the savings banks? Legally everything hangs on the terms on which the money was taken by the seller of these mere receipts. Sold as bonds, the de Valera issue is nothing more or less than a swindle. Truthfully described as a fund for Irish propaganda, with every contribution received and recorded as a gift, the proposition has another and better status although it is still open to severe criticism.'

The Wall Street Journal had been beaten to the punch, a week earlier, by one of it business rivals. Another financial newspaper called *The Street* posed similar relevant questions about the quasi-legal status of the offering, its critique somewhat undermined, though by tired old saws, about perceived Irish ignorance. A small-circulation organ whose voice might not have been heard, at all, beyond its own readership, highlights of the screed were helpfully reproduced for a wider audience by *The New York Times*.

'The new so-called "Irish loan" is very Irish in its confusion of terminology, and has all the originality, the bright disregard of common sense characteristic of the Irish,' went the piece in *The Street*. 'As such it is excellent comedy. Unfortunately, this "Irish loan" has also many extremely disturbing and dangerous aspects for Americans in 1920 ... Irish Bonds or Bonds certificates - call them as you please - are not even a speculative wildcat security. They are not a security at all, and the only motive which would have led de Valera & Co. to lend them the terminology always associated with securities is a desire to confuse the ignorant or inexperienced American citizen and swindle him out of his money. It is passing strange that some of our politicians who have shown such apparent horror of Wall Street, and who have clamoured for "blue sky laws" and about crooked promoters should so blandly place their benediction upon what is in many ways one of the most impudent attempts to swindle Americans in the history of American finance.'

Despite or maybe because of some of that negative coverage, 303,578 individuals eventually bought into the idea of the Irish bond-certificate and raised $5,123,640. The vast majority of those people purchased denominations of $5, $10 and $25, a point underlined by the statistic that the greater New York contribution of $1m stemmed from roughly 100,000 different men and women. The relatively small amounts signify that they were ordinary working folk, probably stretching to invest what they could in the Irish dream. At point of sale, every one of them wrote a cheque payable to Eamon de Valera in whose name bank accounts were now opened across the country. This detail allowed each buyer to feel personally connected with the cause to which they were subscribing. In return they received a document containing the following inscription.

To_____

I, Eamon de Valera, President of the Elected Government of the Republic of Ireland, acting in the name of and by the authority of the elected representatives of the Irish Nation issue this Certificate in acknowledgment of your subscription of $25 to the First National Loan of the Republic of Ireland. This Certificate is not negotiable but it is exchangeable if presented at the Treasury of the Republic of Ireland one month after the international recognition of the said Republic for one $25 Gold Bond of the Republic of Ireland. Said Bond to bear interest at five per cent per annum from the first day of the seventh month after the freeing of the territory of the Republic of Ireland from Britain's military control and said Bond to be redeemable at par within one year thereafter.

Signed by Sean Nunan or de Valera himself

Unfortunately, this also added another complex layer to the already problematic logistics of fund-raising in as vast a country as the United States. The actual selling of the bonds was only the start of a very long and involved process because, while getting people to hand over their hard-earned cash in return for an ornate piece of paper was one thing, ensuring that same cash got back to Ireland without the British government interrupting its progress was another thing altogether. An elaborate stratagem for laundering the first batch of money collected involved using three different banks to remove all traces of its origins and culminated in a draft being written in the name of Fr Denis O'Connor of New York. Pastor of the Carmelite Priory on 28th Street, Irish-born O'Connor's draft was dressed up as a $200,000 gift from him to Bishop Michael Fogarty of Killaloe, who just happened to be one of the trustees of the First Dáil.

If the pace with which the money made its way across the Atlantic proved troublesome for those back in Ireland, who were literally fighting to keep the show on the road, the drive was important on a number of other levels in America. Long after de Valera had visited a city or town, the selling of bonds there and the publicity it engendered in the newspapers kept the Irish question in the national conversation. The very manner in which the scheme was conducted too, using the language and apparatus befitting a government-backed bond held huge significance.

'… the Dail government and its supporters worked diligently to ensure that Ireland carried out all of the motions or all of the roles of an international legal "person", a de jure regime, a legitimate nation-state,' wrote Francis M. Carroll in *Money for Ireland*. 'The bond-certificates had a symbolic value in addition to the money generated. The bond-certificate drive and the money it raised were powerful tools in the struggle to convince people in Ireland, Britain, and the rest of the world that the Irish Republic existed and that Dáil Éireann was its legitimate government.'

CHAPTER ELEVEN

The United States by the Monroe Doctrine made provision for its security without depriving the Southern Latin Republics of their independence and their life. The United States safeguarded itself from the possible use of the Cuba island as a base for attack by a foreign power by stipulating that 'the Cuban Government shall never enter into any treaty or other compact with any foreign power or powers which shall impair or tend to impair Cuban independence, nor in any manner authorize or permit any foreign power or powers to obtain by colonisation or for military or naval purposes, or otherwise a lodgement in or control over any portion of said island'. Why doesn't Britain do with Ireland as the United States did with Cuba? Why doesn't Britain declare a Monroe Doctrine for her neighbouring island? The people of Ireland, so far from objecting, would co-operate with their whole soul

- Eamon de Valera, *New York Globe,*
6 February 1920

O n 6 February the city of Worcester, in central Massachusetts, was battered by a winter storm. When it was over, the streets were piled high with snow drifts, the transportation systems had ground to a halt, and then, to add to the chaos, the heavens opened to spill an icy rain on the mess below. This was the unpromising sight that greeted de Valera when his train pulled into Union Station for the first stop on a brief tour of major New England hubs, designed to whip up enthusiasm and support before the formal commencement of bonds sales in that region of the country on 23 February. It was an auspicious place to start.

'Notwithstanding the fact that the streets were filled knee-deep in places with icy slush, a parade, in which it is estimated about 700 men and women participated, escorted de Valera from his hotel to Mechanics Hall, between lanes of cheering men, women and children, estimated at 40,000 who stood for more than an hour in the driving rain,' went the report in the *Boston Globe*. 'And the vast majority of that great throng had to wade from their homes through drifts and slush to take their places along the lines of the parade because there was no other way for them to reach the centre of the city.'

Having received the freedom of the city, de Valera picked up an honorary law degree from the College of the Holy Cross, before heading west to Springfield. There, another excited parade was soundtracked by army bands, accompanied by World War I veterans, and witnessed by locals, who again appeared curiously unaffected by the severe weather conditions. A similar story ensued in Lowell, where he was met by yet more thunderous ovations, rapt audiences and queues of politicians and dignitaries wanting to shake his hand. It was all a wonderfully choreographed visit to a friendly part of the country, perfectly pitched to capture the imaginations of people and move them to back up that support with money.

It was also seriously out of kilter with the way in which the campaign had just been shunted into the sidings by de Valera's own ill-chosen words. The day before leaving for Worcester, W.J. Hernan, New York correspondent for *The Westminster Gazette*, requested an interview. Figuring this to be a publication that was read by prominent English politicians, bound to reach the desk of Prime Minister Lloyd George, and widely circulated in Dublin too, de Valera agreed. Better yet, he even handed the journalist a draft of a pamphlet he was writing entitled: 'The Moral Basis of the Claim of the Elected Government of the Republic of Ireland for Official Recognition'. He was proofing that work in progress before a planned unveiling of it as his opening speech on his jaunt through Massachusetts.

Hernan was invited to use the paper as the substance of his 'interview' but in his determination to assist the reporter, de Valera didn't realise the journalist's work also appeared in *The New York Globe*. It was that organ which ran the article a day before it hit the streets in London and caused a stir that exacerbated the growing split in the Irish community in America, created consternation back in Dublin, and almost undid all of the good achieved to that point in de Valera's visit. The writer Frank O'Connor perhaps best captured the brouhaha when he wrote of the incident: 'a minute dash of principle provided the excuse for a flood of viciousness and folly.'

The crux of the issue centred on the quote that begins this chapter. *The Globe* decided that portion dealing with the Monroe Doctrine - when President James Monroe warned European countries about interfering in Latin American territories, while asserting America's own right to do so in his 1823

Above: Eamon de Valera and Harry Boland arriving in style

Below: United Irishmen: On top of the Waldorf-Astoria, June, 1919. From left: Harry Boland, Liam Mellows, Eamon de Valera, Dr Patrick McCartan and Diarmuid Lynch. Sitting: John Devoy

Left: Read all about it: *The Kansas City Star* advertises a forthcoming de Valera appearance

Below: Surround sound: Eamon de Valera delivering a speech at Washington Park baseball stadium in Los Angeles, November 1919

Above: Generation gap: Shaking the hand of eighty-four- year-old Sligo native Mary Keelty Sullivan, in Chicago

Below: Money shot: A $10 bond certificate purchased by one Thomas Kennedy, a labourer from Holyoke, Massachusetts

Left: Church and State: Eamon de Valera and Archbishop Patrick Hayes of New York, St Patrick's Day Parade, 1920

Below: Home run: The Boston Red Sox' Fenway Park is packed to the rafters for Eamon de Valera's first public speech of the tour, June 1919

Above: Hear ye, hear ye: Eamon de Valera pointing the way forward at Fenway

Below: Welcome on the mat: American soldiers and sailors are among those excitedly greeting Eamon de Valera upon his arrival in San Francisco, 1919

Above: Hail to the Chief: The Chippewa Indians awarded Eamon de Valera the title Chief Nay-naw-ong-gay-be, October 1919

Right: Comic relief: A Chicago cartoonist comments on de Valera's outsized role at the Republican Convention, June 1919

IRELAND'S
"President"

De Valera Is Not Really a Candidate in This Convention.

LLANUZA—

Below: 'Then and not till then': De Valera unveils a statue of Robert Emmet in San Francisco's Golden Gate Park, July 1919

Above: Mother's Day: With his mother, Catherine Wheelwright, in Rochester, 1927

State of the Union - was the most sensational aspect of the piece because in their interpretation it represented a major shift in policy. 'De Valera opens the door' ran the headline to reflect their belief that this was the extension of an olive branch of sorts to the British.

It was even described as 'a withdrawal by the official head of the Irish Republic of the demand that Ireland be set free to decide her own international relations.' According to his subsequent statements, this is not what de Valera had in mind, but his critics and enemies immediately seized upon it. Suddenly, the cracks running along the surface of the Irish-American movement began to broaden into fissures so large they almost swallowed up the entire campaign.

'The effect of the publication can easily be foreseen,' wrote John Devoy in the *Gaelic American*. 'It opens the way for the discussion of a compromise or a change in objective, while England has her hands on Ireland's throat. It will be hailed in England as an offer of surrender... The Britishers will conduct their side of the controversy in the hope of creating a cleavage among the Irish forces in Ireland and America. England's only hope of triumphing over Ireland now lies in the possibility of creating disunion in the Irish ranks... The Cuban precedent is cited... but he must know that the Cuban Government was kept in a strait jacket by the United States'.

At the very least, it appears de Valera didn't know the ins and outs of the Cuban-American relationship or if he did, either misinterpreted its true nature or failed to properly clarify the point he wanted to make. In his defence, he had been averaging almost four or five public engagements a day for nearly eight months by the time he invoked the Monroe Doctrine. Having to be so constantly on message with every public utterance was bound to be stressful - even for somebody as dogmatic as he. However, the fact he had a reputation for arguing semantics for hours, and that he handed Hernan an actual draft of the speech seriously weakens his defence. This was something he'd spent time thinking about ever before committing it to paper, and had been in the process of rewriting it when the journalist came calling. It wasn't exactly an off the cuff remark that he hadn't thought through first.

At best, de Valera was clumsy in his expression, as he did a far better job explaining his invoking of Cuban-American history in a letter to Griffith in which he argued his comments had been misinterpreted. He contended that he had only been thinking of the first article of the Platt Amendment (a 1901 agreement governing future Cuban-American relations in the aftermath of the Spanish-American War), the one in which Cuba vows not to allow its territory to be used by any foreign power to attack America.

'I quoted the part of the Platt Amendment (the first article) which was germane to the point I was making. I wouldn't personally accept any more of it - but if I accept one or several even of the 39 articles of the Protestant creed surely it cannot be said that that means I must accept them all. I only ask you at home to remember that I never say anything here which I would not say at home,' wrote de Valera to Griffith by way of explanation. 'I do not believe in the old parliamentarian policy of one speech for America and another for Ireland. I am never likely to forget my responsibilities but I admit I do not weigh every word and every sentence of a speech and of an interview as if it were a treaty I was actually signing.'

The problem was de Valera hadn't been specific enough to mention the Platt Amendment by name in the article and, in any case, by the time he sent that missive back to Dublin, a war of words had broken out between his own camp, on one side, and Devoy and Cohalan, on the other. Whether or not the Irish-American duo was merely using the slip-up to try to get rid of this headline-grabbing troublemaker or to finally express jealousies that had been building since June, the pair certainly did a very good impression of being sincerely aggrieved at the content of the quote. They knew that Cuba had been little more than 'a vassal state under American domination'; felt de Valera was now offering to settle for something much less than an independent Ireland, and, using the Gaelic American as a pulpit, Devoy denounced any such enterprise over the following weeks.

The situation deteriorated quickly, exacerbated perhaps by Joe McGarrity's *Irish Press* defending the interview in equally uproarious terms. If the Devoy-Cohalan axis saw this as their chance to finally dispatch de Valera, McGarrity was equally enthusiastic about going to his defence and heading into battle against a pair with whom he'd enjoyed such a turbulent relationship in recent years. That much is demonstrated by the fact McGarrity and Patrick McCartan, the editor of his paper, waded in lustily on de Valera's behalf - even though they didn't agree with his sentiments either. Their motive for doing so was best explained by McCartan.

'We had built up de Valera as the sovereign symbol of our cause in the United States,' wrote McCartan. 'De Valera as president had issued and sold Bonds of the Republic of Ireland, and as President of that Republic had asked the American people to recognise it. Our people had transferred their allegiance from the cause to him. His repudiation would irremediably injure our cause in America, lengthen the fight in Ireland, and encourage England to more murderous measures there. We had either to stand by and see de Valera destroyed, and with him our cause, and our hope of international aid for Ireland, or we had to defend him and to explain away that interview.'

With the publicity surrounding the feud beginning to seriously impact de Valera's status in America, he felt it necessary to send McCartan back to Dublin, in order to give a first-hand account of events to the cabinet. 'It is time for plain speaking now,' wrote de Valera to Arthur Griffith. 'A deadly attempt to ruin our chances for the bonds and for everything we came here to accomplish is being made. If I am asked for the ulterior motives I can only guess what they are.

(1)   To drive me home - jealousy, envy, resentment of a rival - some devilish cause I do not know what prompts or

(2)   To compel me to be a rubber stamp for somebody. The position I have held, (I was rapidly driven to assert it or surrender) is the following

(1) No American has a right to dictate policy to the Irish people

(2) We are here with a definite objective - Americans banded together under the trade name (the word will not be misunderstood) Friends of Irish Freedom - ought to help us attain that objective if they are truly what the name applies.'

While most of the letter was a succinct attempt at explaining his position and clarifying the problematic relationship with the Friends, the last line reads: 'Be assured of this and believe me as ever.' If that sounds kind of desperate it's probably because he was. He wrote those words on 17 February 1920. The previous day, Devoy and Cohalan had tried to capitalise on the fall-out from the interview by effecting a sort of putsch. Larry Rice, an apparatchik of the FOIF, called on Boland in the Waldorf-Astoria to request that Boland break from de Valera due to his comments on the Cuban analogy. Had Boland acquiesced, the damage to his colleague would have been incalculable - given how closely the two were now associated in the public mind of Irish-America.

A split then might also have had a huge impact on de Valera's future political career because by that point, the cabinet in Dublin was growing increasingly antsy on the issue. However, there was to be no parting of the ways. Boland stood by his man. He steadfastly refused to denounce his colleague, wasn't persuaded by Rice's argument that failing to do so represented a departure from the principles of Wolfe Tone, and very nearly threw the messenger out the window of the hotel. A glimpse of the mindset of the opposing faction is offered by the following extract from a personal letter Devoy wrote to a friend at the time.

'I am also convinced that he meant to fight us all along and was only waiting for a good opportunity. He selected the wrong time and the wrong issue because his judgment is very poor, but he is filled with the idea that the great ovations he got here were for him personally and practically gave him a mandate to do what he pleases. His head is turned to a greater extent than that of any man I have met in more than half a century. Every move he has made or that has been made in his name, in my judgment, shows a deliberate intention to attempt to sidetrack both the Clan and the Friends and to substitute for both an organisation subject to his orders.'

The knowledge that his erstwhile allies were prepared to go in for the kill, by even trying to turn Boland against him, really unnerved de Valera. Not to mention his growing realisation they were willing to destroy him, regardless of the impact such an event might have on the cause they claimed to espouse. Throughout the month, de Valera grew so stressed that those around him felt he was suffering from exhaustion and was in danger of falling seriously ill. Eventually, he was persuaded to take a short holiday in March to recuperate from the strain of his schedule and, most likely, the impact of the row.

'Chief very upset and dispirited,' wrote Boland in his diary on 21 February, following that up just over a week later with: 'Chief far from well'. The spat had taken a vicious turn when Boland had hand-delivered a letter from de Valera to Cohalan, addressing the Gaelic American's campaign against him and asserting his own pre-eminence in Irish affairs.

'The articles themselves are of course the least matter. It is the evident purpose behind them and the general attitude of mind they reveal is the menace. I am answerable to the Irish people for the proper execution of the trust with which I have been charged. I am definitely responsible to them, and I alone am responsible. It is my obvious duty to select such instruments as may be available for the task set me. It is my duty to superintend every important step in the execution of that task... I am led to understand that these articles in the *Gaelic American* have your consent and approval. Is this so? ... It is vital that I know exactly how you stand in this matter.'

Cohalan's reply was clinical. After pointing out that de Valera was mistaken to believe anybody but Devoy himself influenced editorial policy at the newspaper, he went on to claim a British Monroe Doctrine would turn Ireland into a buttress of the British Empire, and that his own first allegiance was to his native America above all other lands. Towards the end, the New York Supreme Court judge adopted a tone more suited to a sentencing speech from a rather stentorial bench.

'Do you really think for a moment that American public opinion will permit any citizen of another country to interfere as you suggest in American affairs? Do you think any self-respecting American will permit himself to be used in such a manner by you? If so, I may assure you that you are woefully out of touch with the country in which you are sojourning... I respectfully suggest in closing that you would be well advised if you hesitate before you jeopardise or imperil that solidarity of opinion and unity of action among millions of American citizens which you found here amongst us when you came, which have been the despair of England's friends and have already accomplished so much for America and for Ireland.'

De Valera sent a heavily annotated copy of that Cohalan letter back to Griffith, writing in the margins that the judge was 'a tricky police court lawyer' and somebody guilty of 'a willful misrepresentation of my whole attitude.' That missive was hand-delivered by McCartan, who sailed across the Atlantic aboard the SS *New York* in late February, travelling on the obligatory fake passport. Once safely back in Dublin, Michael Collins summoned him to a cabinet meeting.

'I gave de Valera's explanation,' wrote McCartan, 'which was substantially as follows: First, he had wanted to start England talking, so that some basis of settlement might be considered; secondly, in the interview, he quoted only one paragraph of the Platt Amendment relating to Cuba, to show that Ireland was willing to discuss safeguards for English security compatible with Ireland's independence; and lastly, that only his enemies, and Devoy and Cohalan, had put a hostile construction on the interview, in pursuance of the campaign they had started against him when he arrived in the United States, and which overtly and covertly they had since continued.'

Some at the cabinet table were unimpressed with de Valera's part in the whole debacle. Countess Markievicz, the Minister for Labour, made the point that he hadn't the authority to speak for anybody over there except himself. Cathal Brugha and Count Plunkett, Ministers for Defence and Foreign Affairs respectively, weren't impressed by de Valera's explanations either, but Griffith and Collins, Minister for Finance, put an end to the debate rather quickly, even before McCartan could be questioned at length. All present agreed to accept the version of events being posited by de Valera and such was the desire of the leadership to quell any further discussion, McCartan concluded the President had now successfully 'usurped the right to speak and act for Ireland; and the situation left us without the power to challenge him'.

Whatever the veracity of that, the cabinet resolved to send him a letter of support to be made public in America - if de Valera felt it necessary. Ultimately, de Valera didn't because he figured that might only prolong the controversy and show him to be in a nervous and weakened position.

'Have no fear for Ireland,' wrote Griffith by way of reassuring his colleague on 11 March. 'No such misrepresentation as that you have suffered will shake the national solidarity, but the men responsible for it have little realisation of how England sought to exploit their action over here and how indignant Ireland is at their thoughtlessness.'

Griffith's was a common enough belief among those who took de Valera's side against Devoy and Cohalan in the whole unseemly affair. Bishop Fogarty of Killaloe went farther, describing the pair as 'one of Ireland's greatest afflictions' and accusing them of trying 'to break the people's hearts.' Liam Mellows was even more melodramatic.

'I am thoroughly disgusted with him [Devoy]…The old man can never be the same to me. I regret it for it pains me. As for the Judge - well, the least said the soonest mended… How dare the old man talk of the "young men at home" in view of the treatment meted out to the young men who came over since 1916?'

Against this background of tumult and infighting, the business of flogging the bonds carried on regardless, with fifty cities and towns across Massachusetts participating in a seven-day long sales pitch called 'Liberty Week'. A measure of the fervour for the cause in the state can be garnered from the impressive response on 23 February. On the very first day of sales, the towns of Worcester, Lynn, Brookline, Hingham and Howell alone tallied receipts in excess of $50,000. Working out of American House in Boston, the campaign often ran themes to help boost sales, promoting one pitch as 'De Valera Day' and another as 'Countess Markievicz Day'.

There's no question that the healthy returns had been assisted greatly by de Valera's travelling throughout the state in the most appalling of weather conditions and despite the gathering storm in New York. Snow was falling as he placed a wreath of white roses, tied together with green, white and orange ribbons, on the grave of Captain George Smith Anthony in New Bedford. Anthony was the man who'd sailed the *Catalpa* from his home port to Fremantle, Western Australia, to aid the escape of the Fenian prisoners in 1876. His widow presented de Valera with an autographed photograph of the sailor and invited him to sign his own name in a volume the family kept detailing the expedition.

More solace arrived in the form of the approval and support of the Irish Progressive League, an influential and vocal amalgam of artistic and literary people in New York, whose membership included the actor Brandon Tynan, the poet Padraic Colum, and Nora Connolly, daughter of James, and manager of the Irish Socialist Federation. Having battled for various Irish causes since 1917, the league adopted a resolution regarding de Valera at a meeting on 23 February. The significance of the vote was that many of those then supporting de Valera had shared far more public platforms in the past with Devoy.

'The Irish Progressive League hereby affirm their fealty to Eamon de Valera, President of the Irish Republic and chosen leader of the Irish race in the fight for Ireland's freedom. We recognise in President de Valera a statesman of untarnishable honour, a brilliant and devoted soldier, an uncompromising patriot and a wise guide. Chief of the Irish race, we are confident that the race will follow - and follow to glory - the path he has marked out.'

Amid all of this rancour and division, there was one bizarre and unintentionally comic moment to offer light relief. Shortly after 6.30am on 21 February de Valera arrived at Penn Station, in New York, on a train from Washington DC. As he and his party walked along the platform six NYPD officers led by a Sergeant Oliver approached. One of the policemen walked up to him and asked: 'I beg pardon, Sir. You are the British Chargé d'Affaires, are you not?'

De Valera and his fellow travellers paused a moment as they considered the strange question before erupting into gales of laughter. 'Oh no my good man. I am the President of the Irish Republic.'

Ronald C. Lindsay, the highest ranking British diplomat in America at that point, was travelling on the same train, and had been the original target for the police welcoming party dispatched to officially accompany him on his business. There was no such security detail for de Valera.

CHAPTER TWELVE

*We are the spear-points of the hosts in political slavery - we can be
the shafts of dawn for the despairing and the wretched everywhere.
And those of our race who are citizens of this mighty land of
America, whose thoughts will help to mould the policy of the
leader among the nations - how much of the world looks to you
this St. Patrick's Day, hopes in you, trusts in you. You can so easily
accomplish that which is needed. You have only to have the will,
the way is so clear. What would the people in the old land give for
the power which is yours? May God and St. Patrick inspire you to
use it and to use it well.*

- Eamon de Valera, 17 March 1920

The New York Irish answered the call to arms delivered
in that St Patrick's Day Message by throwing the greatest parade in the history of a city that held its first in
1766. After attending a mass celebrated by Archbishop Patrick
Hayes at St Patrick's Cathedral, de Valera, wearing a black top
hat and overcoat, walked the short distance to the reviewing
stand constructed in front of the landmark church on Fifth
Avenue. He climbed the steps and sat with Mayor John F. Hylan

on one side, and Governor Al Smith and the Archbishop on the other.

Shortly after 2.30pm de Valera rose from his seat, stood to await the first marchers and remained in a standing position for two and a half hours, taking the formal salutes of an estimated 25,000 men, women and children - the largest number of participants then ever assembled. They played their part in a procession loaded with significance and rife with symbolism. The soldiers of the 69th Regiment were among the first to stride proudly in front of de Valera and the rest of the dignitaries, enjoying the best vantage point in town. Some of them were still limping from war wounds, and those unable to walk at all were ferried in two buses, their presence reminding the audience of the significant Irish-American contribution to the conflict in Europe and illustrating the argument behind a banner that read:

'Uncle Sam Vindicate your dead!

OK Irish Republic'

The entire pageant was choreographed and stage-managed to bolster the argument de Valera had been making about Irish-American relations for nine months. Two students from St Gregory's School were dressed up as Uncle Sam and Miss Erin; the green, white and orange clad girl strolling arm in arm with a boy decked from head to toe in the red, white and blue of the stars and stripes. One more colourful attempt to demonstrate the bond between the two countries.

Hundreds of other children from Fr Power's All Saints' Church, in Harlem, marched in full ancient Irish warrior costume, replete with round shields and spears and perfect military formations. If the children were the light entertainment, the

political messaging could be gleaned from the ubiquitous banners being carried.

'Every True American is a Sinn Feiner'

'England Damn your concessions - we want our country'

'Thank God I never made peace with England - John Mitchel'

Those crowding the sidewalks may have come for the festival,
what they got was something far more political.

'This demonstration shows the moral force of New York and
the moral force of America is behind Ireland and Ireland's
constitutionally-elected government,' said de Valera of the display. 'I firmly believe Ireland, recognised by all the world, will
hold great parades of this nature on this day ever year throughout the Republic.'

When a group calling itself the Protestant Friends of Irish
Freedom (PFIF) marched along; their banner invoked the
memory of Charles Stewart Parnell, and reiterated de Valera's
constant plea that the Irish problem was not sectarian. They
reminded the crowd and, more specifically, the journalists present: 'Some of Ireland's greatest patriots were of the Protestant
Faith'. The news reporters were more smitten, though, by a
striking young woman atop a horse, leading a contingent wield-
ing several placards including one that declared: '315,000,000 in
India are with Ireland to the last'.

Wearing turbans and saris of various hues, the Friends for the
Freedom of India cut quite a colourful dash among the various
Irish county associations that otherwise dominated the rest of
the parade. Salinda Nath Ghose, one of their American-born
founders, was the lady on horseback and their presence was a
by-product of a burgeoning relationship between the Indian

activists and de Valera. On 28 February he'd addressed a meeting of theirs at the Central Opera House, in New York, and drew such a crowd that an overflow of hundreds was forced to listen to him from the dining room.

'Like Thomas Francis Meagher, we of today in Ireland will not stigmatise the sword, but there is no people upon the whole earth who so desire that a world condition should be brought about in which the sword should become unnecessary as we do. If those who decry physical force only make half the effort to bring it about that we are making, it will speedily come. But until it comes and while endeavouring to bring it about, we of Ireland and you of India must each of us endeavour,' said de Valera that night, 'both as separate peoples and in combination, to rid ourselves of the vampire that is fattening on our blood and we cannot ever allow ourselves to forget what weapon it was by which Washington rid his country of this same vampire. Our cause is a common cause.'

One of the Friends' marchers carried a large banner in the parade repeating that very last sentence and affirming the mutual bond, but that subtlety was lost on *The New York Times*.

'It became evident that the old Irish flag of green with the harp on it was spending the day in the country, for rank after rank went by with only the Sinn Fein banners and bannerlets appearing,' went the following day's report. 'That was a novelty in itself. But -whist! Some lads from an as yet undiscovered county of Ireland were coming along. Hindus! A whole flock of them… As if surprised by the sight of the strangers, a green lamppost that had stood at 49th Street and Fifth Avenue through many parades fell into the avenue just after the Indians had passed.'

The Times found it interesting too that the Grand Marshal of the parade, Justice Cohalan, had eschewed riding a horse, the usual mode of transport, for an automobile. In spite of the break with tradition, de Valera's nemesis was feted by the thousands lining the sidewalks, leaning out of office windows and peering down over the sides of Manhattan rooftops. In spite of their quarrelling, Cohalan had generously given up the prime spot on the reviewing stand - the privilege of every Grand Marshal - to de Valera.

The magnanimity didn't end there. De Valera went to speak at the Friendly Sons of St Patrick banquet, at the Hotel Astor, after racing around the city attending several different functions that evening. There, it was Cohalan who formally presented him to the crowd. Whether this was a procedural faux pas by an MC ignorant of the feud, a gesture towards reconciliation by the justice, or merely him messing with de Valera's psyche, Colohan delivered the type of encomium that would have been expected by the attendance. 'I have the honour of introducing now as the speaker to the toast of Ireland, a man who is a soldier, who is a scholar, who is a patriot, and who is the elected head of the Republic of Ireland - Eamon de Valera.'

At the end of a day when Ireland held the city in its thrall, the impression may have been that the various combatants had put aside their personal grievances for the greater good. Though de Valera and Cohalan were at the same dinner by evening's end with the appearance all was well, the truth was much different. If the two men were the picture of professionalism on the dais that night, the politicking, scheming and plotting continued backstage. It would all come to the boil very soon. In the immediate aftermath of St Patrick's Day however, there was more good news for all concerned.

On 18 March the US Senate began its final debate on the ratification of the Versailles Treaty. After further months of negotiation and discussion since the November defeat, Senator Henry Cabot Lodge, a Republican and the majority leader in the house, had succeeded in introducing fourteen reservations to the treaty - which would greatly change its meaning once ratified. A fifteenth was added, rather surprisingly, right at the finish when Peter Gerry of Rhode Island, a freshman Democrat, introduced the following addendum.

'In consenting to the ratification of the Treaty with Germany, the United States adheres to the principle of self-determination and the resolution of sympathy with the expectations of the Irish people for a government of their own choice, adopted by the Senate on June 6th, 1919, and declares that when such a government is attained by Ireland, a consummation it is hoped is at hand, it should be promptly admitted as a member of the League of Nations'.

The Gerry Reservation passed by forty-five votes to thirty-eight. Whether senators were seeking to keep their Irish-American constituents sweet or were too tired to obey the party whip after some marathon arguing, its supporters split rather curiously along party lines, twenty-two Democrats and twenty-three Republicans. No matter the make-up of the voters, de Valera regarded this sort of recognition in the US Senate as a genuine triumph for the cause.

'A Te Deum should be sung throughout all Ireland. We thank almighty God, we thank the noble American nation, we thank all the friends of Ireland here who have worked so unselfishly for our cause. We thank the heroic dead whose sacrifices made victory possible. Our mission has been successful. The principle of self-determination has been formally adopted in an international instrument. Ireland has been given her place amongst the nations by the greatest nation of them all.'

There was one slight problem: De Valera sent that grandiloquent message of jubilation by transatlantic cable to Arthur Griffith on Thursday. By Friday night, the situation had changed for the worse and his celebration looked like so much hubris. After agreeing to all the changes, the Senate had voted on the Treaty and the fifteen reservations, including the Irish clause, and failed to ratify it. Forty-nine senators were in favour and thirty-five against - but a two-thirds majority was required for it to pass. The United States failed to sign the Treaty, the genesis of which President Wilson had been so central to, and the League of Nations would eventually start without them.

De Valera had other more pressing issues to deal with as the Treaty, Gerry Reservation and all, ran aground for good in Washington. He was back in New York, fighting for his political life on the stage of the Park Avenue Hotel. How he got there is a tale that demonstrates how duplicitous, clandestine and pernicious the situation surrounding himself, Cohalan and Devoy had become.

'All of the advantages except the scandal of a fight, are on our side now,' wrote Devoy on 26 February in a private letter to John A. McGarry, a prominent member of Clan na Gael in Chicago, about de Valera and the Westminster Gazette affair. 'We'd be worse off in the end than if we fought it out now. I am convinced that he meant to fight us all along, and was only waiting for the good opportunity. He selected the wrong time and the wrong issue, because his judgment is very poor, but he is filled with the idea that the great ovations he got here were for him personally and practically gave him a mandate to do as he pleases. His head is turned to a greater extent than any man I' ve met in more than half a century…His motto is 'the king can do no wrong' and the motto of his heelers is the Wilsonian one 'stand behind the President'. In New York, Brooklyn and Jersey our men are practically unanimous…We cannot permit the continuance of the present intolerable relations without assuming responsibility for very serious danger to the cause.'

Colohan and Devoy's plan to usurp de Valera and expose his failings for all to see was simple. They invited 75 influential Irish-Americans, among them judges, lawyers, politicians and clergy, to a private meeting at the Park Avenue Hotel on 19 March. There, they wanted to effectively put their enemy on trial *in absentia*, since he was conveniently scheduled to travel to Chicago by train that very day. Unfortunately for Cohalan and Devoy, news of their scheme and a copy of the McGarry letter and others on the subject inevitably reached Joseph McGarrity, somebody whose first loyalty remained with the man he'd advised to call himself 'President', the previous June.

Appraised of their intentions to do him in politically, De Valera deliberately missed his train out of town and sat in waiting at the Waldorf-Astoria, while McGarrity went to serve as his eyes and ears at the de facto court set up on the second floor of the other hotel, just blocks away. Attendance at the gathering was by invitation only, a minor caveat that didn't bother the

Tyrone man. Despite master of ceremonies Michael J. Ryan asking all present to register, and pointedly requesting those without invitation to leave, McGarrity refused to budge. He was in his seat as Cohalan and then Devoy formally began their character assassination.

'Cohalan presented his case against de Valera,' wrote Patrick McCartan, 'alleging: de Valera would consult none; knew nothing of American history or politics; alienated by his arrogance those who had spent a lifetime in Ireland's service; lived in royal suites at hotels, wasting money raised to help the gallant people of Ireland; and spread discord in the ranks here, where, before de Valera's arrival, the greatest solidarity and the greatest movement of the race in history had been attained.'

After Cohalan had read extracts from his recent exchange of letters with de Valera for the benefit of the audience, Devoy sang from a similar songbook. He denounced the Irish contingent as 'the enemies of the leaders of the race in America', castigated their prosecution of the bond drive, and returning to the *Westminster Gazette* interview, accused de Valera of lowering the Irish flag with his offer of a perceived compromise.

With the name-calling reaching fever pitch and the charge sheet growing ever longer, McGarrity finally had his say. Rising from his place in the audience, he stood and posed a simple question. 'Where was de Valera and why was he not invited to defend himself?'

'He's in Chicago,' went a reply from the floor.

'No he isn't,' said McGarrity. 'He's at the Waldorf.'

A debate followed about whether or not the plaintiff should be summoned to hear the charges in person. Justice John Goff of the New York Supreme Court, the Bishop of Buffalo William Turner and W. Bourke Cochran pressed the case in favour of halting proceedings until de Valera was in the room.

'It was the business of his friends to set him right,' said Cochran, 'not by what might be considered abuse, but by friendly counsel.'

A phone call was made to the Waldorf. Harry Boland answered, and his initial advice was that de Valera shouldn't grace the proceedings with his presence. Only after a group arrived from the meeting to beseech him to do so, did de Valera finally put on his coat. Within minutes, he strode into the room where his every move had been excoriated, flanked by Boland and James O'Mara. He took a seat on the stage, in close proximity to Cohalan and Devoy, and immediately began a private and animated chat with Michael J. Ryan. Then, without any formal introduction, and presumably briefed on the way across about what had been said, de Valera started to counter the charges.

Looking more anxious than on any podium throughout his time in America, he gave a speech equal parts a defence (of himself) and an attack (on the two older men sitting beside him on the stage). Having praised Devoy's historic role in the fight for Irish freedom, he then declared the old man out of touch with the new leaders in Ireland and the changed situation, accusing the *Gaelic American* of distorting the true meaning of his quotes in the *Westminster Gazette* and doing serious damage by such manipulation. De Valera reiterated that he was in America to fight for the recognition of Ireland on behalf of the Irish people, a mandate that gave him unique standing. Devoy and Cohalan didn't take his ripostes quietly, regularly interrupting, and the back and forth gave rise to an incredible ten-hour long session.

'The Judge made a very clever case,' wrote McGarrity, 'keeping part of the time at least quite cool, and doing everything to irritate the President - walking close to him and pointing his finger etc...The President was always courteous and respectful, and at one point when the Judge told the President he should repeat his assurance that he did not intend to lower the flag, etc...the President pointed out that he had already done so... that he was quite conscious the Judge desired to humiliate him and irritate him by making these requests for him to repeat and repeat; there was never any other thought on his mind that in the Judge's attempts to humiliate him he was only showing his measurement to his assembled friends.'

At a certain juncture, de Valera took issue with the tone being used by his critics and complained to the chairman, Ryan, that he was being treated like a schoolboy. 'You deserve to be treated like a schoolboy,' replied Ryan.

As the evening wore on, the atmosphere grew more heated and manic, with Cohalan even throwing out the canard that de Valera's associate Dr William J. Maloney was 'one of the ablest men in the British secret service'. Ryan also threatened to throw McGarrity out of the room unless he calmed his rhetoric. Boland became so upset when speaking his part that he broke down in tears and had to go outside to regain his composure, before returning to resume a speech.

With any contentious event, eyewitness accounts tend to betray the prejudices of the beholder. De Valera fans regarded it as a daring display of vigour and political instinct, and a few even go as far as to claim he turned the whole event into a trial of

Cohalan and Devoy. De Valera's detractors viewed it very differently, one audience member even interpreted his performance as the bravado of somebody, by then so power-hungry that he had become deranged.

'I attended a conference at New York on March 19, and I confess before Heaven that President de Valera on that day revealed to me as either labouring under some psychopathic condition or that the evil spirit himself had taken hold of the Irish movement,' wrote John P. Grace, Mayor of Charleston, South Carolina. 'I am sure it was the consensus of opinion that whatever President de Valera's qualities might be, his leadership was an accident. He had clearly fallen in the hands of men moved by selfish, and some by sinister motives, and they had convinced him he was the man to lead the movement in America and not Justice Cohalan. For ten hours that day about one hundred of us …were tortured by such an exhibition of intolerance and ingratitude as I have never witnessed before. Justice Cohalan humbling himself under insults repeated constantly during those ten hours…did everything humanly possible or imaginable to bridge the chasm. De Valera had not only been the aggressor, but repeatedly the aggressor, and perhaps encouraged to go a little farther as each new aggression was overlooked. De Valera's attitude was one of infallibility; he was right, everybody else was wrong, and he couldn't be wrong… I thought the man was crazy.'

When de Valera declared it had only taken him one month in America to realise the country wasn't big enough for himself and Cohalan, Bishop Turner rebuked him, asking whether he seriously expected the judge to leave his native land on his account.

'President de Valera stated that he had long been a student of the principles of democracy, and that in his opinion, the Irish-American leaders whom he had met had yet to learn the ABC of democracy,' wrote John J. Splain, chairman of the bond campaign in Connecticut. 'John Devoy retorted that "the exhibition which de Valera had given was the whole alphabet of autocracy".'

The final act of the marathon melodrama came when de Valera accused Devoy, Cohalan and their cohorts of working and plotting to have him sent home from America in disgrace. He knew this he claimed because a letter outlining such intrigue had come into his possession.

'Who wrote that letter?' asked a voice from the floor.

'John Devoy,' replied Boland.

Almost totally deaf by that point in his life, Devoy first shouted: 'What's that? What's that?', though when soon appraised of the substance of the accusation, he was on his feet declaring: 'It's a lie.'

Boland then stirred the pot by teasing the audience with an announcement that the man to whom the letters were written was also present in the room. Following more shouts from the crowd requesting this identity be revealed, Boland responded: 'John A. McGarry of Chicago.' When McGarry - who had apparently been trying to play both sides in the simmering conflict between the two warring factions - made to get out of his seat and refute the charge, de Valera waved his hand theatrically at McGarrity and ordered: 'Produce the letters, Joe.' Cue utter pandemonium and more histrionics, as McGarrity went in dramatic search of the missives.

'The audience became quite excited and I fumbled in my overcoat as though going to produce the letters when a number of persons made an appeal...the incident of the letters was then dropped, in fact there was a general cry for peace,' wrote McGarrity.

Almost certainly choreographed beforehand by McGarrity, Boland and de Valera, the letters were a bold gambit. Certainly there was nothing in them to sustain the contention that they'd been plotting for six months, the bulk of the contents simply dealt with the post-*Westminster Gazette* fall-out.

Predictably, there are differing accounts of what exactly happened next. Some allege that Cohalan actually apologised to de Valera and shook his hand. Others contend this never happened and that the intercession of Bishop Turner, at a point in the meeting when the only next logical step was a split in the movement in America, merely led to an uneasy peace. Prior to the timely clerical intervention supporters from both sides had been asking for a truce from the floor, conscious perhaps not only of an imminent fracture but also of the fact that after a sapping ten hours, somebody had to shout stop.

Arguably the only part of the entire affair on which there is consensus is that it ended with Turner ordering all present to their knees and leading the group in a prayer of reconciliation. It was an extraordinary way to end such a tumultuous occasion; it also may have led to the false impression that somehow a type of unity had been forged in the heat of the argument, simply because it hadn't. Any supposed harmony was shattered almost as soon as they left the room, with Devoy and de Valera quickly accusing each other of reneging on promises made in the Park

Avenue Hotel to unite for the cause.

In any case, there was a far more significant conflict going on than a war of words in a swanky Manhattan conference room. While the most powerful figures in Irish-America grappled with the collateral damage from a personality clash between three of them; Tomás MacCurtain, the Lord Mayor of Cork, had been shot dead by members of the Royal Irish Constabulary (RIC) at his home in front of his wife. A Sinn Féin councillor, MacCurtain had been elected to the office just seven weeks earlier, and his death unleashed a wave of public outrage in Ireland. It also cast the name-calling and the finger-pointing of his colleagues in New York in a very different light.

'I say, advisedly, with the knowledge that I have of the ways of the English in Dublin Castle, that British thugs murdered the Lord Mayor of Cork,' said de Valera, speaking in Chicago later that weekend.

CHAPTER THIRTEEN

Chicago - Patrick King, appearing in naturalisation court this morning, not only renounced allegiance to the British Empire and King George but also, by order of Judge Kavanaugh, to the 'Republic of Ireland' and Eamon de Valera, its 'President'. This is the first case on record, attorneys say, where the 'Irish Republic' has been officially recognised by an American court. Judge Kavanaugh declared later that his action was official recognition of the Irish Republic and its executives. 'It is a de facto government which exists with the consent of nine-tenths of Ireland's people,' he said, 'although it has not been recognised by foreign governments. The same situation existed in the United States in the years from 1776 to 1783.

- The New York Times, 20 March 1920

At the same time that the Cohalan feud sparked so public and spectacular a conflagration, de Valera was busy doing more fire-fighting in the background. On 1 March James O'Mara had submitted his first resignation letter, requesting not only to be relieved of his position in America but also of his dual role as both trustee of, and South Kilkenny's representative in, the Dáil. After successfully putting in place the machinery to handle the bond issue and the loan, O'Mara was worried about the effect the strain of the work was having on his health and wanted to return home. There followed a correspondence between the men that lasted over a month, as de Valera quite simply refused to accept the right of his colleague to depart the scene.

'I dislike to press you in the midst of your strenuous work in Washington,' wrote O'Mara on 14 March, replying to the first refusal, 'but the interest you always take in the affairs of your colleagues, explains if it does not excuse the pressure of my demand that you will allow and assist me to retire from public services to private life. In thanking you for your good wishes and again offering you mine in your great and unselfish work, believe me to be, dear Mr. President, Yours very sincerely, J O'M.'

De Valera's unwillingness to accede to O'Mara's wishes appears to have been twofold. He knew that losing a gifted individual, at such a crucial juncture in the financial process, would greatly complicate the work and force himself to take more of a hands-on role in the minutiae of that. Not to mention, either that the departure of such a trusted lieutenant, and a man who'd garnered so much respect in the American business community, would be perceived as a weakening of his own position, and another sign he was in real trouble.

'Your being at the helm meant…I was able to get far more out of myself; with you steering the responsibility for overseeing the work being done,' wrote de Valera on Easter Sunday. 'I could not have felt like that even with an equally able man - so that you are absolutely irreplaceable. Since you came I have been able to devote myself whole-heartedly to my own side of the Mission without distraction - that ends from the day you leave. My one anxiety henceforth will be to withdraw from my direct political activities - so as to devote myself entirely to the winding up of the Bond campaign... Oh, do not, by unduly pressing your resignation now, spoil the ripe fruit of your devoted efforts hitherto.

'I hate asking you for further sacrifices but, when I consider the interests at stake, I feel I would not be doing my duty if I did not beg you to defer your intended departure for another month or two at least till I return from the South. My entreaty is personal as well as official. You do not need to be reminded of the peculiar difficulties of the moment, you know the campaign that has been taking place underground - and how every opportunity will be seized when it is balked in one direction to renew it in another...Do try and reconsider however - I assure you I am not unappreciative of the sacrifices I am calling on you to make - but I had dreamed that we would see the end of this mission here together.'

At one point, Michael Collins even wrote to Harry Boland on the issue, his tone that of a man growing increasingly exasperated at the all too regular bulletins of rancour from America.

'What on earth is wrong with Mr. O'Mara?' wrote Michael Collins in a letter to Harry Boland during this drama. 'There always seems to be something depressing coming from the U.S.A. I cannot tell you how despondent this particular incident had made me. No doubt I am over touchy in this matter but yet, after a pretty hard year, every little divergence tells heavily. Mr. Griffith is writing to Mr. O'Mara appealing to him to reconsider the question, as his action, if persisted in, would have a really bad effect - very much worse than the 'Gaelic American' difference.'

Although O'Mara's desire to leave had more to do with problems co-existing with Diarmuid Fawsitt, who'd been working as Irish Consul in New York since July of 1919, some have tried to interpret O'Mara's attempted resignation as evidence he could no longer work with de Valera and/or had lost faith in him as a leader. This doesn't appear to be supported by the tone - formal, polite but always laced with a certain affection - of his various resignation letters or by the subsequent testimony of his daughter Patricia. She arrived in New York in early April of that year along with her mother.

Their presence undoubtedly did wonders for O'Mara's state of mind, as he was soon escorting them on sightseeing tours around Manhattan and Washington. His thoughts of resigning were put away; at least until the autumn, when he threatened to leave again to attend to his private affairs and business interests back home. It says much for the nature of the relationship between the pair of them that after one particular row, O'Mara gifted de Valera a mathematics book *The Theory of the Functions of the Real Variable* to replace his own copy, which he'd left in Ireland.

As was now increasingly the routine, the show went on - regardless of the chaos ensuing behind the scenes. In the first week of April, de Valera spoke before the State House of Delegates in Annapolis, was received by Maryland's Governor, Albert Ritchie, performed as guest speaker at a high-powered dinner held by the Lafayette Club in Washington DC, and headlined a meeting at New York's Lexington Theatre commemorating the fourth anniversary of the Easter Rising. There, he took the opportunity to denounce Lloyd George's Home Rule Bill, which a week earlier had passed its second reading at the House of Commons.

'We are not discussing whether it is a good Bill or a bad Bill. We deny his right to have anything at all to say in the Government of Ireland. That is our one and only answer. Britain can have peace the moment she withdraws her troops, her army of occupation from Ireland. We have no motive of revenge and we will not allow our nation to be used as a catspaw by any nation against any other nation.'

During the debate on Home Rule, the British Prime Minister had made waves in America. Under pressure from Edward Carson to do something to counteract the Sinn Féin propaganda making such an impact across the Atlantic, George compared de Valera to Jefferson Davis, President of the Confederate States of America from 1861-65, and threatened to meet the Irish with the same levels of repression visited on the south by the north in the American Civil War. That particular analogy didn't go down well in some parts of America.

'In comparing the Irish Republic to the Southern Confederacy, and de Valera to Jefferson Davis, Lloyd George has offered, perhaps unconsciously, a gratuitous insult to the Southern States in the American Union and to the splendid sons of the Southern Confederacy who fought and distinguished themselves on the fields of France in World War 1,' said NB Forrest, Commander in Chief of the Sons of Confederate Veterans.

'Ireland has not the status of an independent state as was the case with the American colonies. Ireland has not been a self-determining republic. De Valera, without discrediting his status, is not the elected president of a confederation of states, called, as was Jefferson Davis, to the high office. There is no parallel in which the status of the so-called Republic of Ireland and that of its president correspond to the Southern Confederacy and its chief executive.'

Whether by accident or design, the Davis controversy was wonderfully-timed from an English point of view. It came just a matter of days before de Valera embarked on his first sustained foray into the deep south. A region where Catholics were often still on the receiving end of official discrimination and unofficial violence, this southern swing was always going to be one of the toughest trails on the campaign. And so it proved: opposition to his visits often began long before his scheduled stops.

Prominent alumni put paid to a proposed speech and appearance at the University of South Carolina. The appropriately-named Hornet's Nest Post of the American Legion, in North Carolina, formed a committee to protest and to try to prevent him coming to Charlotte. The city's mayor refused to ban de Valera, but denounced his visit anyway as 'an offence to the great majority of citizens.' In New Orleans, the British Consul General, Major Braithwaite Wallis, filed a formal complaint in the name of his government about the reception planned (including an honorary degree from Loyola University) for him in the Big Easy. Newspapers in Jacksonville, Florida, carried advertisements from the America First Association helpfully pointing out: 'Ireland is not on the map of the United States' ahead of his packed house appearance at the Duval Theatre there.

The most vehement resistance, though, came from Alabama where de Valera had been invited to speak in Birmingham on 21 April by the Jefferson County branches of the AOH, the Knights of Columbanus, the FOIF, and the American Commission for Irish Independence. Long before he hit town, the city commission had banned a parade to be held in his honour and the Birmingham Post of the American Legion presented resolutions to Governor Thomas Kilby, asking that de Valera be declared 'persona non grata' in the entire state. Kilby, who'd been elected on the basis of his own fervent anti-Catholicism, hadn't the power to issue such a decree but quenched his visitors' thirst by telling them the State Department should long ago have run de Valera and Sinn Féin out of the country. 'Were I directing official of that department,' said Kilby, 'I would unhesitatingly order the deportation of de Valera without delay.'

This type of sentiment culminated in a mass meeting in Birmingham on 20 April, where a diverse collection of people, including judges, church ministers, businessmen in suits, and working men in overalls, came together to express their outrage at the pending arrival of the man they called 'the Sinn Féin propagandist'. To them, his mission was 'for the purpose of spreading contemptible falsehood and misinformation on behalf of an element in Ireland that stands before the world as notorious traitors, slackers and pro-Germans.'

Following testimony that the American Legion, the Junior Order of Mechanics, the Methodist Pastors' Association, the city commissioners and Governor Kilby himself, were all on the side of the anti-de Valera campaign, a set of five lengthy resolutions were formally adopted wherein, amongst other things, the visit was denounced as 'an affront to our state' and the President and Attorney General were called upon to organise his 'early deportation.'

This vitriol must be viewed in the context of a particularly rampant strain of anti-Catholicism which had infected that city over the previous decade. Over half the Protestant ministers in the area were thought to be members of the revitalised Ku Klux Klan, and nativist vigilantes had even been trying to force employers to sack Catholic workers.

'Birmingham was led to believe that Catholics were plotting to control all government in the name of the pope,' wrote Professor David B. Franklin. 'Their parochial schools would destroy the public education system. Their way of life was a menace to the nuclear family-centred home as the basic unit of society... Kilby promised during the [1918 election] campaign to find legal procedures to force Catholic priests into marriage. His administration enacted a Convent Inspection Law, establishing a state commission to direct sheriffs, upon written petition of 25 citizens, to inspect convents at any hour to determine whether any woman was behind held against her will.'

It was somehow fitting then that the spirit of the pro-de Valera movement in the city was epitomised by a priest. Fr James E. Coyle, a native of Athlone who'd been serving in Alabama for nearly quarter of a century, reacted to all the ludicrous charges being levelled against his religion by offering $1,000 to anybody capable of proving the Catholic Church represented a serious threat to American democracy. Evincing the bravery of somebody who'd been receiving death threats from the Klan for years, and would, just fifteen months later, be shot dead by a

Methodist minister, Coyle loudly countered some of de Valera's critics, labelling the American Legion 'misguided' and lampooning the city commissioners as 'peanut politicians'. Others spoke out too.

'The time is coming,' said Frank J. Thompson, Alabama Chairman of the American Committee on Irish Independence, 'whether Governor Kilby realises it or not, when the same moral law that governs man shall govern nations and when robber nations, like the burglarious individual, will have to realise the truth of the principle and be governed by it.'

In so fractious a political climate, it was inevitable de Valera's eventual appearance at the Jefferson Theatre drew an enormous crowd. Unfortunately for the organisers however, some of those present were opponents who sought to disrupt the meeting at every turn. Even the words of Dr John H. Irwin, a prominent Presbyterian Minister, who had shared many platforms with de Valera all over America over the previous year in an obvious attempt to prove Ireland's cause was a broad nationalist rather than a narrowly Catholic affair, didn't dissuade protesters from shouting: 'Throw him out', when de Valera finally took the stage, and addressed the matter at hand.

'I had seen a number of clippings that seemed to represent the thoughts of the people of this city,' said de Valera. 'So I came to the conclusion that you who live in Birmingham were just like those that Ireland is fighting back in the old country. But after I got to the city, in fact, the minute I got into the depot I understood that a small class of the citizens of Birmingham were against my coming here, and that the largest part of the people of your city were the same kind of square, clear-thinking people that you find anywhere else in the United States…'

He went on to denounce 'the English tyrant' and to lament how that country had squeezed Ireland like a lemon before casting it aside. This was typical of the statements he used to guarantee lengthy applause, though the cheers he received were also punctuated by jeers from the mischief-making opponents who'd gatecrashed the meeting. When voting on resolutions asking President Wilson to recognise the Irish Republic and to stop giving US loans to England, the usual unanimous chorus in favour was distorted by the shouting of 'No' from the fifth column present.

In other parts of the south de Valera fared better. In Atlanta, Georgia, he drew a huge and much less critical crowd to Taft Hall on a Friday night. Governor Hugh Dorsey had entertained him at the State Capitol with tales of his own visit to Ireland, some years earlier, and although Mayor James L. Key refused to formally welcome him to the city as the leader of a nation, he did spend an hour personally explaining his own take on the Irish situation and the reasoning behind his decision. There was a similar welcome down the road in Augusta, where the crowd cheered him to the rafters, despite being three hours late for his own speech.

He was tardy because for the second time in less than a fortnight, de Valera had been involved in a serious train crash. The first took place on 16 April when he was travelling to New Orleans. That train crashed at Bay Minette, Alabama, and initial reports were that de Valera had been injured in the accident. Eventually it emerged that the only damage was his clothes getting wet. The second occurred on the Georgia Railroad, near

Covington, on 29 April but again he emerged unscathed to go on to wow his audience at the Grand Theatre in Augusta, where a large 'Fáilte' sign hung over a stage peopled by, amongst others, former Confederate soldiers in their old uniforms.

'Oh, men of the South, in whose veins runs the warm blood of chivalry, laying aside for a time the question of the justice of his cause, our visitor's courage alone should claim for him your impartial attention and ardent sympathy,' said James B. Mulherin, an officer of the American Legion, charged with the introduction. 'Permit me, therefore, to introduce to you, the head of a government founded on justice, equality and fraternity: the head of a nation that will take its place among the sisterhood of nations and be to all a friend…'

While de Valera was criss-crossing America once more, the British authorities were vainly searching ocean liners in Ireland for him. Word had gone around that he'd left New York, and when the Anchor Liner *Columbia* docked at Moville on 27 April, police swarmed the ship in search of their man. The intelligence was faulty. They'd have been much better served looking for him somewhere between Mobile, Alabama, or Jackson, Mississippi or even up north in Chicago, where he'd detoured briefly the day before his supposed arrival in Ireland.

The purpose of the visit to Illinois was to speak at a banquet in the Congress Hotel to mark the closure of the bond certificate campaign in the city. He used the opportunity to make a point regarding the new British ambassador, who had just come to America.

'We protest against the reception of the British ambassador (Sir Auckland Geddes) to this country as a representative of

Ireland and Great Britain. He does not represent Ireland. We claim recognition for the representatives of the Republican Government, duly and legitimately elected by the votes of the Irish people.'

Geddes had arrived in New York on 19 April, where he was taken off the *Kaiserin Auguste Victoria* (a ship which had sailed from Liverpool with several hundred Irish passengers also aboard) by a Coast Guard cutter, in order to avoid demonstrators awaiting him on the dock. Upon arrival in the city, Geddes issued a wide-ranging statement, about a third of which was given over to trying to spin the situation in Ireland - where the Black and Tans were just finishing their first month of mayhem and terror.

'The British government...is to place fairly and squarely on the shoulders of Irishmen in Ireland the constitutional responsibility of finding for themselves within the framework of the British Empire the solution for their political differences...When [the new Home Rule Bill] becomes operative, it will be the duty of all British subjects, who are not domiciled in Ireland to stand aside and leave those who live there to solve their problem. I venture to add that it will also be helpful if the many in all parts of the world who are not British subjects and who are interested in Ireland, likewise stand aside and leave the Irish alone to grapple with their own political difficulties.'

Geddes was careful not to specifically call out the Irish-American lobby, a group of women from which had picketed the British Embassy, in Washington, earlier that month in protest at the murder of Tomás McCurtain. He'd also resisted the urge to specifically mention the First Dáil or de Valera, for whom the arrival of London's new man in Washington presented a wonderful opportunity for forcing the Irish issue into the national press.

In Lynchburg, Virginia - founded by an Irishman named John Lynch in 1786 - de Valera drew 1,000 people to the Academy of Music, despite the mayor of the town and others opposing his visit. He used the platform available to him that night to emphasise, in a combatively-toned speech, that the mere acceptance of Geddes's credentials represented an overt political act.

'It is said that America should not interfere in the Irish question. You have already interfered in receiving Sir Auckland Geddes as Ambassador for Britain and Ireland. I am not here for sympathy or gratitude. I am here for justice. Why are you so anxious not to offend Britain, yet continue to offend Ireland? Is it because Britain is strong and Ireland weak? Britain has no right to be offended if you act according to the reason for which you entered the war. The act of recognition of Ireland does not mean war. Britain would have to borrow the money from you to carry on that war.'

He laboured the point too about the sincerity of his own credentials.

'I am here as the accredited representative of the Republic, founded in 1919, a Republic functioning, not by poison gas and bombing planes and liquid fire and tanks and all the implements of modern warfare, but functioning by the will of the people. As the American Republic dated from the Declaration of Independence, 4th of July, 1776, and not from the date of recognition by England, 1782, so also will the Irish Republic date from its Declaration of Independence, April 24, 1916.'

While the scale of the receptions and de Valera's audiences had shrunk, and were nowhere near the previous summer and autumn's baseball stadium attendances, and criticism of him had grown louder and more commonplace - another anti-Catholic group demanded action against this 'fugitive from justice' - his shuttling around the south and east of the country in April and May had succeeded in getting the attention of English politicians. After various newspapers published reports he'd already managed to raise the equivalent of two million pounds through the bond certificates, the matter was raised in the House of Commons on 5 May.

Liberal Party MP Captain William Wedgwood Benn (father of Tony) demanded to know what steps the government intended to take to stymie the malicious Irish campaign that was having an adverse effect on relations between Britain and America. Concerned at the news de Valera was being paraded through cities and receiving the imprimatur of Governors as he went, Horatio Bottomley of the People's League wanted the matter raised with President Woodrow Wilson. Bottomley reckoned the welcoming of de Valera represented an 'unfriendly act' in international law, a view shared by Conservative Robert Burton Chadwick.

After denouncing de Valera as 'this outlaw' and asking if anybody in power was aware he'd recently received the freedom of New Orleans, Chadwick described this accolade as 'this deliberate insult by an ostensibly friendly power.' In the absence of Prime Minister Lloyd George, Andrew Bonar Law answered on behalf of the coalition government, plainly stating it had no interest in making any representation to Washington on the matter. A politic answer given eighty-eight members of the US Congress had just written to

Downing Street to express their outrage at the deteriorating conditions in Ireland, a correspondence that had received coverage in the London papers.

One day after the ruckus in the Commons, Ireland was back on the agenda in Washington. James A. Hamill, a New Jersey Democrat, offered a resolution to the House of Representatives, requesting that President Wilson adhere to his own famous principles of self-determination, refuse to receive Geddes as 'Ireland's diplomatic representative' and accept in his stead Dr Patrick McCartan, 'the minister named by the duly elected government of the Republic of Ireland.' A shot across the bows but not anything more than that. No vote was taken on the matter which was referred to and subsequently died in committee.

Another initially promising development that amounted to naught, came when de Valera and W.B. Yeats crossed paths in New York in late May. Travelling around America on a lecture tour, Yeats attended a speech de Valera gave to those working on the bond drive in the city, and later had a private meeting in which it's speculated the politician tried to persuade the poet to use his celebrity and status for the cause; something he was not inclined to do.

'I was rather disappointed - A living argument rather than a living man, all propaganda, no human life, but not bitter hysterical or unjust,' wrote Yeats of his impressions of de Valera in that encounter. 'I judged him persistent, being both patient and energetic but that he will fail through not having enough human life to judge the human life in others. He will ask too much of everyone & will ask it without charm. He will be pushed aside by others.'

Much of Yeats's evaluation would be eerily borne out by events over the following weeks.

CHAPTER FOURTEEN

...and whereas, the conditions in Ireland today endanger world peace: and whereas, in particular, the unrest by these conditions is inevitably reflected in these United States of America, tending to weaken the bonds of amity and the ancient ties of kinship which bind so many of our people to the people of Great Britain and Ireland; therefore, in the interest of world peace and international goodwill, be it Resolved by the House of Representatives (the Senate concurring) that the Congress of the United States views with concern and solicitude these conditions and expresses its sympathy with the aspirations of the Irish people for a government of their own.

- resolution adopted by the Foreign Affairs Committee of the House of Representatives, 28 May 1920

One year after Congressman William E. Mason had introduced a bill calling for the US government to set aside money for the salaries of a consular staff for Ireland, an act that would have afforded the first Dáil official recognition, the above resolution is the sum of what his efforts yielded. Having failed to push through legislation which would have had such a seismic impact, an expression of sympathy for the troubled state of affairs in Ireland amounted to little more than a condescending pat on the head when, all along, the hope had been for a historic hand up. It was a disappointing result made worse by the controversy surrounding authorship of those very sentences

Once the Foreign Affairs Committee had decided to scupper Mason's Bill and to offer him the opportunity to submit a resolution by way of compensation, there arose the matter of drafting something suitable. With every corner of Irish-America unhappy with the final effort that was published, allegations abounded that de Valera, himself, had penned the watery sentences for Mason. At a meeting of the FOIF, Justice Cohalan repeated the charge and when Patrick McCartan immediately went to his colleague's defence, he was handed an incriminating piece of paper. McCartan recognised de Valera's handwriting instantly. 'I went straight to de Valera,' wrote McCartan. 'He explained to me he had tried to draft a suitable resolution, and having failed, threw the paper on the table, and that evidently, Cohalan had finished it.'

Whether de Valera or Cohalan, or both of them, were manipulating the truth of the incident isn't as important as the fact it was one more illustration of how their relationship had deteriorated, to such an extent that the escalating conflict had begun to completely overshadow the campaign. Having co-existed peacefully on the line-up of speakers at the Easter Rising Commemoration at New York's Lexington Theatre, in early April, the pair were also among a group that met in Washington on 22 May to plan how best to approach the Republican

Presidential Convention, set to begin on 8 June, in Chicago. With that party favoured to win back the White House in the November election, it was crucial that a coherent policy be formulated to maximise its interest in the Irish question.

At the conference to decide upon strategy, a request was made for the FOIF to loan $50,000 to be used to make a huge splash at the convention, highlighting the cause with the expressed aim of getting the Republicans to adopt a plank (a formal statement in its election manifesto) in the party platform stating it would recognise Ireland. Cohalan was against giving the money, he didn't think garnering excess publicity was a wise move, and he also didn't want de Valera anywhere near Chicago. Beyond the personal animosity and the obvious turf war involving the pair, at least part of his reasoning appears to have been a very logical concern that Americans generally tend to resent foreigners trying to hijack or impinge upon their domestic electoral business, most especially during presidential contests.

Inevitably, there is some dispute then about the circumstances of the build-up to the convention itself. De Valera's side contend he was quite prepared to allow Cohalan and his cohorts to handle the business of securing an Irish plank. Why the change of heart? The judge was too slow in travelling to Chicago, and word circulated he had no intention of demanding recognition anyway. That was enough to persuade de Valera to hasten there himself. The opposing flank claims de Valera was always hell-bent on attending, regardless of Cohalan's intentions, and ignored the advice of Frank P. Walsh and others about the wisdom of being seen to interfere in America's own business.

Travelling with Sean Nunan, de Valera arrived in the city on 4 June, four days before the convention formally opened at the Chicago Coliseum. Liam Mellows, the master organiser, was already in town, and soon the publicity operation many warned would be ill-advised was in full swing.

'We opened offices with huge circus posters outside, on Michigan Boulevard; headquarters at the Blackstone Hotel - at the Convention Centre,' wrote McCartan. 'We published a daily paper, which was issued from offices opposite the hall where the convention was held. Members of the Irish mission were constantly in the offices and in the Blackstone Hotel. There was no chance of offending America that we did not take. But President de Valera, by virtue of a courtesy unique in American history, was permitted unmolested to carry out this programme.'

From the moment he alighted from the train, de Valera had the media's attention.

'We of Ireland are anxious to point out to all American parties that in Ireland the people, acting on their right to choose their government, have elected to live as a nation with a principle of government which the United States has always been regarded as the foremost champion. We hope to have America recognise the government of a nation which also stands for government by consent of the governed. If the United States wished to remain neutral she should withdraw recognition of British rule in Ireland. It is not a domestic question for England to settle any more than it was a domestic question for Germany to settle when she held Belgium in her grasp. For that reason, we want to see Irish plans in the platform of both the Republican and Democratic Parties.'

This was substantively the same message he'd been delivering for nearly a full year, at that point, but there now was an edge to it too. He was playing a straight bat, refusing to declare any preference for a particular candidate, trying not to throw Ireland's lot in with one party - even if the Republicans were ultimately expected to triumph. When a reporter asked if he'd have to endorse one party, if it came straight out in favour of recognition, he was politic enough to say the voting remained the task of the American citizens. This caution contrasted sharply with Cohalan and John Devoy.

Through the pages of the *Gaelic American*, they had earlier backed the presidential aspirations of California Senator Hiram Johnson, who would compete for that honour at the convention with a whopping fourteen other candidates. The thinking behind their endorsement was that a Johnson administration would then appoint their ally Senator William Borah as Secretary of State and, with that pair of fervent anti-Versailles Treatyites in power, Ireland should duly gain official recognition. It was a wonderful theory, which would be undone by the Republicans instead choosing Warren G. Harding, a compromise candidate from a crowded field.

The competition for commander-in-chief was the least of de Valera's worries. His main concern centred on having the Republicans - and the Democrats too a couple of weeks later - adopt a plank that went farther than the congressional expression of sympathy emanating from the Mason Bill.

'At all times, we have known that the American people were sympathetic,' said de Valera. 'My mission is to get action in accordance with that sympathy.'

The mission was critically compromised and undermined by the feud. Cohalan and Devoy arrived in Chicago, two days after de Valera, and started work on a plank to submit for the approval of the Republican Party's Committee on Resolutions. The pair of veterans believed, with perhaps good reason, if the Mason Bill couldn't get the approval of the Republican-dominated House of Representatives there was no chance of having the party come out in open favour of recognising the Irish Republic at the convention. Thus, theirs was a bland offering which they felt had the best chance of being adopted. It read:

'Resolved: that this Republican Convention desires to place on record its sympathy with all oppressed peoples, and its recognition of the principle that the people of Ireland have the right to determine freely, without dictation from outside, their own governmental institutions and their international relations with other States and peoples.'

In consultation with Frank P. Walsh, de Valera drew up a longer and much different resolution.

'Mindful of the circumstances of the birth of our own nation, we reassert the principle that all governments derive their just powers from the consent of the governed. We will support the continuance of our long established and lawful practice of according recognition without intervention in all cases when the people of a nation, as in Ireland, have by free vote of the people set up a Republic, and chosen a government to which they yield willing obedience. Therefore, we favour the according by our Government to the elected Government of the Republic of Ireland, full, formal, and official recognition, thus vindicating the principles for which our soldiers offered up their lives.'

On 8 June the two warring factions came together in a meeting at the Blackstone Hotel, from which Cohalan had decided to absent himself. Still, he had plenty of surrogates there and what exactly happened in that conference room depends, as is usual in this feud, on which account you believe. One side claim de Valera showed his plank, refused to allow any discussion of it, and even wished to be allowed argue the case himself in front of the Republican Party Committee on Resolutions. The other reckons de Valera had no such wish, received no co-operation from Cohalan's men, and had his attempts at presenting a united front scuppered by their belligerence. Add in to the mix a wild rumour doing the rounds that the FOIF were about to demand de Valera leave America forthwith - and you get a picture of the chaos.

Consequently and bizarrely, the Republican Committee had the pleasure of the company of two separate Irish delegations on the afternoon of 9 June. At two o'clock, a group headed up by Walsh and Congressman Mason (who submitted a letter as well outlining the legal precedent for Irish recognition) pressed the case for the de Valera resolution. At four o'clock, the Cohalan contingent went in to argue their own cause. In between the two appointments, a last-ditch attempt was made to ask the judge to forego his appointment in the interests of at least maintaining the appearance of unity. He refused.

As Senator James E. Watson and the twelve other committee men considered the fate of the two Irish resolutions that night, de Valera was the star turn in a torchlit procession through the streets of the city culminating in a mass meeting at the Auditorium Theatre on Congress Street. Beginning on the North Side,

the parade was led down Michigan Avenue by seventy US servicemen marching in uniform, followed by a car carrying de
Valera. Several state delegations from the convention participated and bands played en route to ensure a noisy and colourful
pageant with a cast of thousands. 'George Washington was a
good Sinn Féiner!' went one banner, 'Our dead in France
demand Ireland's Freedom - Don't break faith with our dead'
went another.

'Most of the marchers carried the Irish Republican flag, and at
the head of each division an American and an Irish flag were carried side by side,' wrote *The New York Times*. 'By this device
nobody in the crowd along the street could escape baring his
head before the Irish banner unless he wanted to keep his hat on
in the presence of the flag of his own country, and there were
plenty of enthusiastic persons on the curb to denounce him as an
unpatriotic American if he did.'

By the time the convoy reached the auditorium, five thousand
people had crammed into the venue, thousands more were
stranded outside the doors, and half a dozen mini-meetings were
quickly convened to keep the crowd entertained. When de
Valera was presented to the crowd, he received a standing ovation, which lasted twenty-nine minutes, before he could remind
his audience of the purpose of his presence in their town. 'I know
all of Chicago wants this. I know the entire country wants this. I
have been all over the country and I know: the Republicans must
promise to recognise the Irish Republic.'

Unfortunately, the large parade and the emotive speech had
all been in vain. The next morning it emerged that De Valera's
resolution was defeated by twelve votes to one. Insult was added

to injury when news emerged that Cohalan's had been accepted by seven votes to six. Apart from being obviously frustrated at the Republicans opting for a formulation that was yet one more expression of sympathy, instead of something approaching full-blown recognition, it's fair to assume de Valera was also seriously miffed at being outsmarted in the committee room by his arch nemesis. Immediately, a statement was given to the press highlighting what he considered the pointlessness of this plank.

'This declaration leaves the Irish question exactly where it was so far as America is concerned... There is no evidence in the declaration of the Resolutions Committee of any intention to act upon the principles embodied in the declaration. It is a pledge of intended action that is needed, not a statement of principles.'

Giving public expression to his anger wasn't de Valera's only response to the setback. By one report, he had John Milholland, one of his more trusted American lieutenants, phone Senator Watson to tell him the plank adopted was not wanted and had to be removed before the resolutions were read to the convention floor. This caused Watson to change his vote and have Cohalan's resolution erased from the platform altogether. An alternative viewpoint contends that the Republicans actually threw out the relevant paragraph of their own volition, after witnessing how the Irish movement was tearing itself apart over it.

In what might be figured to be an objective account, the *Chicago Tribune* of 11 June alleged a larger Republican committee had got rid of the resolution simply because 'it would be inconsistent with the stand of Congress against a mandate for Armenia and also with the declaration against the League of Nations.' It says much for the impact de Valera was having around the place that on the same day the paper ran a cartoon of a bespectacled figure in a morning coat with the text: 'De Valera is not really a candidate at this convention'. McCartan later vouched that this doodle was the only substantive critique of his activities to come from an American quarter during the whole affair.

In a bizarre interlude, as news of the resolutions broke and the house of cards was crumbling around him, de Valera still found time on 10 June to spend more than three hours sitting in the reviewing stand of a religious parade. To mark the diamond jubilee of the Chicago diocese and the twenty-fifth anniversary of the priesthood ordination of its very own Archbishop George W. Mundelein, an enormous procession of 147 religious-themed floats went down Lake Shore Drive. As the participants stopped in front of the guest of honour, they saw de Valera seated on his right-hand side, an esteemed and high-profile position on the dais.

Some might argue his day might have been better spent working the back-rooms of the convention centre, because, at one point, there was speculation that an effort was going to be made to spark a debate on the need for an Irish plank by the delegates on the floor of the Coliseum, though that initiative also came to naught. There was no formal mention of Ireland in the entire Republican platform and indeed, a search of the official report for the proceedings of the 17th Republican National Convention elicits just a single reference to the country over the entire five days. 'We are opposed to the League of Nations,' said Edwin J. Gross of Wisconsin. 'It would make us party to the enslavement of Egypt and India, the rape of China and the ruthless oppression of Ireland.'

In the worst possible outcome, the Irish presence at the convention had degenerated into the oldest national cliché. What time are we having the split? The most powerful and experienced Irish and Irish-American politicians were in Chicago for a week, and had the attention of the party, which would, in all likelihood, take over the White House early in 1921, and yet, they couldn't put aside their personal differences in order to get a job done. It was a missed opportunity that the American Consul, in Dublin, told Washington, in a dispatch, had come as a 'shock to Sinn Féiners in Ireland.' It was principally the fault of de Valera and Cohalan, and their now constant open warfare. The British ambassador offered his take on the whole debacle to London: 'The incident illustrates in an interesting manner the immense influence Irishmen can exert on American politicians if they proceed wisely,' wrote Sir Auckland Geddes, 'and how ready American politicians are to withdraw themselves from that influence if they find some colourful pretext for doing so.'

Worse again than this failure to capitalise on the circumstances available to them in Chicago though was the subsequently toxic fall-out from it.

'The refusal of the Chicago convention to yield to the intrigues and menaces of de Valera shows that the Republicans are not only sensible but consistent, for a party which is so sensitive about interference of foreigners in American affairs cannot be willing to mix itself up in domestic difficulties of other countries,' commented the London conservative daily, *The Morning Post.*

'This does not mean that the Irish problem will not figure in the election but it is formal recognition by party leaders that it is

a British and not an American question and that American interference would only add to their present embarrassments,'
declared the *Daily Telegraph*.

The glee of the English press was the least of de Valera's problems. A delegation of Chicago-based Cohalan supporters
accosted him and formally ask him to leave the country. Soon,
word went round that after attending the Democratic Party
Convention, in San Francisco, later in the month, he was sailing
to Australia. This wasn't true though in actual fact, a tour of
South America was being given such serious consideration he'd
requested and received Dáil approval for it. Speculation about
his next move was harmless enough, compared to the heavy flak
he shipped from John Devoy in the 17 June edition of the *Gaelic
American*.

'This action of Mr. de Valera was most unwise and wholly
unjustifiable and he and his advisers incurred a responsibility
from the consequences of which they can never escape. But they
did worse than that. At an expense of fully $50,000 taken out of
the money subscribed for Irish Republic bonds, and for expendi-
ture in Ireland alone, a nondescript aggregation of individuals
was brought to Chicago from many parts of the country to con-
stitute a rival committee to that of the Friends of Irish Freedom.'

Returning to the theme of financial profligacy, which was
touched on in the Park Avenue Hotel confrontation back in
March, Devoy had hit a nerve and grabbed a headline in *The
New York Times*. De Valera had to quickly counter this accusation that he was playing fast and loose with cash that would have
been better spent bolstering the fight in Ireland. Calling the allegations 'a tissue of misstatement' and the money story 'a

malicious charge', he launched a rebuttal.

'That sum is absolutely exaggerated. We did not spend more than half that sum on expenses at Chicago. When I came to this country, I expected that an effort might be made to control me through the power of the purse and I arranged with the Irish Parliament to vote me appropriations to cover my expenses. That money came out of the Irish Treasury. The bonds were sold with the express understanding that they were for all uses of the Irish Government, and furthering the cause of that Government in this country is a legitimate use of the money.'

As recently as the first week in June, Harry Boland - then back in Dublin - had delivered a message from de Valera to the cabinet, requesting he be allowed to utilise one million dollars to secure recognition. The ministers said they would recommend such a move to the Dáil which, on 29 June, authorised him 'to expend at his discretion such sum not exceeding $500,000 as he may require in connection with the election campaign for the Presidency of the United States of America.'

Apart from addressing the suggestion of financial impropriety being peddled about him, de Valera also attacked the Cohalan resolution without ever using the judge's name.

'I believe it was positively harmful to our interests that a resolution misrepresenting Ireland's just claim by understating it should have been presented. It is not for me to say that the Irish people would be satisfied with something which it was obvious they could not have been satisfied with. Our people are dying in their struggles to maintain their right. We want action which will end the apparent acquiescence of America in British barbarity in Ireland...I believe that the people of Ireland will be thoroughly disappointed with the action of those of the friends of Ireland in America who were guilty of the methods which were used in Chicago to prevent their chosen representative from fulfilling his mission in Chicago.'

His language - blaming America for England's activities - had become as inflammatory as the situation in Ireland, where things were going from bad to worse. The court system was facing collapse because jurors were refusing to participate, the English were ramping up their military presence to cope with increased violent attacks, and taking their cue from a similar strike by the Dublin dockers in January, train drivers were refusing to handle munitions or to operate trains with troops on board. Against that background of social disintegration, Denis Henry, the Attorney-General for Ireland told the House of Commons British soldiers had been instructed to behave exactly as they would on the battlefield. Again, all of that put the name-calling and finger-pointing by de Valera and Cohalan in some context. Still, their proxies continued to do battle in the press.

'Justice Cohalan endeavours to monopolise the term "American" for himself and his adroit political colleagues, just as he monopolised the management of the Irish movement in this country, though not elected to any office which would give him the powers he usurped,' said McCartan in an interview with *The New York Times*. 'The Justice's adherents in dissension are not correctly Irish-Americans or Americans. They are Cohalan-Americans.'

An equally vituperative attack on de Valera came from Daniel T. O'Connell, Director of the National Bureau of the FOIF. 'It is always unwise for those who do not understand American politics to attempt playing with national conventions. Results prove the force of that statement. Facts are facts; specious reasoning, prejudiced views and excited explanations cannot overcome the cold, bare truth which actual, plain, matter-of-fact results disclose.'

Sparring that vicious constituted a lesson in the art of politicking and spin that must have stood to de Valera all his life. It also turned those weeks into arguably the toughest of his time in America. On 23 June William Randolph Hearst, whose papers had been kind to the mission from day one, came to his defence. The newspaper magnate, upon whose life *Citizen Kane* was largely based, sent a telegram from San Francisco to the *Chicago Herald-Examiner* ordering it to reproduce an editorial rebuffing the growing criticism of de Valera.

'If President de Valera had not very clearly and distinctly appreciated his position, and if he had not been conscious at every moment for the past year of the line that divides that which is right to do from that which it would be an impertinence to do, Ireland's enemies would have tripped him up before he had been in this country one month,' wrote Hearst. 'In fact, the most distinguishing characteristic of President de Valera's campaign has been the delicacy with which he trod, never once overstepping the bounds of good sense and good taste. The Hearst Papers have repeatedly congratulated the Irish Republic upon the high character, the tact, the good sense and the diplomatic wisdom of its President. We now repeat and emphasise those congratulations.'

By then, de Valera had already turned his sights west towards San Francisco, where the Democratic Party was convening on 28 June. He'd have to start the fight for recognition all over again there.

CHAPTER FIFTEEN

Dail Eireann assembled in full session in Dublin today unanimously affirmed the allegiance of the citizens of Ireland to your policy, expresses complete satisfaction with the work you have performed and relies with confidence upon the great American nation to accord recognition to the Republic of Ireland now in fact and in law established.

**- Cablegram from Arthur Griffith to de Valera,
1 July 1920**

Having so scrupulously maintained a neutral position in terms of party political loyalties throughout his year in America, Eamon de Valera headed to San Francisco in the last week of June, to try to persuade the Democratic Party National Convention of the merits of Ireland's case. Upon arrival, he was met with the now-obligatory fanfare, including yet one more colourful pageant and parade. However, the cheery reception contrasted with the objective view of his prospects. Even before he'd got off the train, the local papers were speculating his chances of getting the type of resolution he desired were almost non-existent and that he well might end up with no resolution at all.

At least he had a clear run on this occasion. On 25 June the FOIF announced it would not be attending this convention. Justice Cohalan's decision to stay home was inevitable. Having already openly endorsed the (now failed) Republican candidacy of Senator Hiram Johnson, he and Devoy could hardly head west and start up an attempt to make demands on the other half of the political divide in America. It may also just have been incredibly astute on his part, given the gloomy predictions about how the Irish would fare in the dealings there.

Whether chastened by criticism of his spending or simply realising himself that the mission had very little genuine hope of success, de Valera did not launch as coherent or as diverse a publicity campaign in California as he had in Chicago. However, his rhetoric had a far sharper edge. In a statement released to the press on 28 June the first day of the convention, he appeared to accuse America of being complicit in the mistreatment of Ireland by the British.

'Is there any good reason why America should depart from the established custom in the case of Ireland? Has the British Empire got some special licence entitling it to enslave? Or is there some reason why British threats should be heeded where the threats of other tyrannies were not? Before and during the war, through the explicit declarations of its chief executive, the position of America on the right of nations to rule themselves was made clear. The position of Britain was made equally definite through the declarations of its responsible executives. What just cause has

Britain now to be offended or to object if America refuses to betray its dead and insists on applying to the particular case of Ireland the general principle agreed when entering the war? America has given the hostage of the lives of its best - has Britain a right to claim that they be sacrificed?'

The following day, Frank P. Walsh went to the hearing of the Committee on Resolutions, at the Civic Auditorium, to argue the case for a plank remarkably similar to that which had so spectacularly failed in Chicago. It read:

'Mindful of the circumstances of the birth of our nation, we reassert the principle that all governments derive their just powers from the consent of the governed. We will support the continuance of our long-established and lawful practice of according recognition without intervention in all cases where the people of a nation, as in Ireland, have by free vote of the people set up a republic and chosen a Government to which they yield willing obedience. Therefore we pledge our party to the policy of according to the elected Government of the Republic of Ireland full, formal and official recognition by the Government of the United States, thus vindicating the principle for which our soldiers offered up their lives.'

Were they hoping against hope that the presence of Massachusetts' Senator David I. Walsh and W. Bourke Cochran, two stalwarts of the cause, on the committee would yield some sort of miracle? A mistaken assumption because Cochran proved far more interested in fighting against prohibition than for Ireland, a tactic that saw him famously accused of putting rum before his race.

Was the decision to stay with the same controversial formula simply a pig-headed move to avoid admitting Cohalan may have had a better idea of the realpolitik? Whatever the motivation, the meeting degenerated into uproar and controversy that overshadowed Walsh's best attempts to argue the historical precedent for recognising Ireland, and that doing so would not cause a war with England.

The drama began when Demarest Lloyd, President of the Loyal Coalition (an organisation formed to protest against the activities of hyphenated Americans with particular reference to those which threatened Great Britain), rose to oppose Walsh, and accused himself and de Valera of collecting '$10,000,000 from the pockets of American servant girls.' That angered so many in the room, and elicited such a chorus of insults and threats that sergeants-at-arms had to move through the crowd restoring order, so the debate could continue.

'They raised this fund and trickery by the chicanery of one de Valera,' said Randolph Wilford Smith, vice-president of the same Coalition. 'I read in the papers that the Irish bond issue was authorised by the Treasury Department and telegraphed the Secretary of the Treasury. Within five hours, I received a reply that the report was without foundation.'

'It was the Treasury Department of the Irish Republic, ye amadan,' shouted a voice from the floor.

While the committee was considering the resolutions put forward, a 1 July meeting, of what was now called the Irish Caucus, convened to consider its options. That conference grew so animated and angry that one speaker - Judge Michael Sullivan of Massachusetts - declared that the tenor of the discussion lent credence to their opponents' theory that the Irish were incapable of

governing themselves. The whole mêlée culminated in a delegation almost storming the committee room, demanding Senator
Walsh come out to tell them what was going on.

'There is no secret about the fact that the Committee has
voted (by 31 to 17) not to accept the plan on Ireland offered by
the representatives of the Irish people gathered here and that is
has adopted a substitute,' Walsh informed them. It was yet
another resounding defeat for de Valera. Fortunately, the text of
the Griffith cablegram of support (above) was released to the
press, the previous day, by way of proving he still retained the
confidence of his colleagues in Dublin.

There followed an attempt to get a less robust version of the
plank introduced from the convention floor on 2 July. This
effort was headed up by Edward L. Doheny, a California oil
magnate, whose extraordinary life story formed the basis for the
movie *There Will Be Blood*. Having already purchased $10,000
worth of bond certificates, Doheny secured a twenty-minute discussion of Ireland that was a rather tame back and forth, compared to the intense debate among delegates about prohibition
which preceded it.

In the last count of that day, the minority Irish resolution was
defeated by 665.5 votes to 402.5 votes. Still, the final platform
agreed on by the Democratic Party (who decided on Governor
James Cox and Franklin Roosevelt as their Presidential ticket)
did contain the following clause - the substitute mentioned by
Senator Walsh - beneath the heading 'Ireland'.

'The great principle of national self-determination has
received constant reiteration as one of the chief objectives for
which this country entered the war, and victory established this

principle. Within the limitations of the international comity and usage this convention repeats the several previous expressions of the sympathy of the Democratic Party of the United States for the aspirations of self-government.'

This resolution, vague and remarkably similar to what the Republicans had chosen to omit in the final reckoning, looked like nothing more than a sop compared to those the Democratic party issued concerning other countries. Armenia was promised aid in its efforts to maintain a government of its own, the Philippines was guaranteed full and immediate independence from America itself, and a raft of other nations, including China, Persia, Finland, Poland, Czechoslovakia and Yugoslavia, were informed the Democrats admired their newly-established representative governments. It was little wonder that Ireland's failure to get something of that calibre irked de Valera, whose reaction was to question whether the party realised the extent of the Irish vote in America.

'Rejection of the plank pledging the Democratic Party to the recognition of the Republic of Ireland merely indicates it is not yet realised how great is the volume of public opinion in this country behind the demand for justice in Ireland. A more systematic and thorough organisation of the friends of the cause in America is now shown necessary and will be made. An intensive campaign of education will be carried into every State and will reach every citizen.'

Without specifying whether the people would be taught about Ireland herself or how the Democrats (whose ticket of Cox and Roosevelt would be resoundingly trashed in the general election) had neglected her plight, he went on to wax philosophical about the nature of the latest setback.

'I regret, of course, that the Democratic Party has not seen its way to avail of the timely opportunity which the case of Ireland presented for putting its noble principles into practice. I believe in facing positions squarely. Now we know where we are. I am by no means disheartened by the defeat. We have learned to face defeat when necessary and to endure it when it comes. In this case, it simply means we must prepare for a greater effort.'

While his critics on the east coast were positively gleeful at the pointlessness of his trek across the country, de Valera sought solace in the arms of a third political party. The Labour movement and a progressive group called the Committee of Forty-Eight had come together in Chicago, with the intention of forming a leftist Third Party to compete for the White House. De Valera spoke at this convention where for a time Frank P. Walsh was even mooted as a potential presidential candidate. The Farmer-Labour Party - the new entity which emerged from the gathering - underlined its intention to be different from the establishment by giving de Valera exactly what he asked for.

'The third party has unambiguously adopted recognition of the elected Government of the Republic of Ireland by the Government of the United States as the official policy of the party,' he told journalists upon his arrival back in New York on 16 July. 'More, they have pledged themselves to put an embargo on munitions intended to be used against the people of Ireland in their rightful struggle for freedom.'

He stopped short of telling Irish-Americans to vote for the third party ticket, something which would have been pointless any way, because the grouping barely registered on the electoral map come November. That day, he was even forced to admit to reporters this imprimatur was much less than he'd hoped for from his trip to the conventions. Failing to get the endorsement of either of the main parties, he had to settle for the backing of an upstart movement, regarded as extremist cranks by most. A hugely disappointing outcome, it was a miniscule return for six weeks on the road, and to make matters worse, there was more bad news from the other side of the Atlantic, while he was gone.

On 2 July William Barry, an Irish-born fireman on the steamship *New York*, had been arrested at Southampton in possession of two pistols, nearly 300 rounds of ammunition, and an even more incendiary bundle of letters. Some were addressed to code names, but there were enough real names used to allow the British authorities to prosecute Barry under the Defence of the Realm Act and to reveal the substance of the material to the world's press. Witness the report that appeared in *The New York Times* after Barry was sentenced to two months in prison on 13 July.

'The letters presented to the court comprised a covering letter signed "John" and addressed to "Michael", who the police say presumably is Michael Collins, Sinn Fein member of parliament for Cork: three letters addressed to Arthur Griffith, two of them signed "James O'Mara", and the other signed "Noonan", one addressed to "McSweeney" whom authorities identify as the Mayor of Cork and Commandant of the Cork Brigade of the Republican Army, signed Peter who is thought to be the Mayor's brother, and another letter signed "Noonan" and addressed to "Michael".'

From the point of view of de Valera's standing in America the content of the various missives was even more pertinent than the various identities revealed. There were accounts of the failure in Chicago that praised de Valera's efforts, while castigating Cohalan and Devoy. If that was predictable enough, there was also a request for the Dáil to deliver a vote of confidence to its absent Priomh Aire to bolster his position. It may have been a standard political tactic, but not the type of instruction any leader wanted revealed in a newspaper, especially at a time when his every move was being tracked by his rivals.

After so much negativity in both public and private, a wonderful opportunity came along at that time, offering a chance to try to recapture the swagger and the brio of the early campaign. It arrived in the high-profile, outspoken and controversial form of Archbishop Daniel Mannix of Melbourne, Australia. A native of Charleville, County Cork, Mannix was President of St Patrick's College, Maynooth, when it gained university status, and one of his last acts in that role was to have dinner with and appoint de Valera as a mathematics lecturer in October 1912. In his adopted country, Mannix became a powerful political prelate and had never stinted from speaking out on behalf of Irish nationalism.

En route to Rome for an audience with the Pope that summer, Mannix crossed America overland and even before reaching New York, was embroiled in a minor scandal over allegations that he sat through a playing of 'The Star-Spangled Banner' in Honolulu, earlier in his voyage. The subsequent uproar only served to whet the appetite for his appearance at Madison Square Garden, which the archdiocese of New York had booked for the night of Sunday, 18 July. Ostensibly a public reception to formally welcome Mannix, with tickets being distributed, for free, through area churches, the event turned into a 16,000-strong rally on behalf of the cause of Irish independence.

Just at it had been during de Valera's raucous stop there, a year earlier, President Wilson's name was hissed upon every mention, and thousands of Irish tricolours were waved as the NYPD band played 'Amhrán na Bhfiann'. Archbishop Patrick J. Hayes of New York presided over the evening and in his introduction paid fulsome tribute to 'his Excellency, the President of the Irish Republic'. De Valera then opened his speech by reminding his audience of his last appearance at the venue and, in a jab at his enemies, cogently stated he had no intention of leaving America until 'the time comes'.

'It is now a little over a year since I first had the privilege of speaking in this hall, and one of the recollections that I would take back with me to inspire the people of Ireland to be steadfast in their struggle is the recollection of the reception which you gave their representative in your city on the first occasion on which he spoke in public here. I am glad that I can tell the people of Ireland that I did not outstay my welcome in America. It is not an individual you welcomed here on that occasion. It was the representative of a nation that was seeking favours from no nation but bare and simple justice.'

The remainder of his warm-up act for the main man was given over to thanking all those who'd come to his aid in America and to waxing lyrical about Mannix, calling him 'a true champion of the plain people, and of Ireland's mission in the world today.' He then sat back and listened to his former boss laud his work for Ireland over the previous year, and launch into a peculiar take on what might have been at the Versailles Treaty negotiations.

'If our President de Valera had gone over to the Paris conference, and if he had knocked at the door where the great plenipotentiaries were assembled in secret conclave to give us open covenants, and if he had said he had a list of grievances against Germany, the doors would have been flung open to him, and he would have been invited to take a chair at the head of the table.'

Both speeches were punctuated by bouts of sustained cheering and rapturously received. After so much adverse publicity, this was a return to the enthusiasm and the mass meetings that hallmarked the best times in America. It helped that Mannix was an unstinting fan of his and that the archbishop's schedule provided ample opportunity for him to constantly and vocally reinforce his faith in his beleagured colleague.

'I am proud that you have had the good taste and the kind consideration for my feelings to ask President de Valera to sit here at my right hand,' said Mannix, delivering a toast at a banquet given in his honour by the Maynooth Union at the Hotel Astor, the following Tuesday night. 'He has made a place for himself in the Irish nation which entitles him to sit not merely with the laity and clergy, but even on the bench of Bishops. He has gone to more trouble to put himself right before God than those who are his meanest critics.'

There was more praise too.

'We have listened to him here and you could almost see the sincerity of the man's soul while he picked his steps carefully through the morality of the fight that the Irish people have been making.'

Apart from the very eloquent expressions of support and the

headline-grabbing showpieces afforded by such a public figure, de Valera took the opportunity of a joint appearance in Washington on 23 July to revisit the issues raised by the explosive *Westminster Gazette* affair back in February. With a little more clarity than he offered in that seismic interview, he told an audience at Gonzaga Hall that the Irish would specifically be willing to accept a version of the first article of the Platt Amendment. This was the addendum to the agreement between Cuba and America, in which it's stipulated that, in return for independence, Cuba would never allow itself to be used by another power against America.

'I have already indicated my belief that the Irish people would be willing to relieve British anxiety about the future, in so far as that anxiety is legitimate or genuine, by agreeing to a stipulation such as that of the first article in the Platt Amendment. I would have no hesitation myself in recommending such a course to the Irish people, and if a peace were signed on such terms, I would gladly devote myself to the fostering of the same good relations between Ireland and Britain as exist between Ireland and the rest of the world. The whole truth is that the British government does not want peace in Ireland or with Ireland except on terms which no real Irishman will accept - on the basis of Ireland's subjugation as a mere province of Britain…Peace will only come when the last British soldier is removed from Ireland or when Britain is ready to treat with Ireland as a separate and independent national state.'

This time around, the notion barely raised a murmur. That may have been because rumours were swirling that de Valera had written letters to Ireland advising the cabinet to accept the

Dominion Home Rule proposals coming from London. Apart from sending a cablegram to Arthur Griffith, assuring him such reports were 'absurd', he also moved quickly to publicly deny this with a statement to the press that appeared to float the idea such innuendo was the work of the Cohalan faction.

'Stories to the effect that I am secretly in favour of what is called Dominion Home Rule, as it would seem from press dispatches, are being seditiously propagated at the other side of the Atlantic as well as here. These stories originate as British inventions or as the fabrications of those who want to hide purely personal antagonism to me under the cloak of zeal for our cause. They are of the same stuff and for the same purpose as the attempts some time ago to make it appear that I am advocating a British protectorate. The secret whispers, the private letters and the other wily machinations of men who, apparently, from fighting the British, have learned from them to adopt the same base methods, and who now seem scarcely to know what truth is or straight dealing, have shaken the trust of many an honest heart here for the past nine months and sapped the enthusiasm of many an ardent soul.'

The circumstances surrounding the departure of Mannix from New York must have replenished even the most sapped Irish soul. Notwithstanding the British government issuing an order banning him from entry to Ireland, he was booked to sail from New York to Queenstown on the White Star liner, *Baltic*, on 1 August. There were serious concerns that some of the ship's English crew would strike rather than allow such a well-known advocate of Irish Republicanism aboard. They eventually reneged on that idea, but a call in the *Irish Press* for all able-bodied patriots to turn up at the dock to give him a proper send-off, ensured a large crowd turned out at Pier 60 to create a remarkable and explosive atmosphere.

'There were hisses, cheers, fist-fights and the flash of revolvers,' wrote *The New York Times*. 'There were the milling and the shouting of a crowd, estimated at 5,000 persons, gathered both inside and outside the gates to bid the prelate farewell. There were the efforts of police and detectives to settle the outbreak between pro and anti-Irish elements. And lastly, there was the dramatic entry of the Archbishop himself whose "God bless you my men, keep calm" restored order on the liner's deck.'

As he had for much of his sojourn on the east coast, de Valera accompanied Mannix from his accommodation, at Archbishop Hayes's house on Madison Avenue, to the docks. Indeed, when the mob saw de Valera walk onto the ship and then reappear on deck beside the Corkman, word went around that he was going to stay on board and sail back to Ireland too. This added to the frenzied mood and when Joseph Shaw, a *Baltic* coal operator from Yorkshire, leaned over to jeer at those waving Irish tricolours, all hell broke loose. A group of longshoremen working the baggage loading pounced on the Englishman and set about him, until police offers drew their guns and restored a semblance of order.

Throughout the drama, de Valera and Mannix watched from their vantage point atop the promenade deck. On the pier alongside, the mostly English crew of another liner, *Olympic*, then added to the tension by producing a Union Jack, waving it at the crowd and taunting them: 'Here's a flag you can't lick!' A police boat watched it all, patrolling the water, in case, in any ensuing frenzy people ended up going overboard.

Shortly before 1.00pm, the last whistle sounded before sailing, de Valera bade Mannix farewell, and came down the gangway. Perhaps conscious of the potential for trouble and with it a raft of negative headlines, he made to get away from the scene quickly but was stopped by supporters. Despite broiling in the blistering heat of the summer's day, they wanted to continue the festivities. A few of them lifted de Valera off the ground and on to their shoulders, where he was perched as the *Baltic* edged away from its berth and into the Hudson River, from where the archbishop delivered a final blessing to them all from his spot out on deck.

De Valera was then carried aloft down the pier to where the cars had been parked. So many people then gathered around to see him off that the driver couldn't get it started. He was carried again to a different vehicle and finally allowed to leave for the Waldorf-Astoria.

'The American people may need to be reminded that Tuam, Fermoy, Thurles, Kilmallock, Newcastle West, Lismore and other towns that have been bombed, sacked and burned recently are not, like Louvain, in Belgium,' said de Valera in Atlantic City, New Jersey the following day, Mannix still fresh in his thoughts. 'Nor are the forces that are responsible for the outrages Germans, but British. The American people may need assurances also that the Lloyd George that threatens to prevent a patriotic Irish prelate from landing on his native sod is the same Lloyd George who but yesterday lauded Cardinal Mercier (who came to embody Belgian resistance during World War 1) to the skies as one of the greatest of living men because he stood unflinchingly by his people...'

In a dramatic postscript, the *Baltic* was fourteen miles from Cork Harbour on 9 August, when two British naval ships pulled alongside. A pair of Scotland Yard detectives boarded the liner, placed Mannix under technical arrest and forced him to accompany them onto the destroyer *Wivern*, which subsequently sailed to Penzance. By way of explanation, Mannix had been handed government orders informing him that he wasn't allowed to land in Ireland because his presence there would likely cause disorder. It was a strange notion given that over the course of the previous month, the War of Independence had reached such a fevered pitch that Edward Carson told the House of Commons the whole island was in 'a state of anarchy.'

CHAPTER SIXTEEN

To Eamon de Valera, President of Republic of Ireland, care-of Liam Mellows, 504 Grant Buildings, 1045 Market Street, San Francisco. Harry tells me Flanagan and family splendid. Expects Flanagan end of this month, Jim.

- Cablegram from James O'Mara during Democratic Convention, July 1920

When another cablegram reached de Valera, in Washington, in mid-August informing him that Flanagan had finally landed in New York, he assumed this heralded the arrival of Fr Michael O'Flanagan, vice-president of Sinn Féin. The person in question was actually his wife, the former Sinéad Flanagan. The idea for her visit had originated with Harry Boland who, during his trip back to Ireland in May and June, had persuaded her to make the trip. She was reluctant to leave her children for that long and, whether she knew it then or not, her husband wasn't exactly thrilled with the idea of her coming either. De Valera was adhering to such a hectic schedule and battling on so many different fronts - the last thing he needed was one more demand upon his time.

'He (Harry Boland) said that Dev was very tired and worn out in America and that I should go to see him,' said Sinéad de Valera. 'The visit to America was one of the biggest mistakes I ever made. Dev himself had nothing to do with my going. He did not know until I arrived. I went in 1920 and travelled on a false passport. The passport was in the name of Margaret Williams. My dear, dear friend, Máire O'Connor came with me. Mick Collins carried my trunk out to the car. The outward journey was slow, and I was sick for part of the time. I felt lonely and sad thinking of the children at home. I was nervous and uneasy during the outward voyage. When we arrived in New York, there was a bad thunderstorm.'

At this point in their relationship, the couple had been married since 1910, already had six children and yet, due to the vagaries of the struggle, the prison terms and the intermittent spells on the run from the authorities, they hadn't lived together as man and wife since May 1918. Despite carrying the immense burden of raising six children under the age of ten, back in Greystones, Sinéad tried to include their absent father in the parenting. Earlier that year, de Valera received a cable, while in Washington, that reads like the equivalent of a text message from a concerned mother appraising her husband of the latest on the domestic front. 'Children and self very well, have I think temporarily solved schooling problem for Viv, Sinéad.'

Almost immediately upon being reunited, the de Valeras went on holiday together to Greenwich, Connecticut. It was about an hour outside New York, just near enough for him to return, if need arose. Their presence at Edgwood Inns, an exclusive high society retreat, replete with a casino, merited a mention in the *Hartford Courant* and although there is no exact evidence of how long they remained, their stay was substantial enough for the O'Maras to drop in for a weekend visit, from their own holidaying accommodation at the Gedney Farm Hotel, in White Plains.

It's fair to assume the couple had some serious work to do on their relationship after so long apart. For all his attempts at keeping up correspondence from his various locations over the previous years, such a prolonged and stressful absence would have placed enormous pressure on any marriage, not to mention its impact on the children.

'My elder brother and I had of course a vivid recollection of my father and naturally my mother often spoke to us and the younger children about him and the struggle for Irish freedom,' said Máirín de Valera. 'She also worked hard at trying to teach us Irish. The younger children could not remember my father - my mother overheard Brian and Ruairí discussing him. "Who is Dev?" "I think he's Mummy's father." And baby Emer began to know that she could raise a laugh by taking up the newspaper and asking: "Is Mr. 'Lera in the paper today?"'

After so many months of negative headlines, fractious meetings and endless politicking from coast to coast, the arrival of his wife finally forced de Valera to take a sustained break, and the positive effect on his pysche can be gauged from a letter by Harry Boland to Kitty Kiernan. 'Mrs. De Valera is here now and has made a fine impression on every one, "The Chief" is a new man as a result and we are all very happy to have her here.'

Her first public appearance was at the Catholic Summer School of America in Cliff Haven, New York, on 29 August. De Valera was a guest speaker at the gathering, and at the conclusion of his soliloquy, a standing ovation for him mutated into a call from the crowd for his wife to also rise from her seat to acknowledge the cheers and take the plaudits. She did so gracefully, but was reluctant to embrace the spotlight afforded by her husband's fame in these parts. Mrs de Valera turned down repeated requests for interviews from the New York papers. When McGarrity's *Irish Press* did publish a feature with her, she spoke only of the impact of the troubles back home on the educational system.

'The students of the summer schools in Cliff Haven and in Ireland might be compared to the children of two mothers - both good, wise, devoted, anxious for the welfare and happiness of their children. But while in the one case, the mother has every opportunity of protecting the interests and developing the talents of her children to the full, the other has the abiding sorrow of seeing hers crushed and oppressed. This mother does not seek to shirk her responsibilities. She is capable, courageous and strong in her self-reliance. She does not wish that her children would claim anything that is not theirs by birthright.'

The O'Maras were her closest companions during the stay. The two families socialised together so often that upon returning to Wicklow, Mrs de Valera wrote to James O'Mara to thank him for 'all the kindness' his wife and daughter had shown her, and to assure them they remained in her nightly prayers. Notwithstanding the quality of that friendship and the standard of living quarters at the Waldorf-Astoria and other top quality hotels where she was billeted, Mrs de Valera wasn't happy. After the break in Connecticut, her husband had returned to his overbooked schedule, and she found herself either too often alone in her room or unwillingly pushed into the limelight.

The most glaring instance of the latter came in Boston on 12 September. After attending mass at the Cathedral of the Holy Cross, the de Valeras were received by Cardinal William O'Connell, who gifted her an autographed copy of his collected letters. Later that day, she received ovations similar in magnitude to her husband from the crowd, but was clearly discomfited by her role as what locals perceived as Ireland's First Lady. 'Mrs. de Valera was somewhat shy in returning the wild waving of hands that greeted her as soon as she was recognised,' recorded The *Irish Press*. 'But she has a real Irish smile and that compensated many who were keen enough to pick her out.'

The alternative to accompanying her husband on his relentless public outings was no alternative really. At least judging from her own testimony which included telling her children the sojourn represented 'the longest and least profitable part of my life.'

'It was a huge blunder for me to go to America. I derived neither profit nor pleasure from my visit. I am not one who is easily bored but I had nothing really profitable to do and spent a good deal of time in the hotel.'

If that sentiment was expressed many years later, it tallies perfectly with her more contemporaneous opinion. 'I can feel nothing much else but regret that I went to America. It was such a big mistake to go for such a long time for such a short stay. Since I came home I find it hard to be content to get along in the old groove.'

That quote is taken from a letter she wrote in November 1920 to Kathleen O'Connell, a woman who might just be the most under-acknowledged figure in the history of the country. From Caherdaniel, County Kerry, O'Connell emigrated to America in 1904 and had been worked for Cumann na mBan and the FOIF, before being co-opted onto de Valera's staff on 2 October 1919. Over time, she became his confidant, sounding-board and confessor, enjoying unique access to him, and possessing, at least, some influence during most of his political career thereafter.

Far from working for him or with him, she was utterly devoted to assisting him in the prosecution of whatever position, official or unofficial, he held at a given time. She led, as *The Irish Times* put it memorably at the time of her death, 'a life of magnificent unselfishness.' For this loyalty then, including lengthy spells on the lam when they both returned to Ireland, her reward has been to have her good name slandered by the recurring speculation that herself and her boss were also lovers. These rumours were so prevalent that de Valera himself addressed them.

'It went on not merely from platforms and in private, but it was spoken of from the pulpit; it came from the altar,' he said in the Dáil on 22 November 1928. 'I myself was told by a lady in Chicago that a Bishop had told her that my wife had to go over to America in order to keep me straight because I was associating with women… The private characters of individuals on different sides were the subject of propaganda of that particular type. My wife was supposed to have had to leave the country and live abroad because she could not live with me. I was supposed to be living with two or three other women. I am taking my own case because I know it.'

It is impossible for anybody to know whether the smears had any legitimate basis. What can be said for certain however, is that the correspondence between Kathleen O'Connell and Sinéad de Valera betray no evidence of any problems befitting two women in a love triangle. One letter ends with the words: 'love dear Kathleen from your sincere friend, Sinéad de Valera.' This is hardly the way a betrayed wife would write to her husband's mistress. In another dispatch from the Wardman Park Hotel in Washington, DC, which begins 'My dear Kathleen', she asks O'Connell to type up a short story she had written. Again, the tone of the letter, and the request itself, are far from what might be expected to pass between two warring women.

'Please do not think me very cheeky when you hear what I am asking you to do for me. I had nothing to read and nothing to do and so I began to scribble. I don't want to show the enclosed to "headquarters" there. Would you please if you have time type it for me? I don't want to show it to Joe (McGarrity) or to ask for his help. If you can do it will you please give it to Joe to return to me? Don't tell anyone about it. And please Kathleen don't trouble about it unless you have plenty of time and forgive me for being such an awful bother. I suppose you will say I ought to have a little more sense than to write such stuff.'

It may be possible to only parse one single phrase communicated between the women, as potentially illustrative of some row between them.

'I am sure you must have thought I was a real idiot that day I left Washington,' wrote Sinéad de Valera. 'I suppose I was a bit tired and therefore extra emotional?'

A reference to some unsightly clash between the pair or merely an excessively teary goodbye she bade when leaving the American capital? Whatever, this type of imaginative innuendo is hardly enough on which to support any gossip that O'Connell and her husband were paramours.

'Suggestions of this kind are at odds with the tone and content of the surviving correspondence, involving de Valera, his wife, and Kathleen O'Connell,' wrote Patrick Murray in a detailed analysis of the relationship. 'At the time of the American visit, for example, Mrs. de Valera's correspondence with Kathleen betrays no hint of doubt, suspicion, unease or animosity. On the contrary, her letters are those of one trusted friend to another - sincere, confiding and grateful for all kinds of help given, even in trivial matters.'

The presence of his wife - who was also taken to Rochester to meet his mother before sailing for home - may have forced de Valera into deviating briefly from the task at hand, and amplified speculation he would head back to Ireland with her. This was briefly considered but was never a genuine runner, because her stay happened to coincide with the ramping up of the intense faction-fighting between himself and the Friends of Irish Freedom.

A summer which had begun with the unseemly mess that was the dueling resolutions at the Republican Convention degenerated even further into one more miasma of denunciation, repudiation and allegation. The excoriating tone for much of what followed was captured in a report from the Department of Foreign Affairs to the Dáil, back in June.

'The ministry learns that these two men (Devoy and

Cohalan) have never given their whole-hearted support to the President in his campaign. At the very outset they used their utmost endeavour to prevent a launching of the Bond Drive, and they attempted to force the President into the position of accepting their dictation in all matters of policy connected with his mission. The President has definitely refused to allow his judgment or his action to be dictated by these men and the success of his tour and of the Bond Drive are proof of his wisdom in the matter.'

Within weeks, the Dáil was hearing the other side of the argument, reading into the record Diarmuid Lynch's letter of resignation. The Tracton-born veteran of 1916 resigned his seat for South-East Cork, motivated at least in part by some of the explicit criticisms of the FOIF found in the William Barry letters. In choosing his job in that organisation, over his constituency back home, Lynch managed to heighten awareness in Ireland of how dramatically the movement in America was now fractured.

'Differences have arisen since July, 1919, between President de Valera and members of Dail Eireann now in the United States on the one hand, and the recognised leaders of the movement here on the other, as to the proper conduct of the campaign in America for the recognition of the Irish Republic,' wrote Lynch. 'My judgment in this matter, based as it has been upon intimate knowledge of conditions in America, was generally in agreement with the American leaders. This circumstance has governed my actions as National Secretary of the Friends of Irish Freedom, and has furthered my determination to immediately tender my resignation...'

In his capacity as secretary, Lynch also penned a 24 July order expelling the Irish Progressive League - a body which had always been vocal in its support of de Valera, but most especially after the Republican Convention debacle, and one that contained some of his most devoted followers in New York - from the FOIF. On the other side of the row, *The Irish World*, a pro-de Valera paper in the city, accused Devoy of mismanagement of the Irish Victory Fund, and reheated old allegations about him doing likewise with Land League money back in 1882.

With so many public acrimonies leaking into the American press, and inevitably damaging the credibility of the greater cause, there were various back channel attempts to procure some sort of truce between the warring factions. The problem was that throughout the process de Valera was openly trying to overhaul the FOIF structures and word had gone around that if he failed, he'd simply establish a rival organisation which he could control.

His wish was to reconstitute the FOIF, so more power was vested in state committees and less in the national council. In other words, he was looking to weaken the base from which Devoy and Cohalan held so much sway. To this end, he also sought to hold a new Irish Race Convention in Chicago, or some other mid-western venue, later that year, the geographical shift designed to move beyond New York, where his enemies also retained most influence.

'As regards the FOIF, I have indeed thought that Ireland came first among the objectives of the organisation as such,' wrote de Valera to Bishop Michael Gallagher, the newly-appointed President of the FOIF on 6 August. 'It was I thought expressly for the purpose of assisting the people of Ireland in their struggle that the members banded themselves together and subscribed their moneys. It was on that assumption that I relied on it more than any other organisation for the support of my mission here.'

The bitter mood of the time is captured by a comment from Judge Hally, a friend of Gallagher's, who accompanied him to a four-hour meeting with de Valera to discuss his hopes for the FOIF, and to try to find a way for both sides to move forward together.

'His idea of harmony reminds me of Li Hung Chang, who said the harmony he best loved was the ring of the headsman's axe on the neck of his opponents.'

With both parties arguing their cases vehemently in the *Gaelic American*, *Irish World*, and *Irish Press*, indulging in plentiful mudslinging as they did so, the summer of so much discontent finally came to a head on 17 September. The location was the Waldorf-Astoria and the occasion was a meeting of the FOIF National Council. Beforehand, de Valera had supplemented the usual advance notice about the gathering, by personally telegraphing every council member in the country, asking that they do their best to attend. An expensive tactic that might have lent weight to his critics' belief he was profligate with the funds being raised.

Consequently, delegates travelled from as far away as Wyoming and Washington State to be present on an evening when only two motions were passed. One involved giving $15,000 to the longshoremen who'd gone on strike in protest at the treatment of Archbishop Mannix. The other pledged 'as far as possible' to put the resources of the FOIF at the disposal of the Irish President and the Irish delegation. That particular resolution was strangely out of kilter with the way proceedings had gone.

De Valera's hope that the larger than usual turn-out (162 members of the National Council and 63 observers) would help him in the voting proved forlorn. Firstly, he had problems even gaining entry. It took Harry Boland shouldering the doorman out of the way to even get de Valera in the door - hardly a welcome on the mat. Cohalan loyalists then warned the room about being seen to 'take orders from a foreign potentate' and reminded them of the need 'to keep the movement on an American basis'. The fractious atmosphere, the chaotic attempts at debate and the general ill-humour is summed up by Devoy's own (inevitably biased) take on proceedings.

'The whole play was staged last night for a Split. Father Power's attempt to stampede the meeting with his squad of priests marching around shouting "Break it up, break it up", being evidently intended as the signal, but its utter failure knocked out their plans. At an earlier stage of the meeting one of them was heard to say: "We haven't a gambler's chance here" and others said: "See how perfectly the machine works".'

Several eyewitnesses claim de Valera eventually walked out in a huff at hearing one insult too many. Others contend he departed to a soundtrack of cheers, rather than jeers, including attempts by his supporters to create an exodus by exhorting others to 'Follow the President, Follow the President'. What isn't up for dispute is that he did leave the room rather abruptly, knowing full well he wasn't going to get the result he came for that night. Several different deputations left the room later in the meeting to go and ask de Valera to return, but by then he had already retired to his bed, elsewhere in the hotel.

His last significant input had been to leave Boland behind to deliver a message on his behalf, asking all those interested in assisting the Irish Republic to meet him in the East Room of the hotel at noon the following day. Just less than half as many as the previous night turned up for the second conclave, where de Valera outlined his frustrations with the FOIF leadership, and reminded his audience of the damage the split was doing to the country in the eyes of the American public, and the watching British government. Although he was the only significant speaker, resolutions were passed demanding the FOIF call a National Convention for Chicago or Detroit, no later than 6 October and establishing the pre-eminence of the Irish leaders over their Irish-American rivals.

'That until the desired reform of the constitution be accomplished we see to it that in our respective states, all branches, state and local councils recognise as their supreme and primary guiding principle the needs and wishes of the Irish people as expressed through the Irish President or other duly authorised spokesmen of the Republic of Ireland.'

Aside from that statement of allegiance, the big news to come out of the meeting was the pronouncement that a rival organisation (a more democratic entity according to de Valera) might have to be established to usurp the place of the FOIF. That notion had been gestating for a while and within a month it came to fruition. On 20 October de Valera went public with the new body, the American Association for the Recognition of the Irish Republic (AARIR). He personally insisted upon the unwieldy title to clearly outline the movement's aims, and the arrival of the AARIR (newspapers immediately began using the acronym) confirmed the split was now irrevocable.

As an addendum to the final break, Harry Boland, in his role as a member of the Supreme Council of the IRB, dismissed Clan na Gael - Devoy's American arm of the movement - from that body. There ensued the usual bout of name-calling from both sides, much of it, yet again, carried out through the press. Even those back in Ireland became ensnared in the fall-out.

'Let it be clearly understood finally that we all stand together,' wrote Michael Collins in a letter to Devoy outlining where the government stood in this battle, 'and that here at home every member of the Cabinet has been an ardent supporter of the President against any and every group in America who have either not given him the co-operation which they should, or have set themselves definitely to thwart his actions. There is no necessity to name anybody as supporting him more ardently than another. We have all been as one on the question.'

Only the formation of the insults had changed, the tenor of them remained the same. On both sides, it was all rather pathetic, predictable and ultimately, embarrassing. Even many of those involved could see the damage being wrought by the constant in-fighting.

'To Ireland in her agony it mattered less than nothing whether de Valera or Cohalan was the more responsible for our fighting in the United States,' wrote McCartan. 'To Ireland all that mattered was that we were fighting, that by our fighting we had shattered our power to influence the American Government to restrain England's murderous intent and that the only defence against extermination now left to the Irish was the valour of her sons, the matchless men of the army of the Republic of Ireland.'

Yet again, this bruising and sapping carry-on was taking place at a time when all involved might have better served devoting their complete energies to the cause. Most especially since Ireland had actually recaptured the American national imagination and the front pages of its newspapers in the most dramatic fashion.

'Oh dear!', wrote Liam Mellows. 'How small do we all appear in the face of this terrible tragedy. How little indeed are the ambitions that have brought the movement to such a pass here, compared with the great principle for which MacSwiney is giving up all.'

As de Valera and the FOIF bickered, Terence MacSwiney was dying on hunger strike in Brixton Prison in London.

CHAPTER SEVENTEEN

The whole case is epitomised in the determination of the Mayor of Cork to starve himself to death in an English prison. His suicide - for such it would be - would make him at once a martyr and a hero in Irish eyes. And Ireland has ever craved heroes and martyrs. She would rather have a long roll of them than the largest degree of self-government possible within the empire. But the English government cannot, without ceasing to be a government, allow convicted criminals to go free simply because they will not eat. And there, in little, we have the entire Irish difficulty. Ireland makes impossible demands.

- *The New York Times* editorial, 27 August 1920

On 12 August 1920 Terence MacSwiney was arrested at Cork City Hall by British soldiers from the Hampshire Regiment. For possession of a cipher key to decode Royal Irish Constabulary (RIC) messages, a Cork Corporation resolution recognising the legitimacy of the first Dáil, and a copy of the speech he made at his inauguration, MacSwiney was charged with sedition. Less than four and a half months had

passed since he'd been elected to succeed his friend and former colleague, the murdered Tomás MacCurtain, as Lord Mayor of his native city. Apart from that office, MacSwiney was also Commandant of the Cork Brigade of the Irish Republican Army.

Appearing before a military court-martial, at Victoria Barracks in Cork, four days later, MacSwiney invoked his position as Chief Magistrate of Cork, declared the court illegal and threatened all involved with arrest. It was a bold, symbolic gesture from a man who'd started a hunger strike protest immediately after being taken into custody, in order to highlight the illegitimacy of the authorities. Nevertheless, the proceedings culminated in the Lord Mayor being given a two-year jail sentence.

Before dawn the following morning, MacSwiney was walked onto a British sloop at Custom House Quay and sailed to Pembroke, South Wales, from where he was brought by train to Brixton Prison, in South London. The dramatic and almost instantaneous impact of his refusal to take food can be gauged by *The New York Times* publicly denigrating his protest, barely a fortnight after it began. De Valera was quick to respond to the *Times's* characterisation. At a protest meeting called for New York's Lexington Opera House, the following day, in order to inform the American public about why an Irishman was starving himself to death in an English prison, de Valera dismissed such talk.

'If I were in MacSwiney's place, I would like to have some one speak for me. MacSwiney will die if he does not get his liberty. If MacSwiney dies in an English prison, 100,000 Irishmen are ready to do the same thing. They tell us it is a suicide. But he dies like a soldier and his death is at the hands of the enemy. He is offering his life just as would a soldier on the battlefield. England may do what she will with MacSwiney's body, but MacSwiney's spirit will triumph over that brute force and make Ireland's cause victorious. MacSwiney doesn't want to die, as no sane man looking on the sweetness of life does but he is making a sacrifice for the greatest principle in the world - liberty.'

On this and many other occasions during this episode, de Valera also sought to explain the Corkman's motivation by invoking the memory of Patrick Henry, an icon of the American Revolution, who delivered the famous 'Give me liberty or give me death' speech urging action against the British forces in 1775.

'He (MacSwiney) is acting as a faithful soldier of the Irish Republic, daring death for his country's sake. The British and pro-British press is preparing the way to make it appear that his death will be suicide. *The New York Times* has already taken up the British cry. Yet I have no doubt that the editor who penned the lines deprecating MacSwiney's action would write columns proclaiming the nobility of the sentiment "Give me liberty or give me death". Why not apply to MacSwiney the standard by which you measure Patrick Henry?

'Why not apply to Irishmen fighting for their country's liberty the same standards you would apply to yourselves in a similar case? MacSwiney does not selfishly or cowardly desire death. His young, joyous manhood lies before him. If he dies, it is not because he wants to die but because death is forced upon him as the alternative of an ignoble slavery, not for himself alone, but, under Lloyd George's new Coercion Act, for every Irishman and Irishwoman who thinks as he does.'

The new Coercion Act had been approved in the House of Commons on 6 August, and effectively replaced Crown Courts in Ireland with Court-Martials, operating without the need for juries. Barely a week later, MacSwiney was prosecuted at one such military tribunal, and under a new provision allowing the transfer of Irish prisoners to England, he was subsequently billeted at Brixton. The circumstances of his trial, the location of his cell in London, and the hunger strike itself prompted a letter from Arthur Griffith asking President Wilson to intervene. Several American bishops also contacted the State Department in Washington, in the hope of getting the US government to do something to ameliorate the situation.

With all such entreaties coming to no avail, de Valera kept the case in the public eye. On 9 September he released the contents of a cable he received from Fr Dominic OFSC, then serving as MacSwiney's chaplain at Brixton Prison, in response to his own missive to the Corkman.

'Lord Mayor expresses deep gratitude on behalf of self and comrades. Your generous tribute will sustain them in carrying on their struggle to the end. They put their trust in God and are satisfied that if they die the recognition of the Irish Republic will be advanced near to victory. God Bless and guard you in your noble work.'

By that point, ten men arrested with MacSwiney were also on hunger strike in Cork Prison, two of whom, Michael Fitzgerald and Joseph Murphy, fatally so. With its mayor incarcerated and apparently doomed, Cork hummed briefly with a rumour that de Valera - by a curious transatlantic sleight of hand - was somehow going to bring an end to the protests before any of the men died.

'Such a thing has never occurred to me,' said de Valera on 10 September. 'The rumour circulated in Cork that I would intervene at the last minute is far-fetched. Lord Mayor MacSwiney is fighting his own battle and knows what he's doing.'

Three days later, de Valera was paraded through the streets of Boston, where a crowd, of almost half a million, witnessed his journey towards an outdoor speaking engagement on Boston Common. Later that night, he was the star turn at a gathering in Mechanics Hall, where 8,000 loudly approved two different resolutions pertaining to MacSwiney. The first declared the 'Government of Great Britain has resorted to the slow, deliberate murder of Terence MacSwiney', the second demanded his 'immediate, unconditional release and repatriation'.

As the month wore on, and the reports from London worsened, de Valera wrote Muriel MacSwiney a letter on 26 September that read more like a political tract than a personal note of support.

'We grieve with you in the tension of your long agony. The silent masses now dumb at the outrage on humanity being committed by the British government cannot storm your husband's prison. They will not, however, forget. They now see in its nakedness, the hypocrisy of the plea which that government recently called on the millions of the noble-minded of the world to assist it and they will yet rock that Bastille of the subject nations - the British Empire. Please tell your noble husband and have conveyed to his comrades suffering with him the heartfelt gratitude of the Irish nation and the Irish race and may God give you all his consolation.'

That missive was also given to journalists; a move underlining the fact that despite so much energy having been diverted to the internecine squabbling with the FOIF, de Valera made good use of the MacSwiney hunger strike as propaganda. Almost every and any private correspondence between himself and London, at the time, was given to the press to keep the Lord Mayor, in particular, and Ireland, in general, in the international spotlight. If it would have been bad politics and a disservice to MacSwiney not to maximise his plight in this way, some of de Valera's activities in America, during this period, inevitably look kind of trite by comparison with his colleague's dire situation.

How else could they appear when one member of the Dáil (MacSwiney held the seat for mid-Cork) was on hunger strike, and another was rooming at some of the finest hotels up and down America's east coast? In de Valera's defence, he was fighting the war too - just on a very different front. Still, it hardly seems proper that he was taking day-trips by train to the seaside, while on the other side of the ocean, his colleague was drifting towards an increasingly certain death.

'We reached Long Beach and walked on a promenade below which crowds bathed,' wrote Patricia Lavelle, describing an afternoon on which she accompanied her father and de Valera to a local New York resort. 'Terry MacSwiney, Lord Mayor of Cork, had gone on Hunger Strike in Brixton Gaol, and they argued about hunger strikes and then about international politics. The promenade dwindled into a sandy rut and we walked on and on. They argued about high finance, and then back to Irish affairs, and then to Irish-American politics, switching occasionally to domestic American politics and still we walked and walked ...long stretches of sand with slow waves rolling in, wind blowing sand in our faces, a feeling of high tension and the slight discord of the arguments pervading everything.'

Having fallen into a coma on 20 October MacSwiney died five days later. De Valera was in Washington, when he received the news, busy preparing a submission to President Wilson formally requesting recognition for Ireland. He responded by releasing the contents of a cable of condolence he had dispatched to Mrs MacSwiney, and then issuing his own statement to the press. Having spent almost a year and a half visiting sites across America pertaining to the country's battle for independence from Britain, he now had one more poignant comparison to draw between that struggle and his own.

'The principles that Mayor MacSwiney, like his comrade, Fitzgerald, has given up his life to uphold - the principles for which the remaining comrades are giving up their lives in British jails - are the principles of the American Declaration of Independence and President Wilson's war aims - the inalienable right to liberty, "the privilege of men everywhere to choose their own way of life and obedience." Like Patrick Henry and his comrades, these Irish patriots were forced by the tyranny that would deprive them of liberty to make death the alternative.'

He also used the opportunity to remind Americans - who had, like much of the world, been tracking MacSwiney's demise via their daily papers - of Ireland's plight compared to other countries in the spotlight in recent years.

'Belgium is free, Poland is free, the subject peoples of Austria, Czechoslovakia, Jugoslavia are free. Ireland is now the one last white nation that is deprived of its liberty. England asked America's material aid. America gave it, and because of that aid alone

England is strong. Ireland asks only America's moral support, and the fair-minded liberty-loving people of the United States who sent their sons across the seas on a crusade for right will, I trust, not deny it.'

On 31 October 40,000 people filed the Polo Grounds, a baseball field that was then New York's largest open-air stadium to commemorate MacSwiney's death. An estimated 10,000 more were stranded outside, as the city's Irish community gathered to mourn his passing together, carrying tricolours and a collective wish to pay tribute to his sacrifice. They were joined in this rite by many of other nationalities, who had simply been touched by the story over the seventy-four days, during which he had refused food.

'As de Valera stood with bowed head amid cheering that already had lasted five minutes, three turbaned Hindus darted across the baseball field, waving a large Irish flag and the flag of their own aspirations,' wrote *The New York Times*. 'They rushed to the platform and draped the flags about de Valera's shoulders. The cheers were renewed, and although de Valera waved for order, ten more minutes had elapsed before a band struck up "Soldiers of Erin" and the crowd chanted the Irish Republican hymn'.

This was the last great meeting of the American tour. The spectacular and awful circumstances of MacSwiney's demise had energised de Valera's constituency in America once more, and brought out an impressive roster of New York politicians and clergymen. It was a hastily-arranged affair that succeeded in keeping Ireland on the front page of the country's newspapers, for one more morning, but the gathering itself was a rather chaotic affair. Four separate stages had been erected to cater for the huge crowd and this led to cheers from one section, often making it difficult to hear a word in another.

'Terence MacSwiney did not die to put spirit into his own people,' said de Valera, whose hoarseness didn't help amid the cacophony. 'He knew that they had spirit; that they were willing to make sacrifices as he did. In other lands, patriots have had to teach other people the spirit of sacrifice by such an example but MacSwiney knew that his people had spirit...We are not complaining at MacSwiney's death. He did as much for American principles as he did for Irish principles. We want America's support- her moral support. I know that the plain people of this country are in entire sympathy with us. They have told me wherever I have gone throughout this land.'

There were other protests across the country that weekend. A gigantic parade of people, of all ethnic groups, marched behind three empty caskets, draped in the Irish flag that coiled its way through the streets of Philadelphia, to the soundtrack of bands playing funereal music. Similar obsequies were attended by tens of thousands in Chicago, Los Angeles, Washington, San Francisco and Boston, where an estimated quarter of a million people lined the streets to witness the passing of a cortege in near-perfect silence.

The propaganda boon which resulted from the Corkman's death wasn't lost either on a company called Creation Films, which was about to release a movie titled: *For the Freedom of Ireland*. Ever the canny businessmen, the producers realised the heart-rending death of an Irish patriot made the timing perfect. Hence the following politically incorrect quote from a marketing memo advising cinema-owners how best to sell the film.

'Exploitation angles: The only sincere way of exploiting this picture will be to put it over as propaganda. The story, while interesting is decidedly subordinate. You should be able to stimulate interest by linking MacSwiney's case with the facts involved. In Irish communities, the picture will be a whiz and it should be lavishly advertised.'

From the moment he announced himself in the Waldorf-Astoria, de Valera had received umpteen offers to put his name, and the stamp of his office, on songs and films about Ireland. One writer asked his permission to dedicate a vaudeville number he'd written 'To the cause of Ireland'. Permission was refused. A pair of Ohio authors offered to sell de Valera a film script that would finally bring the complete history of Ireland from before the English arrived to the big screen. While that idea was also dismissed out of hand, he was smart enough to realise that at a time when almost 90 per cent of Americans went to the movies at least once a week, motion pictures represented a particularly slick form of propaganda.

Eamon de Valera made his Hollywood debut then in November 1919. Back during his fractious trip to Los Angeles, towards the end of his speaking tour, he went to the Capital Film Studios to pose for a series of special pictures that formed the conclusion of this movie called *For the Freedom of Ireland*. Written by Hal Reid, a 'dramatic love story' in six reels was directed by Roy Sheldon and starred Vincent Coleman - whose other credits that year included an anti-syphillis commercial - as Robert Emmet Corrigan. There is no explanation why de Valera got involved in this particular project, while eschewing so many others, although the breathless publicity material might hint why.

'"For the Freedom of Ireland" is claimed as probably the greatest photoplay championing the cause of Ireland ever attempted. It is the pictured oppression of a nation striving to gain its release from the yoke which clamps it to earth. It is the plea of a smaller nation for an equal freedom, an equal right to national growth. The picture deals with the questions of today, the democracy we fought for, and the motives actuating the League of Nations. The fact that the events portrayed spring spontaneously from the hearts of a people is enough to ensure its enthusiastic reception.'

The lead character, Corrigan, is an Irish-American who - inspired by de Valera's own escape from Lincoln Jail, achieved on screen, via clever mirrored communication and wire lock picks - returns to Ireland to assist in the fight against the English. He ends up being arrested and sentenced to death by firing squad, escaping due to the intervention of Sinn Féin. His girl-friend joins him in Ireland, where she is also imprisoned before dying, while fighting off the unwanted attentions of a British soldier. At the end, Corrigan decides to leave Adair (presumably Adare) and to head back to America to assist de Valera there in his quest to gain recognition for Ireland.

A rough cut was shown to an invited audience at Orchestra Hall, Chicago, on 10 November 1919. The two and a half thousand present that night were suitably impressed, even if the final scenes involving de Valera weren't shot until later that month. Contemporary reviews weren't exactly kind. One critic said 'the laurels of Fairbanks, Chaplin et al are safe', another highlighted problems with continuity and subtitles that were on the preachy side.

The time lapse between the Chicago premiere and the general release of *For the Freedom of Ireland*, nearly a year later, was down to problems with the censors. Ironically enough, de Valera's first personal experience of the cinema business involved men with scissors insisting certain scenes ended up on the cutting-room floor.

'Some members of the board received the impression that America is somewhat derided at points,' commented an official from the Chicago Censorship Board. 'Touching these things we cannot act but the entire picture savoured of the extreme melo-drama with lust, murder and bloodshed predominating. The rules of the board point to the members' duty and we must act accordingly.'

Amid the long, slow agony of MacSwiney, his own pending debut in the silent movies, and the ongoing schism with the FOIF, de Valera still had to play the role of statesman on occa-sion. At the end of September, Viscount Grey, Britain's foreign secretary at the outbreak of World War I and a former ambassa-dor to the US, advocated a solution to the Irish problem in which Ireland became a self-governing dominion sharing one foreign policy, one army and one navy with Britain. A notion that split opinion in London, the proposal generated enough coverage in the American papers to prompt de Valera to respond.

Within twenty-four hours, he sat down with a journalist from *The New York Times*, conveniently forgetting its 'suicide' jibe of the previous month, to refute the proposals. He opened by querying whether Grey even understood the nature of the issue he had addressed.

'Those who really want to solve a problem will first make clear to themselves what the problem is. I take it that the problem to be solved is the ending of the quarrel between Britain and Ireland, or more properly England and Ireland, for it is the English throughout history who have been our real opponents, so that the same good relations might exist between the Irish and British as exist between the Irish and the people of the United States or the Irish and the people of France. The point of the dispute is the point of the problem. What is that point? It is simply this, that the British government insists on claiming a right to circumscribe the legitimate liberties of the Irish people and to deprive them of the independence to which sovereign states are entitled.'

Then, for the umpteenth time since arriving in America the previous summer, he tried, once more, to place the Irish struggle in the context of the conflicts which had pockmarked World War I.

'The Irish do not admit the right to force them into any schemes of the kind. The Irish do not admit that Britain has any more right than France would have or Germany or any other power. The Irish people deny that Britain's superior military power gives her a moral right to insist on any such demands. The superior military might of Britain no more entitles Britain morally to force her will upon the Irish people than it entitled Germany to force its will upon the Belgians. Ireland has a right to the control of her own destinies, subject only to a due regard for the similar rights of other nations. So long as Britain insists on claiming the right of might, so long will the conscience of the

Irish people continue in revolt and so long will the people continue to contest English authority in their country - and so long will the problem remain unresolved.'

In between taking Grey to task for, yet again, trying to compare the situation of Ireland in the British Empire with the dispute between the southern and northern states in America's Civil War, denouncing him for an implied comment about the Irish being unable to rule themselves, and reiterating the claim of the first Dáil to legitimacy, de Valera raised the matter of the Black and Tans and the carnage that was, by then, becoming commonplace in Ireland.

'Who is it that lacks a sense of responsibility? What of Lloyd George and his Cabinet, who have turned loose on an unarmed people as guardians of "law and order" miscreants over whom, he admits, he has not control, who shoot up whole towns and villages, loot, murder and destroy indiscriminately? ... the British always approach the Irish question with the feeling that owing to their superior brute force they can really dictate the terms of settlement. They hope even now by persecution of our civil population and the pressure of military duress they can force a definite surrender of our people's rights. They are mistaken.'

CHAPTER EIGHTEEN

*You are hereby authorised to advance to the representative of the
Russian government the sum of $20,000 on condition that
arrangements are made so that its equivalent may be made
available later for the duly accredited representatives of the Irish
Republican Government at Moscow*

**- Letter from Eamon de Valera to Harry Boland,
27 October 1920**

Almost from the moment Eamon de Valera stepped off
the *Lapland*, Dr Patrick McCartan had been bending
his ear about the possibility of Ireland gaining formal
recognition from Russia. McCartan had developed an especially
good relationship with Ludwig Martens and Santeri Nuorteva, a
pair of officials at the Russian Information Bureau in New York.
With their own Bolshevik government, an administration still
unrecognised in the US, busy fighting a long and costly civil war
back home, the Russians in Manhattan were amenable to the
idea of signing a treaty with the Irish Republic. For his part,
McCartan was anxious to go to Moscow to negotiate the finer
points of the deal.

CHAPTER EIGHTEEN

However, the Russians were also desperately short of cash and tapped the Irish contingent for two loans of $20,000 in the space of six months. On the first occasion back in April, Harry Boland had famously taken possession of some of the Russian 'crown jewels' as collateral for the money given. That package eventually made its way back to the Boland family home, on the northside of Dublin, and while the gems were turned out to be worthless, the Soviet government did pay the money back decades later. If the willingness to help their eastern European colleagues out financially was obvious evidence of de Valera's interest in working with them, he was careful at all times to be non-committal in terms of formal treaties. Most especially since one of the terms included the possibility of the Russians supplying arms and training to Irish soldiers.

'I have not finally made up my own mind on the question of a published agreement,' wrote de Valera in one memo, 'but I certainly am of the opinion that the mission should go and that the whole question be taken up very seriously.'

De Valera realised that whatever good could have come from inking a treaty of co-operation with Moscow, it might also have been costly in terms of relations with America and Washington, as always, had to remain the primary focus. That much was underlined by the amount of time he spent in the city during September and October, and by a particular piece of business conducted there on the same day he signed off on the second Russian loan.

A delegation headed up by Frank P. Walsh met with US Secretary of State, Bainbridge Colby, in the Diplomatic Room of the State Department. Watched by journalists and with his every word recorded by stenographers, Walsh delivered an hour-long address, pleading the legitimacy of the Irish government. Colby had rearranged his schedule specifically to sit down with Walsh's group, but let it be known beforehand that he would only meet American citizens, a very obvious proviso designed to keep de Valera away from the encounter.

Even by sitting across the table from him, Colby would have been conferring a degree of legitimacy on the Irish cause. That this was obviously something he was extremely keen to avoid is a poor reflection on how the campaign had failed to impact in the higher echelons of the American government. In any event, de Valera submitted his own case in writing, sending a lengthy document direct to President Woodrow Wilson at the White House.

Dated 27 October, 'Ireland's Request to the Government of the United States of America for Recognition as a Sovereign Independent State' represented an amalgam of many of the arguments in favour of Ireland that he had delivered on podiums all across America over the previous sixteen months.

Equal parts history lesson and contentious position paper, it was a spectacularly wide-ranging document in which he attempted to present a persuasive argument by invoking Wilson's own statements about nation's rights, pertinent quotes from various English politicians stretching back decades, and the legal precedent of America's historic quest for independence from Britain.

'The people of Ireland are a people and the Government of the Republic of Ireland is a government exactly such as described,' he wrote. 'Hence, as it is not to be believed that the

United States would abandon the principle of "government by the consent of the governed", which has always been a fundamental guiding principle of its national policy, reiterated with special emphasis during the war by you, Sir, as the necessary basis of any peace which the United States would feel justified in guaranteeing, the people of Ireland and their government are confident that their claim to recognition will not be refused or ignored by the Government of the United States.'

By way of establishing the bona fides of the government he represented, de Valera also offered a lavishly detailed account of how the Dublin administration had already performed under so much duress during its brief period of existence. This extended, even as far, as pointing out the Fisheries Department was keen to help in the purchase of more motor-boats for fishermen, the Department of Agriculture had instituted an Arbour Day, with the intention of planting trees on waste lands, and the Minister of Labour, Countess Markievicz, was concerned about the provision of suitable housing schemes for workers.

'Neither Czechoslovakia, nor Yugoslavia, nor Finland, nor Armenia, nor Poland itself, nor any of the newly-established states of Europe, whose independence is now rightly recognised, even approach the perfection of nationhood manifested by Ireland, nor can their claim compare with Ireland's on other grounds,' he continued. 'These nations, for instance, had no elected or organised government of their own to point to, as Ireland has, ready to discharge the duties of a responsible government, not only but actually discharging the most essential of them.'

A Herculean effort in many ways, the request was little more than a grand symbolic gesture. Wilson remained so incapacitated he was playing no role in government and even if he had been in the prime of his health, he was hardly likely to antagonise his British allies, especially so near to the end of his presidency. With America still hoodwinked into believing Wilson was working away diligently from his sick bed, the official line emerged that the president had forwarded the de Valera brief to the State Department for further consideration. Apart from satisfying the desire of his colleagues, back in Dublin, for the Irish case to be formally presented to the highest office before de Valera left the country, nothing at all came of the document.

Even after running into that bureaucratic dead end in Washington, de Valera continued to command a high profile and to attract fresh controversy. He'd begun November publicly reaffirming his desire to continue fighting the Irish cause in America, and he was as good as his word. Ten days later, he excoriated the British actions in Ireland over the previous month.

'The people of America have no idea of the desperate situation impending in Ireland this winter. A systemised effort is being made to paralyse the larger cities, and transportation is being stopped and employees being discharged by British orders. Within six months of the withdrawal of the British army of occupation, Ireland would be the most peaceful and prosperous country in Europe...The system of the Kitchener concentration camps in South Africa where the women and children of the little African republics were carried off and packed together like animals and left to die by the tens of thousands in order to break the spirit of the brave Boers was not more pitilessly cruel than the system employed against the Irish in the effort the British are making to destroy the government set up by the people of Ireland…The uniformed bandits known as the Black and Tans whose indiscipline and lack of responsibility to any authority but their own passions and whose barbarities contrived at by the British Premier and sustained by his parliament have caused them to be likened even by British generals to the Bashi-Bazouks and have led their own officer-in-chief to resign are now roving through Ireland carrying murder and destruction to whole towns and villages, killing and torturing the most representative of citizens, burning their property, driving the womenfolk and children of whole countrysides homeless into the fields.'

By drawing comparisons with the Kitchener concentration camps, where an estimated 27,000 Africans died, and the Bashi-Bazouks, savage irregulars in the Ottoman Army who were paid in loot stolen rather than wages, de Valera had ratcheted his rhetoric up a notch to match the escalation of violence in Ireland. As the daily reports of fresh carnage from back home filtered in, he responded by becoming more and more outspoken. When British troops killed fourteen unarmed people at Croke Park on 21 November, in what became known as Bloody Sunday, he was unequivocal in his support of the way Michael Collins and his colleagues had earlier that morning assassinated twelve secret service agents and two auxiliaries in Dublin.

'The Irish people have learned again the old lesson that as long as the patient will suffer the cruel will kick, and having no other avenues of redress they naturally pursue the individuals of those forces who are responsible for outrages and are, as enemy spies among them, rightly deserving death if any human beings deserve death, for they provide the alien government with knowledge and the strength to persecute and inflict endless misery upon a whole nation.

'When armed soldiers attack an unarmed populace, it is a massacre. There is no comparison between the guilt of the British soldiers, who from tanks and armoured cars in full war outfit, with machine guns and rifles mow down unoffending civilians as they walk the streets intent upon their ordinary business or attend a football match - or murder prominent Irishmen in the bosoms of their own families - and the Irishmen who kill these British soldiers engaged in an armed campaign of violent aggression against the Irish people's rights. No British soldier has a right to be in Ireland.

'Those who are there are guilty of making war, not a civilised war, but a barbarous war on people who are guilty of no act of aggression against England. If the British withdraw their forces from Ireland, every individual of those forces will be unmolested so far as Irishmen are concerned. As long as the British forces remain in Ireland, no Irishman is safe either in his person or his property. The aggression of the British and their invasion by force of Ireland's rights is the root cause of all the bloodshed.'

The comments were regarded as justifying murder and provoked outrage in some quarters. *The New York Times* trashed de Valera in an editorial, calling into question his Catholic credentials and denouncing his 'apology for the Dublin assassins' as 'a frightful blunder in tactics.' De Valera's comments had started to match in tone and intensity the situation back home. Not only had he raised his game to reflect the changed circumstances in the War of Independence, there was also a sense of a man speaking more freely now that he realised his time in America was coming to a close, and that the attempt to gain formal recognition had come to naught.

Freed up, perhaps, by no longer having to worry about the grander political implications and the risk of offending those in power, he was less guarded than ever before in his remarks. He was also very adept at placing the Irish situation in a wider historical context and reminding his audience that the British weren't exactly innocents abroad.

'The conduct of the British troops in swooping down and firing their machine-guns on unarmed people, attending a football match in Dublin, is simply a repetition of the Amritsar Massacre in India, [when hundreds of unarmed Sikhs were shot in 1919] and whatever British officer was in charge in Dublin will be commended for it and rewarded as (Brigadier-General) Dyer was, and later when that officer is made to feel by Irish Republicans that, although he may commit these crimes with impunity so far as his own government is concerned, he may not do with impunity so far as Irishmen can secure it, his death will be classed by a British-controlled press as "another murder by the Sinn-Feiners".

'While the spokesmen of Ireland have been appealing almost in vain to moral forces, the British government has been goading the Irish people to the limit of human endurance. When it was announced that Mrs. MacCurtain, widow of the former Lord Mayor of Cork, was to come to America to give evidence of the brutal murder of her husband, she was shot at. Today the body of a priest who was about to come here to give evidence of the murders he saw committed by the British in Galway was recovered from a bog where he had been taken and shot by Black and

Tans - Lloyd George's own. Ireland does not fear but invites investigation of her case by the whole world.'

The first priest to be murdered in Ireland since the days of Oliver Cromwell, Fr Michael Griffin, of Barna, had been scheduled to testify at an investigation into the Irish crisis launched by *The Nation*, an American current affairs weekly with a liberal slant. First mooted by its editor, Oswald Garrison Villard, back in September 'as a Committee of One Hundred American citizens to hear evidence about the goings-on in Ireland', the response from invitees had been so overwhelming it grew in size to 150. Intended to be deliberately non-sectarian and non-partisan, the roster included state governors, US senators, congressmen, mayors, Catholic and Methodist bishops, rabbis, sociologists, academics, business people, lawyers and editors.

Although it strove to give off the air of objectivity, the Commission had the look of a War Crimes Tribunal about it, albeit one with no legal redress. From the larger number of those involved, a group which included representatives from thirty-six states, a committee of eight under the chairmanship of Dr Frederic C. Howe, a renowned economist, held hearings in Washington from 18 November 1920 to 21 January 1921. De Valera and the British Embassy were both furnished in advance with lists of events likely to be investigated, and invited to have official representatives present at every meeting. The day before the start of business, the embassy refused that opportunity and dismissed the whole thing as 'not impartial and prejudiced'.

The British also reneged on an earlier promise (also made by de Valera) not to interfere with the safe passage or testimony of any witnesses called. Donal O'Callaghan, Terence MacSwiney's successor as Cork's Lord Mayor, eventually had to stow away to America to attend. Following evidence from, amongst others, O'Callaghan, former members of the RIC, and MacSwiney's wife, Muriel, the Commission published a damning report in March 1921 laying the blame for the deterioration in Ireland squarely at Britain's door. Even more pertinently from de Valera's point of view, they accepted the legitimacy of his government.

'In spite of the British terror,' went the report, 'the majority of the Irish people have sanctioned by ballot the Irish Republic, given their allegiance to it; pay taxes to it, and respect the decisions of its courts and of its civil officials.'

On November 16, two days before the Commission opened its doors, de Valera had presided over the birth of the AARIR at the Raleigh Hotel, in Washington. A week earlier, he'd invited a hundred prominent Irish-Americans to attend a conference, designed to further the cause of the recognition of the Irish Republic, and from this gathering sprang forth the new organisation with Edward L. Doheny, the oil man, as its first president, and de Valera's words about the urgency of the task ahead ringing in their ears.

'I have called you here today in order that you may plan concerted action, so that this great current of sympathy and good will may be harnessed and made effective. This action on our part is, I know, long overdue…By February 1, you should have enrolled the bulk of your membership. The State conventions should be scheduled for a date between February 1 and February 15 so that within a week or two of the latter date the organisation could assume a permanent form with the permanent officers elected for the ensuing year... Action cannot be postponed - the situation in Ireland is such that if you delay it will be but a devastated land and to the remnant of a people you will bring succour, for the English government is ready to advance from horror to horror and the Irish people on their side can never surrender their birthright.'

Within a year, the AARIR had a membership dwarfing that of the FOIF. By some (almost certainly exaggerated) estimates, 800,000 people signed on to the new organisation, although that number may have been reflective of a scheme by which people were paid for bringing aboard newcomers. Others place the sign-up at a still wildly impressive half a million. Both figures are even more significant when considered next to the fact that Devoy's outfit had shrunk to 20,000 in the same time frame. Even if he departed the country within weeks of the formal announcement, de Valera must be given credit for this logistical triumph, a victory that of course, represented a lingering slap in the face to his, by now, sworn enemies in the FOIF.

A day after the inaugural conference, a mass meeting was also held at the Coliseum on Ninth Street, in Washington DC, to promote the new departure. Beforehand, thousands participated in a march along Pennsylvania Avenue that took them past the White House. With a group of ex-servicemen at its head, and three bag-pipers blaring a soundtrack, the size of the procession was remarkable given that cold rain fell throughout. Pointedly, de Valera didn't join the convoy until it had first wended its way past the Presidential accommodation. He spoke at the meeting however, and then set off on a mini-tour to publicise the venture, conscious of the fact this initiative was going to cause serious ructions.

'We are as much for Irish freedom as President de Valera is, and we stand loyally behind him,' said an un-named member of the FOIF, at its New York State Convention later that month. 'But there are certain elements which enter into the situation which he must recognise. One of them is that as the spokesman for Ireland he loses weight in this country because he is not an American citizen. Then again, it must be remembered that the American citizens of Irish extraction are for America first while de Valera is for Ireland first....We do not want de Valera as President of the Irish Republic to dictate the policy of American citizens.'

With reports emerging of loyal members of the FOIF clashing with de Valera supporters and would-be acolytes of the AARIR at meetings in various cities, walk-outs and shouting matches were now commonplace events. To some in the older body, de Valera's sponsoring of the new outfit was regarded as outright treachery.

'...President de Valera deliberately split the Irish movement in America, and all the energy of his followers has been wasted in the struggle to destroy instead of being expended for Ireland's cause against the common enemy,' wrote Bishop Michael J. Gallagher. 'I nourished the hope that the friends of Ireland would soon see the folly of thus playing England's game, but it has been all in vain. The new organisation is still spending thousands upon thousands of dollars trying to wipe out the Friends of Irish Freedom. Anybody who suggests that de Valera is not master of the people of Irish blood everywhere, or that, like ordinary mortals, he ever made a mistake in his whole life, is overwhelmed with billingsgate and foul abuse in the de Valera press.'

Against that background, de Valera did his best to promote the AARIR with a brief foray through Massachusetts, upstate New York and into Ohio.

'This new organisation is being formed for the purpose of helping me to carry out the objects for which I was sent to this country by the people of Ireland, in the manner in which they wish them to be carried out,' he said before an audience of 1,000 at the Hotel Bancroft, in Worcester, Massachusetts on 26 November 1920. 'Those who differ from us cannot stand in our way. We hold no grudge against those who remain in the old organisation.'

That last line was undermined a little, just two nights later, when a hundred of his supporters stormed out of a meeting, in the same town, when it came time for Justice Daniel Cohalan to speak. Those who stayed heard Cohalan make the outlandish and totally erroneous claim that if de Valera had went along with his plank at the Republican Convention in Chicago, Ireland would not be in the midst of such terrible strife.

The arrest of Arthur Griffith - who had now been acting Priomh Aire in de Valera's place for over a year - by the British on 26 November also prompted renewed speculation that de Valera, himself, would not be long for America. He dismissed the idea that this would impinge on his plans in any way, while explaining the motive for the imprisonment of the leader to American journalists.

'The arrests seem to me simply to be for the same purpose that they arrested all of us back in 1918. They hope by doing so to disorganise the forces of the republic, but as these forces are a co-ordination of the Irish people, and as this movement comes from the heart of the Irish people, it does not depend upon fixed leaders for its success. There are plenty of substitutes ready to take the places of Griffith, MacNeill and the rest.'

De Valera gave that quote while speaking at his mother's house in Rochester. He'd stopped there, en route to Cleveland, for another meeting. Whether he'd dropped in to the city specifically because he knew - despite his public protestations to the contrary - that he was heading home soon and wanted to bid farewell to his mother, is open to debate. According to press reports, he spent only two hours at the house and much of that was given over to addressing the Irish activists from the region, who'd gathered there to hear first-hand about the AARIR.

That certainly didn't leave much time for a lengthy visit with his mother and her husband. Catherine was by then sixty-two years old, an elderly woman in an era when the average life expectancy was in the mid-fifties. The brevity of the goodbye is shocking too, given de Valera knew the moment he left America he was going back to either be imprisoned or to participate in the war. Both options contained the built-in danger of having his own life cut short.

CHAPTER NINETEEN

I will not write the sentimental things I feel lest I lose your good opinion - for thinking over the companionship of the year and a half, the recollections of various sorts that crowd upon me are such that what I am tempted to write you would count as womanish. God bless and guard you always and give to your eyes the supreme joy of seeing the Republic recognised by all the nations. Your Comrade for Ireland, Eamon de Valera.

**- Letter to his personal secretary Sean Nunan,
10 December 1920**

Conscious of the clock ticking down on his return to Ireland, the quest to try to quickly ensure the primacy of the AARIR took Eamon de Valera through Chicago and as far west as St Paul, Minnesota. There, on 3 December, he was forced to deny a Lloyd George charge that the British had documents linking him to a pro-German conspiracy, material they claimed to have found on his person during his 1918 arrest. It was also in St Paul where, after so much travelling, de Valera's body finally shouted stop. He was confined to bed with a billious attack so severe it threatened to keep him there for weeks.

His critics may have wondered whether the liver condition was a byproduct, as it can be, of the patient eating too much rich food at so many luxurious hotels. Whatever the prognosis, he managed to make it back to New York in a somewhat diminished state. On 5 December he was too ill to attend a high mass at St Patrick's Cathedral, where Mrs Muriel MacSwiney (whose arrival on the *SS Celtic*, the day before, had been greeted by 3,000 people) was guest of honour. She later dropped by the Waldorf-Astoria to visit the patient, and declare herself available for whatever tasks he wished during her stay in America.

Three days later, the relentless Horatio Bottomley MP raised new questions in the House of Commons about whether the time had come for the British government to protest to Washington about the way it had allowed de Valera to run amok in America. Bottomley complained that by conferring honours on him, several cities were guilty of committing unfriendly acts towards London.

'I think there is no doubt that we would, from the diplomatic point of view, have the right to take the course suggested,' answered Andrew Bonar Law, the government leader in the house. 'But it is not the question of what is a right, but of what is expedient. Undoubtedly a very severe campaign is being conducted against this country but so far we have found the Americans can be trusted to look at the matter from a reasonable point of view.'

De Valera responded swiftly enough for his riposte to be carried alongside the original American newspaper accounts of the debate in Westminster. Allegedly dictated from his sick bed at the hotel, the statement represented the last grand pronouncement of his stay in America as the *Celtic*, the ship that would take him back, was preparing to depart from New York. It was a robust effort.

'I do not think that the British government will in fact make any official representations to the American government, because even the British government well knows that my activities have been not anti-British, but pro-Irish. I have simply advocated Ireland's right to justice. If there are forces disturbing Anglo-American relations, they are not of Irish origin, but fundamentally of English origin... The instigation by Bonar Law and Lloyd George of the assassination of Irishmen and the murder of women and children, the wholesale burning of Irish towns and villages, the general destruction of property, and of crops, and the attempted dislocation of the whole civil and economic life of the country, through anarchy and starvation, the surrender of Ireland's right to liberty - those are the things that are causing the disturbance of Anglo-American friendship....'

The following day, de Valera and James O'Mara travelled to Philadelphia, so that he could say goodbye to Joe McGarrity and sort out the logistics for handling the money raised through the bond-certificates, the eventual tally for which in 1921 would reach $5,123,640. He wished McGarrity to act for him as a trustee of Dáil Éireann with regard to the funds, and it says much about his mindset that when he eventually signed over powers of attorney to his friend, he wrote about the possibility of being 'incapacitated by imprisonment or death'. He also drew up a quasi-legal document witnessed by his two colleagues in which he offered his opinion about ownership of the money.

'...I regard the funds collected through the issue of Bonds of the Irish Republic as national and party funds. At the same time the party that stands for independence and in particular for the idea of an independent Republic has a very special claim on them. Should the Irish people then by vote depart from the present position and the Irish parliament other than an independent or Republican parliament be set up by the vote of the majority so that Irish representatives would be in a minority - I think that the funds in the hands of the Trustees of Dail Eireann should be partly retained in trust so as to be available to enable the Republicans to again secure a majority in Ireland through elections or to equip them to drive out the BRITISH by arms...'

Their meeting in Philadelphia dragged on so long that in the end, McGarrity had to get the train back to New York with the pair of them that night so they could continue the discussions. On that leg of the journey, the talk turned to what awaited de Valera back in Ireland and the extremes he might have to go to if captured by the British.

'I told him I should consider it a serious blunder for him if caught to adopt hunger strike; that I thought McSwiney's death had served all purposes of the method,' wrote McGarrity. 'He said that he must keep an open mind on that; it might be again necessary to use it. That at times great sacrifices were necessary of performance as they at certain times brought results which could not be brought about by other methods.'

The arrangement put in place for handling the money, not already sent back to Ireland (near enough $1m) or spent on the drive itself (roughly the same amount), was especially convoluted. A sum of about $1.5m was to be deposited in bank accounts under the names of de Valera (with McGarrity now acting in his stead), Boland, as Irish envoy in America, and Diarmuid L. Fawsitt, as trade consul. Two signatures were necessary in all cases to make withdrawals. That left another $1.5m to be invested in United States Liberty Bonds. Those would be placed in deposit boxes under three different combinations involving John. J. Hearn (who had distinguished himself with his work on the Connecticut bond-certificate campaign) Boland, McGarrity and Sean Nunan.

'The securities were held in four New York City banks: Guaranty Safe Deposit Company, Central Union Safe Deposit Company, Garfield Safe Deposit Company and Harriman National Bank,' wrote Francis M. Carroll. 'The keys to the boxes were left in the possession of O'Mara. This procedure provided for de Valera's return to Ireland, but it made the bond revenues accessible to people who were American citizens and beyond the reach of the Dail government and all three of the trustees, thus creating enormous difficulties in the future.'

Within weeks, the difficulties began to manifest themselves. The FOIF went public with an attempt to access the money raised through the bonds and that was only the start of the drama surrounding the funds. The labyrinthine mechanism by which multiple people had responsibility and access to the money, was subsequently complicated further by political events in Ireland, when the Treaty and ensuing Civil War split the movement there down the middle.

The battle for the bonds eventually wound its way through the New York courts for several years, before Judge Curtis A.

Peters issued a ruling in 1927 disallowing the various claims to the funds and appointing receivers to begin the process of returning the cash to the purchasers of the bond-certificates. In December of that year, de Valera was back in America running a rather gauche campaign trying to persuade bond-certificate holders to turn over their return to him, in order to help with the establishment of the Irish Press newspaper in Dublin.

In this way, he may have received as much as £100,000 from original subscribers, who then received shares in the new venture. Nine years after that, de Valera was in power, himself, when the Irish government took over from the receivers the task of ensuring, where humanly possible, the original subscribers received $1.25 for every dollar paid in to the fund. Opposition politicians were quick to label the government's bill to authorise this as 'the Irish Press Bill, second edition' given the obvious impact it would have on the fledgling newspaper's fortunes.

All of that murky business lay in the future on 10 December 1920 when de Valera, McGarrity, Nunan, Boland and others convened in Room 228 of the Waldorf-Astoria for what was, essentially, their last supper together. Following an emotional get-together during which eulogies were delivered and gifts exchanged, it came time for final farewells before de Valera, escorted as ever by Boland, headed down to the White Star Line pier where the *Celtic* was docked. One of his last acts before leaving was to warn McGarrity to look after his health problems, and his friend then cautioned him to 'stand firm and not to compromise.'

'Never fear,' replied de Valera. 'There is only one path. We will keep to it.'

'God guard and keep you,' said McGarrity as they shook hands and then gave each other military salutes.

Within an hour, he'd been given the coat of a crew member, smuggled aboard the *Celtic* and placed deep in the bow of the forecastle. Almost exactly eighteen months had passed since he'd sailed into American waters in similarly clandestine circumstances. In that time, he'd succeeded in garnering swathes of publicity for the First Dáil, raising an enormous sum of money (not enough of which had got back to Ireland when needed), and managed to sample some of the finest hospitality at the country's best hotels. Even if he'd ultimately failed to get official recognition from Washington, the scope and ambition of the entire campaign, from the slick pr machine to the hard lessons learned dueling with John Devoy and Justice Cohalan, ensured de Valera was returning as a savvier and more battle-hardened politician.

As the noise all around indicated the ship was readying to leave New York, he found a piece of paper on which to write a letter to the people of America. With 'a full heart', he composed the following message, which was smuggled off before the *Celtic* left the dock. It appeared in the American newspapers on New Year's Eve, more than a week after he'd made it safely back to Dublin.

'Land of the free and home of the brave, Farewell! May you ever remain, as I have known you, land of the generous-hearted and kindly. May you stand through time as they would have you who love you - Liberty's chosen champion; and Oh! may you never know, yourself, the agony of a foreign master's lash.

'I came to you on a holy mission, the mission of Freedom; I

return to my people who sent me, not, indeed, as I had dreamed it, with the mission accomplished, but, withal, with a message that will cheer in the dark days that have come upon them and that will inspire the acceptance of such sacrifices as must yet be made.

'So farewell- young, mighty, fortunate land. No wish that I can express can measure the depth of my esteem for you, or my desire for your welfare and your glory. And farewell, the many dear friends I have made and the tens of thousands, who for the reason that I was the representative of a noble nation and a storied, appealing cause, gave me honours they denied to princes-you will not need the assurance that Ireland will not forget and that Ireland will not be ungrateful.'

APPENDIX

During a visit to the United States and Canada in 1964, Eamon de Valera was officially welcomed to the country by President Lyndon B. Johnson. He had been back to America many times, in the interim, but almost exactly forty-five years after strolling into the Waldorf-Astoria Hotel and asking to be called president, it was finally the title he bore. On 28 May 1964 President Eamon de Valera addressed the joint Houses of Congress, in Washington DC, with the following speech.

- Mr. Speaker, Mr. President pro tempore of the Senate, Members of the Congress of the United States: my first word to you must be to thank you from my heart for the great privilege you have granted me in permitting me to appear before you and to address you. I was here some forty-five years ago, and I toured throughout this great country. You may remember on that on the 21st of January, 1919, the national assembly of Ireland - Dail Eireann - declared Ireland independent and a republic, just as the Second Continental Congress here declared the independence of America.

President Wilson, during the First World War, had put the rights of people to self-determination as a fundamental basis for peace. We in Ireland took advantage of the fact that that principle had been enunciated by the head of this great nation. There was a general election due at the time, and we took advantage of that election to make it clear that the people wanted independence. The elections were held under British law, and therefore there could be no suggestion of any interference in our favour. The results of the elections were such that it would be impossible for anyone to deny what was the status of the nation and what was the form of government that the Irish people desired.

I was sent here some months later - in June of 1919. I have told you that our Declaration of Independence was made on the 21st of January, 1919. That is our Independence Day, as July 4 is yours.

I was sent here to the United States with a three-fold mission. First, to ask for official recognition of the independence and the Republic that had been declared in Ireland in full accordance with the principles of self-determination. I was sent here also to float an external loan for the uses of that Republic. And finally, I was asked to plead with the American people so that, if the Covenant of the League of Nations and the Treaty of Versailles, which were under discussion, were to be ratified, the United States would make it clear that, notwithstanding Article X of that Covenant, the United States was not pledging itself to maintain Ireland as an integral part of British territory.

Some weeks after we had declared our independence - I think it was on March 4 - the House of Representatives here passed a resolution by some 216 votes to 41, asking the Peace Conference that was sitting in Paris and passing judgment upon the rights of nations to favourably consider Ireland's right to self-determination. A few months later, on June 6, your Senate passed a resolution earnestly requesting the American Peace Commissioners, then in Paris, to endeavour to secure that the representatives who had been chosen in Ireland for that purpose, would get a hearing at the Peace Conference in order that they might present Ireland's case.

But the Senate went further. Nearly a year later, when the ratification of the Treaty of Versailles was under discussion, it passed a resolution which was intended to be a reservation to the Treaty, if adopted, reaffirming its adherence to the principles of self-determination and its previous vote of sympathy with the aspirations of the Irish people for a government of their own choice, and went further and expressed the earnest hope that once Ireland had got self-government it would promptly be admitted as a member of the League of Nations.

You know that on account of the articles in the Covenant and circumstances of the day the Treaty was not ratified. But the resolutions here in Congress, supported as they were and mirroring as they did the attitude of the American people as a whole, were made manifest by immense demonstrations in all the principal cities throughout the United States. Recognition was given by the mayors of your principal cities, by the governors and legislatures of many of your states, so that Congress here was expressing accurately the will of the American people in regard to Ireland. It is not necessary for me to tell you how heartened our people were by these expressions of sympathy and friendship. We were in a very difficult struggle, facing very great odds. And it was a comfort and an earnest of ultimate success that this great freedom-loving nation of America and its people were behind our efforts.

What was the gratitude of the Irish people was clearly evident to anyone who saw the reception that was given to your late President, President Kennedy. He was welcomed not merely because he was of Irish blood, not merely because of his personal charm and his great qualities of heart and mind, nor even because of the great leadership which he was giving to the world in critical moments; but he was honoured because he was regarded by our people as the symbol of this great nation, because he was the elected President of this great people. In honouring him they felt that they were in some small measure expressing their gratitude to the people of the United States for the aid that had been given to them.

The United States, since the Declaration of Independence, has been looked upon by all freedom-loving peoples as the champion of true human liberty, the liberty of nations and the liberty of individuals. We in Ireland have constantly looked to you as such a champion. We all know that the former League of Nations came into being as the result of American initiative - although, as I said, for reasons which seemed good at the time to the American people they did not ratify the Treaty or become members of the League. But the idea came from America, in modern times anyhow. And the successor of the League - the United Nations Organisation - also came into being as a result of American influence. Most thinking people will admit that, if we are to look forward to peace, to anything like a lasting peace in this world, it can only be secured by the working of such an organisation - an organisation that will purposely devote itself to bringing about the rule of law and, where other means have failed, judicial determination of international disputes, and enforcement of peace when that becomes necessary.

Now, you all know that we are far from being at that goal at present. But there is no one who has read the speeches of President Kennedy or the speeches of President Johnson or the speeches and statements of your Secretary of State or of the chairman of your Foreign Relations Committee, but must be satisfied that American leaders are thinking at the highest level and that they are facing realistically the complicated situations that confront them and also the social evils that have to be remedied. It is a great comfort to know that a nation like yours is thinking at that level. And we have the hope that, as long as there is thinking at that level and as long as this nation is guided by the Divine Spirit, ultimately the peace and the conditions which we all wish for will be realised.

But freedom and peace are but the foundations. They are the necessary foundations. The United States as a great nation and ours as one of the smaller nations, working in our complementary ways, are endeavouring to build, to secure that these foundations will be well laid. But that is not all, of course. An Irish poet [James Clarence Mangan] thinking, some 120 years ago, of the role he would wish his nation to play addressed us in these words;

Oh, Ireland, be it thy high duty

To teach the world the might of moral beauty

And stamp God's image truly on the struggling soul.

President Kennedy in his address at Amherst College, thinking of the future that he would wish and that he foresaw for America, said he wished an America whose military strength would be matched by its moral strength, the moral strength of its people; its wealth by their wisdom; its power by their purpose - an America that would not be afraid of grace and beauty - in short, he said, an America that would win respect not because of its strength but because of its culture. I am sure that is the America that ultimately you would want, as it is the Ireland that we would want. But these things can only be secured by undeviating pursuit of the foundations that I have mentioned and pursuit, ultimately, of the higher ideals that mean the mental life, the full life of the people.

Mr. Speaker, I would like to confess, and confess freely, that this is an outstanding day in my own life, to see recognised, as I have here in full, the rights of the Irish people and the independence of the Irish people in a way that was not at all possible forty-five years ago. I have longed to come back, and say this to you and, through you, to the people as a whole. I would indeed be fully happy today where there not one serious setback that had occurred in these forty-five years. When I was addressing you here in 1919 and 1920, our ancient nation, our ancient Ireland, was undivided. Since then, it has been divided by a cruel partition. As my predecessor Mr. Sean T. O'Kelly, when he was addressing you here said, partition is one of our serious problems, but, please God, that too will be solved.

And I salute here, in prospect, the representative of Ireland who may be permitted to address you as I have been permitted, and who will be able with full heart joyfully to announce to you that our severed country has been reunited and that the last source of enmity between the British and Irish peoples has disappeared and that at last we can be truly friends.

And now, Mr. Speaker, I would like to renew to you and to

the Members of Congress, my thanks for this great privilege - and, of course, to the President of the United States, without whose generous invitation I could not be here. I am deeply grateful. I hope that the close ties which have kept our countries together for centuries will continue into the future and that the representatives of Ireland may be able to talk to the American people as close friends, and representatives of the United States to talk to the people of Ireland as their close friends.

May I pray in our own language, the Irish language, that this may be so:

Go dtuga Dia gur mar sin a bhéas, agus go stiúraí an Spiorad Naomh na daoine a bhéas mar threoraithe ar ár ndá thír, agus taoisigh an domhain fré chéile, ar bhealach na síochána agus leasa an chine dhaonna.

ENDMATTER

BIBLIOGRAPHY

Beaslai, Piaras, *Michael Collins and the Making of a New Ireland*. London: GG Harrap & Co, 1926

Carr, William J., *The Irish Carmelites of New York City and the Fight for Irish Independence, 1916-1919*. Middletown: Vestigium Press, 1973

Carroll, Francis M., *American Opinion and the Irish Question 1910-23*. Dublin: Gill and Macmillan, 1978

Carroll, Francis M., *Money for Ireland*. Westport: Praeger, 2002

Coogan, Tim Pat, *Eamon de Valera: the Man who was Ireland*. New York: Harper Collins, 1995

Cronin, Sean, *The McGarrity Papers*. Tralee: Anvil Books, 1972

De Valera, Terry, *A Memoir*. Dublin: Currach Press, 2004

Doorley, Michael, *Irish-American Diaspora Nationalism*. Dublin: Four Courts Press, 2005

Dwyer, T. Ryle, *Eamon de Valera*. Dublin: Gill and Macmillan, 1980

Fanning, Ronan, *Documents on Irish Foreign Policy Volume 1*. Dublin, Royal Irish Academy, 1998

Ferriter, Diarmuid, *Judging Dev*. Dublin: Royal Irish Academy, 2007

Fitzpatrick, David, *Harry Boland's Irish Revolution*. Cork: Cork University Press, 2001

Foster, Roy, *WB Yeats: A Life Vol.2* New York: Oxford University Press, 2003

Golway, Terry, *Irish Rebel*. New York: St Martin's Press, 1998

Greaves, C. Desmond, *Liam Mellows and the Irish Revolution*. London: Lawrence and Wishart, 1971

Hart, George L., *Proceedings of the 17th Republican National Convention*. New York: The Tenny Press, 1920

Jensen, Joan M., *Passage from India*. New Haven: Yale University Press, 1988

Longford, Earl of and O'Neill, Thomas P., *Eamon de Valera*. Dublin: Gill and Macmillan, 1970

Macardle, Dorothy, *The Irish Republic*. New York: Farrar, Straus and Girous, 1965

MacManus, M. J., *Eamon de Valera*. New York: Ziff Davis, 1946

McCartan, Patrick, *With De Valera in America*. New York: Brentano, 1932

McCullough, David, *1776*. New York: Simon and Schuster, 2005

Moynihan, Maurice (ed), *Speeches and Statements by Eamon de Valera 1917-1973*. Dublin: Gill and Macmillan, 1980

O'Connor, Frank, *The Big Fellow*. Dublin: Poolbeg, 1979

O'Doherty, Katherine, *Assignment America: De Valera's Mission to the United States*. New York: De Tanko, 1957

O'Mara Lavelle, Patricia, *James O'Mara: A Staunch Sinn Feiner, 1873-1948*. Dublin: Clonmore and Reynolds, 1961

O'Toole, David Sex, *Outing the Senator: Spies and Videotape*. Worcester: James Street Publishing, 2005

Russell, Francis, *The Knave of Boston*. Boston: Quinlan Press, 1987

Sperber, Murray, *Shake Down the Thunder*. New York: Henry Holt, 1993

Tansill, Charles, *America and the Fight for Irish Freedom*, New York: Devin-Adair, 1957

Tarpey, Marie Veronica, *The Role of Joseph McGarrity in the Struggle for Irish Independence*. New York: Arno Press, 1970

Journal Articles

Duff, John B., 'The Versailles Treaty and the Irish-Americans'. *Journal of American History* 1968 55(3)

'Eamon de Valera: Newport ties of the man who was Ireland'. *Newsletter of the Museum of Newport Irish History*, Winter 2005

Franklin, David B., 'Bigotry in 'Bama: De Valera's Visit to Birmingham, Alabama, April, 1920'. *History Ireland*, Winter 2004 Vol 12, No. 4

Maxwell, Kenneth R., 'Irish-Americans and the Fight for Treaty Ratification'. *Public Opinion Quarterly*, Vol 31. No. 4.

Murray, Patrick, 'Eamon de Valera's Indispensable Secretary: Kathleen O'Connell, 1888 - 1956', *Eire-Ireland* (winter 1996)

Murray, Patrick, 'Obsessive Historian: Eamon de Valera and the Policing of his Reputation'. *Proceedings of the Royal Irish Academy*, Vol. 101C, 2001

Nunan, Sean, 'President Eamon de Valera's Mission to the United States of American, 1919-20'. *Capuchin Annual*, 1970

Silvestri, Michael, 'The Sinn Fein of India'. *The Journal of British Studies,* Vol 39. No. 4 (October 2000)

Newspapers

Billings Gazette, Boston Globe, Capital Times, Chester Times, Chicago Daily-Herald, Chicago Tribune, Daily Kennebec Journal, Decatur Review, Evening Gazette, Evening State Journal, Fresno Republican, Gaelic American, Hartford Courant, Helena Independent, Irish Press (Philadelphia), *Irish World, Kansas City Star, Kingsport Times, Kingston Daily Freeman, Los Angeles Times, Lowell Sun, Mansfield News, Middletown Daily Herald, Modesto Evening News, Montreal Gazette, The New York Times, The Newark Advocate, Newport Mercury, Notre Dame Scholastic, Oakland Tribune, Ogden Examiner, Ogden Standard, Racine Journal News, Renwick Times, Wall Street Journal, Washington Post, Wellsboro Agitator*

Archives

Dáil Debates

Eamon de Valera papers, UCD Archives

Kathleen O'Connell papers, UCD Archives

Joseph McGarrity collection, Villanova University

Library of Congress, Washington DC

Websites

Celticcousins.net, Wildgeese.com, Cankuota.org,

SOURCE NOTES

PROLOGUE

City of Chicago sailing – *The New York Times*, 1885
De Valera, Terry – p149
Longford, p3

CHAPTER ONE

Would one not say – Dáil debates, 16 November 1943
The scene of the *Lapland* coming into New York composed using photographs, contemporary accounts and shipping logs
Details of de Valera's crossing on the *Lapland* are gleaned from 'Deverant's Story', an interview with the seaman who arranged his passage – UCD Archives P 150/668
Rather unexpected this – Fitzpatrick p124
McGarrity's sartorial and semantic influence – Tarpey p111
Tarpey, P111 – McGarrity's sartorial and semantic influence
'Mrs. Charles E. Wheelwright…' *The New York Times*, 22 June
De Valera and his mother – De Valera, Terry, p150
Mary Connolly story – Longford and O'Neill p97
De Valera's trips to his brother, Senator Borah, Cardinal Gibbons – p150/118 UCDA
Boland in the Waldorf-Astoria – *The New York Times*, 23 June

CHAPTER TWO

Press reports indicate …Tansill, p341
De Valera arriving at Waldorf-Astoria – *The New York Times*, 24 June;
Golway, Terry, p 259-261, *Irish Press*, June 28

John Devoy's career, Golway, Terry,
Story about Devoy and de Valera's first meeting – McManus, p80
Friends of Irish Freedom – Doorley, p 38
Cohalan's introduction of de Valera – O'Doherty, Katherine, p16
De Valera quotes – *The New York Times*, June 24
Dev in horse drawn carriage – McCartan, Patrick, p140
Middletown incident – Middletown Daily Herald, 23 June
De Valera and the loan, *The New York Times*, 25 June
Reverend Irvine, *The New York Times*, 28 June
Sir Charles Allom incident, *The New York Times*, 28 June
De Valera and the Carmelites – Carr, William J, pXXX
Sean Nunan, Capuchin Annual, p 239
Tumulty, *The New York Times*, 30 November 1921

CHAPTER THREE

Resolution – *Boston Globe*, 30 June
Scenes at South Station and details of train journey, *Boston Globe*, 29 June; *The New York Times*, 29 June; *Lowell Sun*, 29 June; *Irish Press*, 5 July
Fenway Park scenes and quotes, *The New York Times*, *Boston Globe*, *Lowell Sun*, June 30; *Irish Press*, 5 July; O'Doherty, p46-47
Character portraits of Mayor Peters and his colleagues, Russell, Francis, *The Knave of Boston*
David Walsh's sexuality and battle with the British, O'Toole, David, *Outing the Senator*
Article X and de Valera, Longford and O'Neill, p99
Visit to Washington Elm, *The New York Times*, 1 July; *Boston Globe*, 5 July
Washington Elm history, McCullough, David, 1776, p24
Massachusetts State Legislature, *Lowell Sun*, 1 July
Bunker Hill, *Irish Press*, 5 July

CHAPTER FOUR

'The whole trouble…' – Fanning, p35

Wilson's homecoming – *The New York Times*, 9 July

De Valera in restaurant – Longford, p99

Wilson, Versailles and Ireland – Maxwell, Kenneth, and Duff, John B.

Wilson's unofficial assurance, *The New York Times*, 12 June

Madison Square Garden, scene and quotes, *The New York Times*, 11 July; Hartford Courant; *Irish Press*, 19 July

Sinn Féin and *Lusitania*, *The New York Times*, 1 September

'I would be deeply humiliated…' *The New York Times*, 13 July

Mary Keelty Sullivan – *Chicago Herald Examiner*, 13 July

De Valera's Chicago itinerary – *Chicago Daily Tribune*, 13, 14, 15 July

Mundelein quote – Doherty, p55

Edward Carson quote – *Decatur Review,* 13 July

Cubs' Field meeting scene and quotes – *Chicago Daily Tribune*, 14 July;

Irish Press, July 19

British Consulate dispatch – Coogan, Tim Pat, p151

Ulster map – *The Newark Advocate*, 16 July

De Valera Chicago City Council, *Ogden Examiner*, 15 July

CHAPTER FIVE

De Valera arrival in San Francisco scene – *Oakland Tribune*, 18 July

'We hail you…' – *Oakland Tribune*

'The Lord is the strength …– *Irish Press*, 2 August 1919

Jerome Connor statue story – www.celticcousins.net

'I thank the citizens…' – O'Doherty, p 56

Snagge incident – *Oakland Tribune*, 18 July

'Never witnesses say…' – *Oakland Tribune*, 22 July

'In speaking to labour here…' – *Oakland Tribune*, 22 July

De Valera itinerary – O'Doherty, p 57-58

'Speaking as an outsider – *Daily Kennebec Journal*, 19 July

De Valera in Salt Lake – *Ogden Standard*, 25 July

Reception and speeches in Butte – *Irish Press*, 9 August; *Billings*

Gazette, 26 July

'If Mister de Valera…' – *Montreal Gazette*, 29 July

De Valera in Helena – *Helena Independent*, 31 July; *Irish Press*, 9 August

Meagher and the flag – www.wildgeese.com

'It was hard for the…' *Helena Independent*, 31 July

CHAPTER SIX

'The reception accorded…' – Dáil Debates, 19 August

De Valera audiences – O'Doherty, p44

'I have a mandate…' – O'Doherty, p44

Roosevelt meeting – Longford and O'Neill, p100

Irish Victory Fund details – Tansill, p345

'I remember him coming..' – McCartan, Patrick p143

'Considerable difficulty…' – Fanning, p39

'Of course you know…' – *The New York Times*, 13 September

'A half Spaniard…' – *The New York Times*, 24 September

'I recall how….' – *The New York Times*, 25 August

'The Mayor of Newport…' – Fanning, p40

'The war front is…' – *Chester Times*, 13 September

De Valera in Newport – *Newsletter of the Museum of Newport Irish History*, Winter 2005; *The New York Times*, 14 September

De Valera in Providence – *Lowell Sun*, 15 September

'We will resist…' – O'Doherty, p79

'I ask the American people …' – O'Doherty, p79

James Wilson meeting – *Newport Mercury*, 27 September

'The latest development…' – Golway, p267

CHAPTER SEVEN

'The American Legion…' – *Wellsboro Agitator*, 8 October

'This shrine is not a shrine…' – *Irish Press*, 9 October

'I think the greatest…' – P150/1121 UCDA

'We Irishmen know the meaning…' – *Irish Press*, 9 October

'That means will...' – *Irish Press*, 18 October

'The patriots of Ireland...' – O'Doherty p94

Scenes in Philadelphia – *Irish Press*, 9 October; O'Doherty, p 96

Washington's message to Ireland – O'Doherty, p95

Youngstown, Ohio reception – *The New York Times*, 5 October

Cleveland reception – *Mansfield News*, 7 October; *Evening Gazette*, 9 October

Valparaiso – P150/666

'Mr. de Valera will...' – *Notre Dame Scholastic*, 5 October

Notre Dame reception – *Notre Dame Scholastic*, 11 October

'In the first place...' – *Notre Dame Scholastic*, 18 October

'His personality made...' – *Notre Dame Scholastic*, 15 November

'De Valera's visit...' – Sperber, p81

Henry Ford meeting – Longford, p102

Chippewa meeting – Fitzpatrick p133; de Valera Terry p16; O'Doherty p103; *Irish Press* 1 November; *Oakland Tribune*, 18 October

Chippewa history – www.cankuota.org

'Chief of Ireland...' – *The Renwick Times*, 19 October

CHAPTER EIGHT

'Robert E. Lee...' – *The New York Times*, 17 October

'British propaganda...' – *The New York Times*, 1 December

De Valera adverts – *Kansas City Star*, 23 October

De Valera's diary – p150/666 UCDA

TW Drumm – Doherty, p109

'I have no objections...' – *Kansas City Star*, 23 October

Murder trial – *Kansas City Star*, 26 October

Portland flag incident – *Los Angeles Times*, 15 November; *The New York Times*, 16 November; *Oakland Tribune*, 16 November

'The flag of the Irish...' – *Modesto Evening News*, 17 November

'He is the self-styled...' – *Los Angeles Times*, 16 November

'I think de Valera is here...' *Los Angeles Times*, 19 November

De Valera at Washington Park – O'Doherty p118, *Los Angeles Times*,

24 November; *Irish Press*, 6, 13 December; *Fresno Republican*, 24 November

'It is said here…' *Los Angeles Times*, 24 November

'We stopped off at Williams…' – Nunan, p 242

'For Mellows…' – Greaves, C. Desmond, p211

CHAPTER NINE

'To James O'Mara…' – Lavelle, Patricia p139

O'Mara biography – Ibid

'I wish O'Meara…' – Fanning p43

'Dad had his own kind…' – Lavelle, p 139

'Bonds by day…' – Fitzpatrick, p144

'In Ireland, O'Mara…' – McCartan p144

JP Morgan – *The New York Times*, 30 November

'It is admitted by…' – *Lowell Sun*, 9 December

'The case is before…' – *The New York Times*, 11 December

'To crush the…' – *Irish Press*, 13 December

'We stand for…' – *The New York Times*, 30 December

'As far as himself…' –Tansill, p351

'Peace…' – P150/666 UCDA

'The claim of… – *Washington Post*, 13 December

'Representative Tom Connally…' – Tansill, p355

'We point out that…' – *The New York Times*, 13 December

'Would be fought…' – *Oakland Tribune*, 22 December

'I have not seen…' – *Kingston Daily Freeman*, 30 December

'There is ample evidence…' – de Valera, Terry, p155

'Greetings to the persecuted…' – O'Doherty, p124

'Another New Year's night…' – *The Irish Times*, 23 November 2004

Michael Collins and de Valera kids – Coogan, p167

CHAPTER TEN

'We, the members…' – *The New York Times*, 27 June 1919

Scenes at City Hall…' – *The New York Times*, 18 January; *Irish Press*,

24 January; Doherty p127

'It is a privileged...' – *The New York Times*, 18 January

'Mr. Mayor...' – Ibid

'After a very...' – *The New York Times*, 19 January

'We have issued bonds...' – *The New York Times*, 19 January

'I feel it somebody...' – *The New York Times*, 19 January

'It did not shock me...' – *The New York Times*, 12 January

'The Republic of Ireland...' – *Irish Press*, 24 January

Bond subscriber details, – *The New York Times*, 20 January; *Irish Press*

'The near illegality...' – Carroll, FM, p152, *American Opinion and the Irish Question*, 1910-23

'More than one...' – *Wall Street Journal*, 4 February

'The new so-called...' – *The New York Times*, 29 January

Bond subscription details – Carroll, Francis M., *Money for Ireland*, p21

'To _____...' – Noreen Moriarty copy

'The Dail government...' – Carroll, *Money*, p23

Bond funds transfer – Fitzpatrick, p145

CHAPTER ELEVEN

'The United States...' – *The New York Globe*, 6 February

'Notwithstanding the fact...' – *Boston Globe*, 7 February

Worcester reception...' – *Irish Press*, 14 February

'A minute dash of...' O'Connor, p97

'The crux of the issue...' – *Gaelic American*, 14 February

Varying interpretations of the Gazette interview are available in every book on de Valera, as the mouthpieces for de Valera and Devoy respectively, the *Irish Press* and *Gaelic American* also offer wildly divergent views on what happened.

'I quoted the part...' – Fanning, p58

'A vassal state...' – Golway, p 270

'We had built up...' – McCartan, p152

'It's time for plain...' – Fanning, p54

Boland putsch – Fitzpatrick p 154; Fanning, p 58

'I am convinced...' – Tansill, 364

'Chief very upset...' –Fitzpatrick, p154

'The articles themselves...' – Doherty, p135

'Do you really think...' – Tansill, p 364

'I gave de Valera's...' – McCartan, p153

'Have no fear...' – Longford, p108

'I am thoroughly...' – Greaves, C Desmond, p216

New England itinerary – *Boston Globe*, 7-24 February; Doherty p140

'The Irish Progressive League...' – O'Doherty, p 143

Ronald C. Lindsay incident – *Hartford Courant*, 21 February

CHAPTER TWELVE

'We are the spear-points...' – Moynihan, p35

Patrick's Day parade scenes – O'Doherty p144; *The New York Times*, 18 March; *Irish Press*, 27 March; *De Valera and Friends for the Freedom of India* – Jensen, Joan M. p242

'Like Thomas Francis Meagher...' – Silvestri, Michael, p460

'It became evident...' – *The New York Times*, 18 March

'I have the honour...' – Tansill, p365

'In consenting to...' – *Irish Press*, 27 March

'A Te Deum...' – *Boston Globe*, 19 March

'All of the advantages...' –McCartan p165

'Cohalan presented his case...' – Ibid, p168

The Park Avenue Trial details – Tansill, McCartan, Golway, Doherty, Cronin,

'The Judge made a...' – Cronin, Sean, p79

'I attended a...' – Tansill 367

'President de Valera stated – Ibid.

'The audience...' – Cronin, p80

'I say advisedly...' – *Evening State Journal*, 22 March

CHAPTER THIRTEEN

'Chicago – Patrick King...' – *The New York Times*, 20 March

'I dislike to…' – Lavelle, Patricia, p177

'Your being at…' – Ibid

'What on earth is…' – Beaslai, Piaras, p15

'We are not…' – O'Doherty, p150

'In comparing…' – *The Kingsport Times*, 23 April

'An offence to…' – *The Capital Times*, 23 April

'Were I directing official…' – *The Racine Journal News*, 20 April

'For the purpose of…' – *The New York Times*, 21 April

'Birmingham was led…' – Franklin, David B. p31

'The timing is come…' – Ibid, p32

'I had seen a…' –Ibid p33

'Oh, men of…' – *Irish Press*, 8 May

'We protest against…' – *Irish Press*, 1 May

'If it be…' – *The New York Times*, 20 April

'It is said…' – *Irish Press*, 15 May

House of Commons report – *The New York Times*, 7 May

Hamill Resolution…' – *Irish Press*, 15 May

WB Yeats – Foster, Roy p168

CHAPTER FOURTEEN

'and whereas the…' – McCartan p187

'I went straight…' – Ibid p188

Washington conference details –Tansill, 374

'We opened offices…' – McCartan 1919

'We of Ireland…' – *The New York Times*, 6 June

'At all times…' – O'Doherty p154

'Resolved: that this…' – Tansill, p375

'Mindful of the…' – Beaslai, p16

Parade details – *Chicago Tribune*, 10 June

'Most of the marchers…' – *The New York Times*, 10 June

'I know all of…' – *Chicago Tribune*, 10 June

'This declaration leaves…' – *Chicago Tribune*, 11 June

'..it would be…' – *Chicago Tribune*

'We are opposed…' – Hart, George L., p110

'shock to Sinn Feiners…' – Carroll, *American Opinion*, p155

'The incident illustrates…' – Doorley, Michael, p129

'The refusal of…' – *The New York Times*, 14 June

'This action of…' – *Gaelic American*, 17 July

'That sum is…' – *The New York Times*, 20 June

'I believe it…' – McGarrity Papers p81

'Justice Cohalan…' – *The New York Times*, 22 June

'It is always unwise..' – *The New York Times*, 20 July

'If President had…' – *Chicago Herald-Examiner*, 23 June

CHAPTER FIFTEEN

'Dail Eireann assembled…' – Dáil Debates, 29 June 1920

'Is there any good reason…' – *Oakland Tribune*, 30 June

'Mindful of the…' – *The New York Times*, 29June

'They raised this…' – *The New York Times*, 30June

'There is no secret…' – *The New York Times*, 2 July

'The great principle…' – O'Doherty p168

'Rejection of the…' – *The New York Times*, 5 July

'The third party…' – *The New York Times*, 17 July

'The letters presented…' – *The New York Times*, 14 July

Mannix tour details – *Irish Press*, 24 July-7 August, Doherty, p171-173

'It is now little…' – *Irish Press*, 24 July

'If our President…' – *The New York Times*, 19 July

'I am proud…' – O'Doherty, p172

'I have already…' – *The New York Times*, 24 July

'Stories to the…' – *The New York Times*, 30 July

'There were hisses…' – *The New York Times*, 1 August

'The American people…' – *Irish Press*, 7 August

CHAPTER SIXTEEN

'To Eamon de…' – Lavelle, p172

'He said that…' – de Valera, Terry, p131

Sinéad de Valera visit details, *Irish Press*, August, Sep; de Valera, Terry, p131/132; *Hartford Courant*, 8 Sept; Lavelle, Ch. 9

'Children and self…' – UCDA P150/1058

'My elder brother…' – Longford and O'Neill p113

'Mrs. de Valera…' – Fitzpatrick p191

'The students…' – *Irish Press*, 18 September

'It was a…' – de Valera, p131

'I can feel…' – UCDA P155/ 4

Kathleen O'Connell biography – Murray, Patrick 111-133

'It went on…' – Dáil debates, 22 November 1928

'Please do not…' – p150/236 UCDA

'Suggestions of this…' – Murray, Patrick p130

'The ministry learns…' – Fanning, p70

'Differences have arisen…' – Dáil debates, 6 August

'As regards the FOIF…' – Doorley, p132

'His idea…' – Tansill, 387

'The whole play…' – Ibid 392

'That until the…' – *Irish Press*, 25 September

'Let it be…' – Nunan, p247

'To Ireland in…' – McCartan p198

'Oh dear!…' – Greaves, C. Desmond p 218

CHAPTER SEVENTEEN

'The whole case…' – *The New York Times*, 27 August

'If I were…' – Ibid, 28 August

'Lord Mayor expresses…' – Ibid, 9 Sept

'Such a thing…' – Ibid, 10 Sept

'We grieve with…' – Ibid, 27 Sept

We reached Long…' – Lavelle, Patricia. P177

'The principles that…' – *The New York Times*, 26 October

'As de Valera…' – Ibid, 1 November

'Terence McSwiney…' – Ibid

'Exploitation angles...' – Library of Congress, Washington
movie and song offers – p150/1067 UCDA
'For the freedom...' – Library of Congress, Washington
'Some members of...' – *Chicago Tribune*, 14 Nov 1919
'Those who really...' – *The New York Times*, 1 October
'The Irish do...' – Ibid
'Who is it...' – Ibid

CHAPTER EIGHTEEN

'You are hereby...' – P150/108 UCDA
'I have not...' – Cronin, p87
Colby meeting – *The New York Times*, 28 October
'The people of...' – Moynihan, p37
'Neither Czechoslovakia...' – Ibid p38
'The people of America...' – *The New York Times*, 10 November
'The Irish people...' – *The New York Times*, 23 November
'The conduct of...' – Ibid
'apology for the...' Ibid 24 November
Commission workings and report – *The New York Times*, 1 April
1921
'I have called...' – *Irish Press*, 20 November
AARIR membership – McArdle, Doorley, Tansill, Carroll
Washington march – Ibid
'We are as...' – *The New York Times*, 29 November
'...President de Valera...' – Tansill p394
'This new organisation...' – *The New York Times*, 27 November
'The arrests...' – Ibid, 28 November

CHAPTER NINETEEN

'I will not...' – P150/954   UCDA
'I think there...' – *The New York Times*, 9 December
'I do not...' – Ibid
'I regard the funds...' – Cronin, p92

'I told him…' – Ibid, p91

'The securities…' – Carroll, Francis M., *Money for Ireland*, p25

Bonds certificate money aftermath, Ibid p49-95

'December 10th meeting – Fitzpatrick p192; Cronin p191

'Land of the free…' – Moynihan p48

APPENDIX

Moynihan, p599

INDEX

www.obrien.ie